Your Backyard Birds

DR GRÁINNE CLEARY

With a foreword by Robyn Williams AM

Your Backyard Birds

ALLEN&UNWIN
SYDNEY • MELBOURNE • AUCKLAND • LONDON

First published in 2019

Allen & Unwin
83 Alexander Street
Crows Nest NSW 2065
Australia
Phone: (61 2) 8425 0100
Email: info@allenandunwin.com
Web: www.allenandunwin.com

NATIONAL LIBRARY OF AUSTRALIA
A catalogue record for this book is available from the National Library of Australia

ISBN 978 1 76029 735 0

Internal design by Stella and John Danalis/Peripheral Vision
Index by Puddingburn Publishing Services
Internal illustrations by Estee Sarsfield
Set in 11.5/17 pt Adobe Garamond Pro by Post Pre-press Group, Brisbane
Printed and bound in Australia by Griffin Press

10 9 8 7 6 5 4 3

FSC www.fsc.org MIX Paper from responsible sources FSC® C009448

The paper in this book is FSC® certified. FSC® promotes environmentally responsible, socially beneficial and economically viable management of the world's forests.

For my heart's best treasure and partner in everything I do, Bill Coleman.

'The beat goes on . . .'

CONTENTS

FOREWORD

I met Robyn Williams while being interviewed by him about bird feeding on ABC's *The Science Show*. Robyn's love for birds shone brightly as he recounted a tale about a cheeky magpie who he had come to know. This magpie would enter his sitting room to land on the coffee table in order to chew on whatever book Robyn was currently reading! I invited Robyn to foreword this book with stories about the birds who share his garden.

BIRD CENTRAL

Robyn Williams

I parked the car on the steep drive to our cottage high up overlooking the ocean on the South Coast of New South Wales. Within one minute The Family had turned up on the deck, four magpies, in a row, one of them singing the trills and warbles as distinctive to the Oz ear as the smell of eucalypts to our noses when we're overseas.

The Family is two parents, attached to our territory and its surroundings, plus young offspring, still with grey plumage rather than white. They were waiting for meaty snacks from me and I provided them *even before* unpacking our gear.

We had just returned from Italy and Greece, staying at exquisite locations, but strangely bereft of bird life. Indeed, it was disconcerting when by the 'Med' to see gulls winging past making baby-like noises, yet not looking towards our house, let alone visiting. In Australia, from our cottage, we can see parrots and corvids coming from afar and most of them are heading our way, wheeling and diving, then landing smartly on our deck where lunch is always offered. After our maggies were served, a butcher-bird arrives, waiting confidently. I throw a piece of fat towards him and, knowing the game, he zooms upwards, catches the morsel and flicks off into the bushes to devour it. Then back for more. Such an acrobat!

It was windy that day, but crystal clear, with pale blue sky and hardly a cloud. The dishes we have for the birds are wide and solid, the ones usually used under very big flower pots. Several birds can perch on the rims and share. Rain had obviously been scarce, so I put water out and was rewarded immediately with a customer. Why is it so satisfying to see a bird like a magpie dipping its beak in the drink, raising its head to let the water run down its throat, and then to swallow?

Next, out with the seed. Crested pigeons come quickly, followed by two rainbow lorikeets (there are fewer blossoms around for them in the winter season) and, inevitably, a bunch of galahs with their chubby cheeks and soothing plumage of pink and grey. These are the standard neighbours; they come every time.

More unpredictable are the king parrots, usually in pairs, he with his crimson head and deep green body and wife with red undercarriage and more cautious approach. As the deck is invariably overcrowded, I reach for some china, a posh tea plate, fill it with seed, and place it on the table. The kings gracefully walk to each side of the dish and begin to eat, gurgling slightly as they do so. If a parrot twice their size barges in, I lift the dish and prepare to leave, but sometimes (thrill!) the male leaps on to my wrist and from there continues to feed from the plate I'm holding. I freeze, often for long periods—this is especially trying in the winter—while these exquisite native parrots have lunch. The Greek family next door look, nod and say, 'How good is that!'

Sometimes we have crows, more flighty than the rest, eventually settling, but flying off at the slightest disturbance. We miss old Pegleg, who was a regular years ago, with his one stump still displaying coils of fishing line which we longed to remove, but could never get close. Red-browed finches used to visit in packs of ten or twelve, but no more.

Pegleg, like other corvids (and I include currawongs and magpies here, though the latter are in a different classification), bring their offspring to our smorgasboard and teach them that it is safe. They do this by flying down off the rail and demonstrating that it's okay to browse. We delight in the varied and subtle behaviour we've seen over the years: maggies taking hard bread to water to soften it; the patience of mothers with demanding chicks; the ranking of aggressiveness among species with lorikeets and corellas at the top (corellas—have you seen their eyes?—just like ET). Some birds are obviously used to humans and try to come into the house. This gets me into trouble: I'm too lenient.

Sulphur-crested cockatoos are obviously the most outrageous at home invasion. One or two walk solemnly through the open doors from the deck, leap up onto the back of the sofa, look at me and nod, giving a small squawk. This is the signal for me to fetch a shortbread biscuit. This is grasped by one foot and brought to the beak for consumption, crumbs liberally dropping to the floor. When one biscuit is finished—another nod and squawk, and I oblige with another.

On one occasion I had no treats handy so the cockie leapt on to the coffee table and solemnly began to devour pages from the large atlas lying there. I also get told off about their habit (though the galahs are worse) of chewing the framework of the deck—the railings especially. Deep gouges now line the woodwork. I take it as a natural souvenir from our visitors. My partner Jonica Newby does NOT agree.

Magpies, of course, were quick to come through the doors. Within a metre of the entrance they would, without fail, need to drop another kind of souvenir, a white splat with black and grey. I would leap to clear it up to keep the avians and me out of trouble. But never quickly enough. Jonica would shoo them out and train them, loudly, to respect the clear boundary between inside and outside. The magpies are immensely smart and learned the lesson almost instantly, but are often willing, as time passes, to test our vigilance.

But it is instructive to talk to Jonica about *how* she approaches training. The magpie, having been chased out a few times with shouting or a flung soft pillow, comes towards the open French windows and stands on one leg just before the shining floor of our lounge. Then it slowly lowers the other foot just *inside* the house—barely a centimetre over the line clearly marking the start of 'inside'. As that trespassing toe hits the floor, Jonica shouts very loudly. At that instant the bird learns the lesson, it knows exactly what the limits are. They are smart creatures, Oz birdies.

The wider garden has a different population than the deck where we feed birds does. Once we had a pine tree (which the neighbours next door had removed) into which black cockatoos would regularly perch and cavort, chewing the cones. We miss them. And, again, the sheltered back garden, with its almost English shrubbery and calm, has birds we never see at the front: finches, blue wrens, silver-eyes . . . and was that a rare robin?!

All this abundance makes us so much more aware of what we need to look for. We are primed for a bush alive with coloured creatures, flying and singing and enriching our surroundings. As we look from the deck down to the long beach, we see ospreys, sometimes in pairs doing a training run with offspring, squadrons of pelicans and even more 'nowras' (as yellow-tailed black cockatoos are called), hence the name of the local large town. Down on the beach itself are oyster-catchers and fast running terns, that's a distance from our cottage, about which I am supposed to be rhapsodising, but it does give an idea of the territoriality of our birdlife.

All this attention to our birdlife, for us, began when our precious border collies and Burmese cat died. The collies were much too lively to allow birds to settle and Babo the cat frightened them off despite, himself, turning out, to our surprise, to be something of an ornithologist. We would take Babo from Sydney on our laps to stay at the cottage as he pushed into old age. He was a survivor—with feline AIDS (worry not, it's common), arthritis and diabetes. Babo would sit on the steps that led from the deck, watching birds and yowling soundlessly in what I inferred was frustration, but he made no attempt to go for them. When he died (run over by a crazed Sydney driver trying to break 100 kph in our street barely 200 metres long), we decided to concentrate on our feathered friends instead. We did, after all, travel too much to be able to commit to cats or dogs properly.

So, it's been about ten years since Fine Dining On The Deck opened and we were stunned by how quickly a vast clientele emerged. But what do I mean by 'friends'? I don't for one minute imagine that any bird regards me with any affection nor that they 'appreciate' how much I spend on seed and sundry bird foods. I take them as they are, not as I would imagine them to be. And they give me and Jonica profound puzzles to consider. Do the corvids, maggies and parrots have a Theory of Mind—do they know that Jonica and I will respond to their signals as, for instance, they sit outside looking through the window singing, even tapping on the glass, both indicating they want grub? You could say, as Descartes did, that they are merely little machines programmed to react to simple signals. I appear, food often follows, so they approach. They don't necessarily think that I think and therefore want to prompt me to think about them.

I am convinced that Descartes was wrong. He should have met sulphur-crested cockatoos or crows whose intelligence matches that of four-year-old humans, though, being a cussed Frenchman, he would have thought of some mechanistic, Jesuitical means to evade the obvious.

And, again, are they consciously working out solutions to problems? Why, just now, did I notice that several pieces of corn had found their way into the water bowl? Answer: crows or magpies had put them there to soften the seeds. Every day we discover something new.

It is a continuing feast of enjoyment watching our visitors, our 'neighbours'. We are away from the cottage at least five days a week, so they'll never be locked in to our service, dependent on our supply. And we keep the deck clean, so there are few dangers of disease.

So, it's a relief to be back from Europe, at least from an avian point of view. Scientists such as Dr John Krebs in Oxford have shown how depleted the birds of Britain are from the hedgerows where they once flourished, and the story's the same on the Continent where shooting is still rife.

But then I was delighted when staying at a posh hotel resort in Tuscany to find the open air breakfast tables were constantly being raided by sparrows. I, of course, naughtily began to drop them bits of bread—until Jonica gave a low scowl to stop me. Being a vet she knew exactly when to give the 'NO!'—just as I raised my hand to fling the crust. The sparrows waited. Jonica went to the loo. Both the sparrows and I were ready.

PREAMBLE

There is a cartoon that illustrates a scientist full of hope that he can teach a monkey to say 'apple'. He soon realises that the monkey is the classroom dunce when a parrot vocally identifies the apple variety as 'Golden Delicious'[1].

When we think of evolution, we often think of Darwin's teaching. It was Charles Darwin who famously suggested that there is 'no fundamental difference between man and higher mammals in their mental faculties'[2]. But what about birds? For a long time birds were ignored when we thought about our own evolution. We think of evolution as being a straight line; from higher apes to humans. Maybe it is not too surprising that much of Darwin's principle explaining the descent of man inspired much of the research into animal parallels with human speech and language. However, in our family tree (primate tree) that we share with Gorilla (gorillas), Pan (chimpanzees, bonobos) and Homo (humans), we are the only complex vocal learners. That is, we have the ability to modify acoustic and syntactic sounds and acquire new sounds through learning from others. In stark contrast the avian family tree, hummingbirds and the common ancestor of parrots/cockatoos and songbirds show immense complex vocal learning[3]. But why would birds have the same type of intelligence or even evolution as primates? The last common ancestor of primates and birds lived 300 million years ago.

To make sound, humans and other animals rely on the larynx, an organ located in the neck close to the mouth. While, like humans, birds have a larynx, their main vocal apparatus is called a syrinx. The syrinx is hidden deep in the body at the end of the trachea, close to the forking of the bronchial branches that go into the lungs on each side of the body[4]. This means birds have two exhaling airstreams impinging on their vocal organ rather that one as in humans. The syrinx varies in complexity from species to species.

In Australian magpies, for instance, song development is related to the development of syringeal muscles and the brain, with audible vocalisation beginning a few days post-hatching. Full song is only produced once the syringeal muscles have fully grown. Depending on the social context, song sequences can vary; for example, magpies have many different call types sending different messages. The calls may be short and harsh or, in full song, tuneful, melodious and very extended depending on the message the bird wishes to communicate[5].

While attempts to teach apes speech have failed, their symbolic communication through gestural movements has exceeded expectations. Chimpanzees have learned to manually combine several visual symbols in order to 'sign' with humans[6]. However, their ability to learn vocalisations is considerably more limited. In all cases where vocalisation has been achieved these abilities have required extensive training[7]. We are still unsure to what extent vocal learning may depend upon a gestural motor system.

Primates and birds can both produce emotional and/or spontaneous sounds, apparently innately. However, only humans and song-learning birds seem to rely primarily on a forebrain motor system for learned vocalisation[8]. Birdsong is a complex learned behaviour involving the song system region of the brain. Similar to the motor cortex part of the brain in humans[4]. Again, similar to human speech but unlike most other animal vocalisations, birdsong is a culturally transmitted behaviour. For example, a particular song is widely accepted and copied by others in the group.

As songs are typically learned early in life, how well young birds learn greatly affects the efficacy of their signals as adults[9]. There is increasing evidence that female preferences, like male song repertoires, are influenced by cultural transmission. Among the few species studied, it has been found that the type of songs females experienced when young are generally preferred over unfamiliar songs in adulthood[10]. Learned preferences thus influence which songs within a population are attractive. Cultural preference for a particular song can guide mate choice and even lead to mimicry of the song by all males.

Vocal imitation appears to be an important precursor in the evolution of spoken language. It is a trait we share with certain marine mammals, parrots, hummingbirds and songbirds, but it is absent in non-human primates. Juvenile songbirds learn to sing in a process that is strikingly similar to the development of speech learning in humans[11]. In the first few months of their lives, juvenile songbirds listen to and memorise one or more songs from their parents. These memories can be stored for many weeks or even months before being recalled[12]. Different bird species vary considerably with respect to learning strategies during song development. To what extent songs change in adulthood varies greatly among bird species. In human infants and juvenile birds of many species, there is a listening phase preceding a production phase[13]. We listen before we learn to speak. When speech or song production starts, both humans and songbirds produce vocalisations that are quite different from those of adult conspecifics[14]. During well-defined stages, starting with babbling in human infants and subsong in songbirds, vocalisations gradually come to resemble adult forms[15].

Despite our 320 million years of separation and looking very different, Australian birds and humans have an important trait in common. We both can live in family groups and are constantly interacting with other individuals from other groups close by. Like us, birds can form long-term partnerships and their offspring can find it hard to establish territory so spend longer at home. The parent birds make them pay rent by helping to gather food to stay at home! Working in cooperation and respecting social rules is what determines survival. Working in sync with others and at times living in high density with others means a need for communication. Did language evolve in humans and birds to address a need for social communication, to tell another what one is thinking? To master a language, one has to learn the correct use of words by interacting with other members of the community. Such interactions fundamentally shape the way individuals think and act in the world[1,16]. Many joint behaviours, such as mating, predator avoidance, and putting the kids to bed, depend upon accurate production of social signals and others' understanding of them. Development of these behaviours is strongly influenced by interaction with other group members, as a story sent to me by Linda shows.

SLEEPY RED-BROWED FINCHES

Linda Kendall

I was watching a somewhat frazzled-looking, adult red-browed finch shepherd his fledged brood of five up to their old (I assume) nest and put them to bed. The nest was right outside my window but unsuspected. The parent supervised while each of the young crawled through the walls of the nest and settled for the night. This at 6 pm in summer so the parent clearly believed in early to bed. The young

> were very young, with white still at the corners of their mouths and not much red on them. I had the pleasure of seeing this performance twice and will be looking out for it again next year.

To maintain group harmony, individuals must be able to meet their own requirements as well as coordinate their behaviour with others in the group. They need to be able to defuse any direct and indirect conflicts that may occur in group living, for example when many group members are foraging in the same small area. When living with others, a bird needs to show flexibility in its behaviour and at times give way to more dominant birds. To show behavioural flexibility within a social situation—that is, the ability to flexibly adjust behavioural responses depending on external conditions—may be essential for individuals in making the most of group living.

Social complexity derived from living with others has long been considered to have an important role in the evolution of a flexible and intelligent mind[17]. Birds that live in social groups (in contrast to solitary species) have evolved particular cognitive adaptations for maintaining relationships with others[18]. Group living favours an individual's ability to interpret, predict and respond flexibly to change.

In 1963 a Louisiana State University business professor, Leon C. Megginson, said during a lecture:

> According to Darwin's *Origin of Species*, it is not the most intellectual of the species that survives; it is not the strongest that survives; but the species that survives is the one that is best able to adapt and adjust to the changing environment in which it finds itself. Applying this theoretical concept to us as individuals, we can state that the civilization that is able to survive is the one that is able to adapt to the changing physical, social, political, moral and spiritual environment in which it finds itself.

Australian birds have been living by this rule for a long time and we could learn from them! In terms of our own lives, to be cognitively flexible is to change the way we think or feel about a situation or an indivdiual. Since its emergence in the 1970s, this simple concept is a key principle of cognitive behaviour therapy. Changing the way a person thinks has been used as a therapeutic approach in psychological therapy and stress management programs all over the world. Many of us can get anxiety and even depression from living in a social world. Cognitive behaviour therapy has been used for management of daily life stressors, from minor hassles to major psychological challenges. While we may not be able to change people or alter our life circumstances, we can change the way we think about them. We are capable of changing our thinking to help us adapt better to our social surroundings. We can, for example, try to see things from another's point of view, especially if they are a stable individual in our lives.

Science is discovering more and more evidence of intelligence in birds who share our urban environment. Ravens and crows (family corvidae) and magpies (family artamidae) are shining examples. Being adaptable helps birds to survive in an unpredictable world. It is unpredictable with regard to finding food sources and having to interact with others to learn about them, but also unpredictable in terms of living with other personalities in the group. Whether it is a lifelong partner you see every day, a neighbour you see occasionally, or an unknown individual, like us, a bird encounters a range of individuals with whom it shares a variety of relationships.

Very much like birds, we live in an unpredictable social world. As long as other individuals are involved, there are aspects of our lives we cannot control; so, like birds, we need to think and behave flexibly in order to work with others. Long-term relationships, such as social monogamy, foster an enhanced ability within individuals in a pair to read their partner's behaviour and possibly to read their mental states. To maintain group harmony, individuals must be able to meet their own requirements as well as coordinate their behaviour with others in the group.

Social monogamy with bi-parental care is the most common breeding pattern in birds, occurring in 75 per cent of species, but we are still unsure how a bird chooses its mate[19]. If we think about the peacock's tail as a display of good genes, we would expect all female birds to mate with the highest-quality male. A bird might show mate preferences based on bringing together combinations of good genes. What about birds in long-term relationships with another though? Where they bring up the chicks depends on both the male and female working together cooperatively. Could mate choice, similar to us, arise from behavioural (phenotypic) compatibility of two partners? Could compatibility of the pair in terms of personality type affect breeding success?

Compatible partners could, for instance, be better at coordinating tasks and sharing them, or better at complementing each other's performance on various tasks. Mate choice for such behavioural compatibility might be especially important in species with intense bi-parental brood care (it takes two to raise offspring) and important in sustaining long-lasting monogamous bonds that persist even when not caring for young. In the next story, Saluay describes a partnership between two butcherbirds raising their offspring.

POLITE BUTCHERBIRDS

Saluay Hall

We have been in our house for twenty years now, and have fed butcherbirds since we arrived. We are now feeding the fourth generation of six families which we have observed over the years. We can recognise individual birds via small beak markings, etc.

> They are currently feeding hungry nestlings, and each year at this time they become bolder. They arrive at dawn on my kitchen window ledge and sing beautifully until I bring out some food for them. This continues for a couple of weeks until the desperate struggle to feed young families eases. Then they return to more usual patterns of singing in the lilli pilly tree where I have bird feeders hanging for the daily ritual feeding of many kinds of feathered friends.

There can be a risk in committing to one individual. This includes the risk of bearing a disproportionate share of the costs of reproduction, for example in having to make more feeding trips because your partner is too busy attending another female's nest. Individuals must be especially careful in choosing good-quality mates who will be reproductively loyal and play their full part in vigilance duties, ensuring they are time-shared appropriately[20]. Could social monogamy be more valuable than sexual monogamy? Let him play away from home—you might too!—as long as he comes home to feed and help look after the chicks, even if they are not his.

A study of socially monogamous species with bi-parental care focusing on zebra finches found that females showed little consensus regarding the most attractive males[21]. Behavioural compatibility was important, possibly because offspring mortality, once offspring are hatched, primarily results from the behaviour of the caring parents[22]. Divorce (switching partners) or pair disruption (due to the death of a partner) has been associated with decreased reproductive success, suggesting social monogamy is a strategy that may maximise reproductive fitness via coordination between partners. The assumption that offspring mortality depends on parental behaviour supports the idea of mate choice based on behavioural compatibility, with behavioural compatibility among pairs offering benefits in mate choice.

The study found that when females were *assigned* partners—in other words, when a bird is forced into partnership (to mate and raise young) by the experimenters—the female responded less positively to courtship and tended to copulate less frequently with her partner[21]. The males in these forced partnerships showed poorer nest attendance during the egg-hatching period. The lower nest attendance during hatching by males in forced partnerships could indicate a reduced motivation to care for the young or defend the nest, leading to greater offspring mortality and egg loss.

Evidence to support the benefits of pair coordination comes from studies showing an increase in breeding success with time spent together. It is suggested that individuals choose each other based on their respective personalities which would determine their behavioural compatibility[23]. Individuals that show similar behavioural typology or similar flexibility (and therefore predictability) could be better at negotiating or coordinating their actions, therefore having fewer conflicts over parental care and higher reproductive success[24].

Social relationships are crucial for living in cooperative groups but are also prone to generating conflict which can damage relationships. Losing a conflict can lead to a higher possibility of additional attacks by the same aggressor. Flexibility in forming groups does not mean that flocks are simply anonymous crowds that aggregate near resources such as food. In fact, flocks may consist of different social groups with familiar and/or related individuals forming subgroups. Social support through having positive nurturing relationships with others may help to reduce the effects of unpredictability in others and to alleviate stress. Social support is not directed towards random individuals but rather specifically towards close affiliates or bonding partners, and the quality of the social relationship determines the amount of social support given and received. Individuals thus engage in various affiliative interactions with others. The formation of social bonds is valuable because, in times of conflict, bonded birds tend to support each other during fights. They win more fights than non-bonded birds.

Ravens, for instance, form non-breeder groups that are characterised by close social bonds shown through affiliative interactions and selective cooperation. Affiliated birds give each other support and console one another after conflict with other individuals[25]. Recent findings have further revealed that ravens are able to remember such relationships, even for years. Ravens' social bonds are pivotal in daily social life, and whether or not individuals can rely on a bonding partner affects their status in the group and their ability to secure resources such as food. This is because they have more bonding partners with whom they share more positive interactions[26]. A bird may have different types of valuable relationships simultaneously, which requires the bird to be highly flexible in its behaviour when negotiating social relationships. In our next story, Johann describes social bonding and knowledge sharing in a cockatoo.

INJURED COCKATOO

Johann Stewart

I am a wildlife carer and one day a friend rang to say she had an injured cockatoo in her yard. When I arrived there must have been at least 100 cockatoos in surrounding trees, on roof lines and along fences, all watching as I picked up the injured one. He had a broken wing which an avian vet pinned, then sent us both home with several weeks of physio. At the end of the 'course of physio', the vet cleared him and the pin was removed.

I asked my friend what time the cockatoos gathered around her house and we returned at this time. Again there was a huge flock and they all went silent as I set the cage in the centre of her backyard and opened the cage door.

> The injured cockatoo hopped out and two cockatoos came down beside us. He looked at me and the three flew off and then the flock all rose and circled above, the noise was deafening. I stood in the yard and cried.
>
> For months afterwards, I had to rewire my cage doors for all my birds in care because a cockatoo came in every day at 3 pm to try and open the cages. I often wondered if it was my injured one visiting and had learned how to open the cage while I was looking after him.

It seems likely that the injured cockatoo had shared his knowledge and experience while in care with others. Did the injured cockatoo show others where he was kept and how to open the cage? Is this story an example of social learning through sharing knowledge in a group? That is, other birds learning a new behaviour from an individual who has had a unique experience. Very much like us, when we find a new trick that could be helpful to others we care about, we share the experience to add to our knowledge base for future reference.

Johann's story tells of a new behaviour being shared and practised by others. Was this learning motivated by finding new food? The cockatoos visited at the same time each day. I wonder whether this was when Johann was providing food for other birds in their cages. An interesting question might be: could the cockatoos use this knowledge about opening a cage and apply it to other cages they may encounter? We can only speculate.

The idea for this book came from the stories sent to me by people who notice the behaviour of birds around them. A major theme in these stories is birds showing personalities. The fact that our common urban birds have intelligence and show unique behaviours that make a bird more than a bird, an individual in fact, is a further theme. Throughout this book I hope to share knowledge with you that will help you to understand some of these behaviours.

The magic of this book is that, while it might answer some of your questions, it will leave you with new ones to ponder. I hope these questions will inspire you to find answers through supporting further studies of the birds around us. I feel we still have a lot to learn, that we might even be underestimating the birds that have adapted to and are even thriving in urban areas—those birds that share our space and are always watching us.

In the next few chapters, we will learn how and why birds differ in their behaviour and what causes personalities to form. In chapters 4 and 5 we will investigate how the changing Australian environment has led to intelligent birds who survive by learning from others and by working as part of a team.

In chapters 6 and 7 we will learn how Australia as a country of resource boom and bust makes finding those resources, such as food and water, vital. These resources can disappear as fast as they appear. Birds need to find them quickly and communicate their finds to others. With this information shared, the birds work as a team to find the water or food.

In chapters 8 to 10 we will move from why birds need to communicate to *how* they communicate. We will explore how a bird interacts with others to learn from its experience and to form memory.

Chapters 11 and 12 show how working as a team is vital in Australia, home to the most diverse group of cuckoos in the world—birds must communicate and cooperate to outwit these cuckoos. We will examine what happens when a bird doesn't play by the rules and cheats instead. Is the cheat punished?

In chapters 13 and 14 we will explore how birds often display human behaviours, such as grieving, conducting funerals and engaging in play. Are birds really saying their last farewells to the fallen, or is something else going on, such as gossiping about the dead bird? And do birds play for fun, or are they playing in order to learn how to interact with others and use tools?

Chapters 15 and 16 consider the old English saying, 'Necessity is the mother of invention'—and urban birds are inventors! Given that an urbanised Australia may well be the future, birds are learning how to live with us and us with them in that environment. And working with others leads to innovative behaviour.

In the final chapter we will discuss the most controversial way in which people interact with birdlife: by providing food. Do birds become so dependent on our handouts that they would starve if we stopped? There is no doubt that we live in a country ruled by birds who live in societies very much like our own. Is it any wonder we want to connect with them?

Chapter 1
THE FRIENDLY BIRD

Do you ever wonder what birds are talking about as they fly by? The sounds and songs of birds constantly surround us as we go about our lives. But what are they talking about? Or are they even talking or just mindlessly squawking and chirping? Is there a message in what the birds are telling each other? Compared to European cities, birds in our urban areas are much bigger and louder in their vocalisation. One of my personal favourite calls happens between bonded magpie larks. When you hear one call, you always hear its mate answer. Why are birds so loud? A possible reason could be birds have more to talk about in Australia and there are more individuals who are motivated to listen.

When compared to the rest of the world, Australia has a high number of birds living in groups made up of individuals. These group members work together to survive in a country with unpredictable food and water. Just like us, the lives of birds such as parrots, cockatoos, honeyeaters, crows, ravens and magpies are filled with social interactions. And, just like us, they need to communicate with each other: to let one another know what they are thinking.

The white settlers' fascination with Australian birds began very early on. In 1788 naval officer and surgeon Dr Arthur Bowers Smyth, on board *The Lady Penrhyn*, reported in his journal that: 'The singing of various birds among the trees, and the flight of the numerous parraquets, lorrequets, cockatoos and macaws made all around appear like an enchantment.' In 1837 Charles Darwin and birdman John Gould had a conversation about this:

'You're not alone in your fascination. These birds do exercise a strange power over us,' said Darwin. 'Were you aware that when New South Wales was colonised, convict, surgeon, redcoat—no matter what class—all shared a passion for the penal settlement's birdlife?'

'Everyone, it appeared, was in a rush to pick up a pencil and capture the bright creatures flitting about,' John Gould replied. 'I'm not surprised by the colonials' interest in their unique birdlife. Who could resist such distracting beauties?'[1]

Like us, many Australian birds are highly social creatures, living in cooperative societies with others. We share similar life trajectories to corvids, parrots and artamidae families (such as magpies, butcherbirds, currawongs) in terms of having a relatively long childhood before gaining independence and living long lives. We don't start our own families until later in life, instead putting learning and survival above having babies early. This seems to be a common trait in Australian birds compared to European birds, who breed earlier and have shorter lifespans.

Breeding age can, however, vary with birds. Budgies, for example, can breed at three months, while satin bowerbirds wait until they are seven years old. But just because a bird can breed doesn't mean it will. Among superb fairy-wrens, for example, a study found that lack of available territory and/or willing females often means that the male remains a bachelor for years[2].

In order to live in harmony with others in your group, you must be able to change your behaviour and even learn from another individual—this is a show of behavioural flexibility. In science, this ability has long been viewed as an indicator of intelligence[3]. For example, research has found that birds can learn to manufacture and use tools to solve problems insightfully and even plan for future needs. This shows birds are capable of using their own experience to anticipate the future behaviour of others, including humans[4].

We share similar characteristics with birds such as vocal learning, and we have individuals in our lives with whom we interact at different times and share information with them. These characteristics, while uncommon in most primates, are found in birds including parrots/cockatoos, corvids and the artamidae family[5]. Understanding how birds form and maintain relationships in complex social groups can aid our understanding of social behaviour in these cognitively complex species.

In this book we will explore the different relationships birds have with each other, and how they convey their messages. A bird has relationships of different status, from neighbours to life-partners and offspring. It needs to convey different messages to each of them. Duetting, for example, is used to help reaffirm bonds between individuals, playing an important role in the vocal communication system of birds[6]. Duetting is a specific form of communication in which one bird initiates a call and another one answers. Another type of vocalisation are contact calls, which are short and used to stay aware of each other's presence while flying and feeding (for example, magpie larks). This call usually consists of a short, high-pitched sound, recognised and duplicated exactly by mates. Very much like children playing the Marco Polo game!

Magpies produce some of the most complex songs and have one of the largest range of vocalisations of any songbirds. They can project sound at very high decibels and may be able to produce entirely different sounds simultaneously. In our next story, Bill tells of a magpie whose song had him wondering if the bird had listened to jazz legend John Coltrane.

JOHN COLTRANE, THE MUSICAL MAGPIE

Bill Coleman

While listening to our local neighbourhood magpie doing his morning warbling, I realised that he was making two notes at once! Not only this, but both notes moved together and appeared to make complex patterns in harmonic thirds. Similar to the music of saxophone legend John Coltrane, this bird's cascading notes overlapped in a way that seemed to reflect a mathematical symmetry. I've been totally blown away by this, and every time I hear a magpie I'm now listening closely to his call and wondering if there is more to it than we've given them credit for!

Birds that live in family or cooperative groups are constantly interacting with each other. This means you need a brain that is capable of learning (that is flexible), and driven to trying new things. Groups or families can change in size, structure and composition so birds need to learn who is who in their group and recognise new individuals.

Being social and having others to rely on is thought to have played an important role in the evolution of intelligence[4]. This may be due to the complicated social pressures that come from group living. One such pressure is the need to understand and adapt to a mate and to others in the group. This requires a flexibility of behaviour that is particularly important in societies in which individuals have a history of interactions with others.

A number of Australian birds have cognitive abilities that match and even surpass those of mammals[5]. Corvids and parrots/cockatoos, for example, appear to be cognitively superior to other birds, rivalling great apes in many psychological domains. Cognition has been described as 'the mechanism by which animals acquire, process, store, and act upon information from the environment'[7]. Biologist Irene Pepperberg provides a helpful analogy in one of her papers: 'The structural differences between mammalian and avian brains are like the wiring and processing differences between PCs and Apple Macs. However in both cases the resulting output (i.e. behaviour operations) is similar.'[8]

Although there may be fundamental differences in the size and structure of avian and mammalian brains, recent evidence suggests that they share advanced cognitive abilities[4, 5]. While our brain neurons were sorting themselves into cortical layers to generate complex behaviour, birds were developing another neural architecture altogether[9]. Some bird brains are packed with very high numbers of neurons where it counts, with densities akin to those found in primates and with connections much like ours[4,5]. They have the ability to replace old brain cells with new ones that help the brain to be flexible so it can constantly learn. New neurons provide increased behavioural flexibility permissive for learning new and/or overwriting old memories.

You might be wondering how humans and birds, who are separated by a 320-million-year gulf of evolution, can have similar skills and abilities when it comes to social interactions? As we discussed in the preamble, the common ancestors that we share with birds were reptilian-like stem amniotes that lived more than 320 million years ago. During the course of this long, independent, evolutionary divergence, birds evolved in Australia while it was still part of Eastern Gondwana, while humans came out of Africa in Western Gondwana. In both environments, working together in cooperation was the winning trait for species survival.

Surviving in Eastern Africa and Australia required dealing with the unpredictable appearance and disappearance of food and water, while watching for predators[10]. While we were evolving to stand up and walk on two feet, birds were perfecting lightness and flight to move between patches of food and water. We both felt safer in groups as we crossed the landscape in search of food and water. Bigger numbers in your group means more individuals to help you find what you are looking for. But you need to tell others if you are looking for food, water, or somewhere to raise a family. Constantly interacting with others means trying to predict their moods and behaviours as social environments are ever-changing and largely unpredictable[5]. Group living requires considered and flexible responses to others, not just on some occasions but on a regular basis, even over lifetimes[9].

The size of a bird's social group can influence the information a bird chooses to transmit and the mechanism by which information transfer happens, for example a loud call for all to hear or a soft call just for one individual. How efficiently information is understood and used by others can also depend on group size[4,9]. Therefore group size is connected to social complexity which influences the cognitive demands placed on the bird. This may be the reason birds have evolved a flexible brain: to allow them to process and retain information about social relationships, such as those with flock mates[5,9].

The social intelligence hypothesis supports this and suggests that the social pressures of group living have driven the evolution of a flexible, intelligent mind[4]. Observations of social interactions among captive chimpanzees first prompted the hypothesis that social living and interacting with others plays an important role. The hypothesis suggests that those who are good at keeping track of the identities and interactions of numerous individuals within large social groups will do better than those who are less proficient[10]. In other words, a charismatic and outgoing personal type works well when interacting with others to make alliances.

Birds from the corvid, parrot and artamidae families have relatively extended periods of juvenile development. That is, they pass through a long childhood before they reach/start breeding[5]. It is during this time that birds have the opportunity to learn from others and explore their environment. The bird could learn through social learning from watching others, such as offspring observing parents[11]. Another type of learning is through individual learning while exploring the world around it. Similar to us, long-lived birds appear to accumulate knowledge throughout their lives from interacting with others and from their own experience[5]. They can use such knowledge to make better decisions and be better prepared to solve and adapt to future problems. It allows food to be found even if it is in a novel environment, as our next story tells.

OUT OF THE RAINFOREST

Dave Tribe

A couple of years ago I was over from England to visit my daughter. We spent a couple of days in the Daintree area of Queensland where we spent our time walking the various rainforest tracks and looking for cassowaries. A bit disappointed on our final day not to have seen one, we paid a visit to another of the local attractions, Daintree Ice Cream Company. The place was very good with a nice selection of flavours made from native ingredients. Anyway, we noticed a small crowd forming by the orchard, and, being human, went over to see what was going on. Well, who would have expected to see a male cassowary at the ice cream shop, let alone with his three chicks! They got a lot of attention as they poked around the fruit trees until they made their way back to the rainforest where they belonged.

As I said earlier, many of the stories sent to me ask the same question—Can a bird have a personality? In humans, is it our personality that makes us an individual, makes us who we are? Our personality or phenotype is a combination of our genetic material and life experiences. For example, how people interact with us and how we interact with them over long periods of time can help shape our personality.

When a bird is long-lived with a long childhood of interacting with others, it too could develop a personality. A bird who is a shy individual in comparison with others would have had different experiences that affected how it interacted with others[12].

Birds, such as parrots, cockatoos and even wrens and thornbills, can form groups that are stable yet break up over the course of a day. We call these fission–fusion societies; societies in which numerous individuals move into and out of groups at various times of the day and night. A fission–fusion society is one in which size and composition change throughout the day. Do we live in a fission–fusion society? We move from our family group to a work/education group where we learn and contribute to society, then back to our smaller group at the end of the day where we share our day's events. As birds in pairs or small groups move through their environment, they merge into a larger group (fusion) at certain times such as when feeding or roosting at night. During fusion, learning happens. The birds talk to each other to find out who is present and who is not, and who are the dominant individuals and where they are in the roost. In the morning these groups might split (fission) into smaller groups to go about their business.

For instance, at night-time roosts or midday napping roosts, birds in these groups not only need to recognise other individuals but also understand intergroup relationships, for example the social status of individuals relative to other group members (dominance rank)[13]. They do this through communication, as Hannah found one morning.

SCREECHING CORELLAS

Hannah Tribe

One Sunday morning I was abruptly awoken by a raucous screeching flock of white parrots (little corellas) who had decided to interrupt my only lie-in of the week. I peered out of the window at the

> neighbouring garden, and thought, 'Heavens! There must be over a hundred birds in that gum tree!' Considering my own half-awake state, I wondered what matter could be so pressing, firstly that they needed to jabber so aggressively over each other and secondly, at six o'clock in the morning!

Possibly what Hannah was hearing was the birds discussing who the dominant birds were, re-establishing bonds from the previous day, and asking who knew where breakfast could be found! Birds maintain their place in fission–fusion societies in a number of ways, including special bonding calls, drumming, and even dancing[5]. Individuals in long-term partnerships can evolve to match each other's state, to be in sync with another bird by changing body state. By doing this, the bird is sending information to another bird such as, 'I am thirsty, let's find water now.' They can do this through coordinating behaviours, such as synchronising their body movements, social displays and vocalisation. This allows messages to be shared between two bonded birds, possibly about what is happening in the moment.

Birds can also use a wide range of body postures for communicating a particular message and magpies are a great example of this. Some of the body postures issue warnings not to approach, such as an outstretched neck or sleeked-down head feathers. Others postures convey appeasement or submissiveness messages. A distinct submissive/appeasement gesture by magpies, also used by currawongs, is the flutter of the wings involving not the entire wing but mostly the primary feathers. Submissive behaviour can also be expressed by magpies; by falling down and rolling over on the back and exposing the belly[6].

Birds can use social cues, such as head and eye direction and pointing, that we can understand. So is it no wonder that when we meet we want to communicate, as our next story shows.

JULY THE MAGPIE

Anthea Tomkins

I have a great story to tell about birds, one in particular, a magpie named 'July'. She was a wild bird living at Aireys Inlet in Victoria. July was hand-fed prime minced steak. Mother would give her some meat saying, 'Did you have a nice day today?' July would reply as only a magpie can. 'That's nice,' Mother replied. July was named 'July' because that was the month in which they first met.

One day when my friend and I were visiting, we walked upstairs towards the lounge room where we could hear Mother talking to July, and July's song in response. We presumed Mother had left the glass door to the balcony open. Indeed she had! And the flywire screen door as well . . .

There sitting in the house on the back of a dining room chair was July 'talking' as only a magpie can and Mother saying, 'Have you had a nice day, July?' July responded. 'How are your babies? Did you enjoy the nice warm day?'

Birds can behave in ways we are hard-pressed to understand yet seem so similar to our own. They seem to communicate with us and challenge us to understand what they are saying. Birds being very vocal reflects their need to communicate with and connect to others, especially their need to communicate the importance of working for a common goal, such as raising young or finding food. Both birds and humans rely on mates to navigate the harsh environment of post-rainforest Australia.

Throughout this book we will explore how this helps a bird to make friends and to live in cooperative societies. Like us, birds have different levels of mateship, different for those with whom they interact on a daily basis, such as neighbours, and those they see occasionally, like an old friend. Birds use these relationships to gather information from various individuals, perhaps about food or water in new and different habitats. However to gain this information, a bird must work cooperatively with others and maintain relationships. How a bird does this is the topic of our next chapter.

Chapter 2
THE COOPERATIVE BIRD

For a bird, life in Australia means having mates. Others who they can trust and work with to locate food and water that can disappear as suddenly as they appear. A bird flying over Australia sees a flat continent, so working as a flock high in the sky means more eyes to locate the resource. If a bird works with others and shares knowledge about important resources, the bird, in turn, can rely on information from others. In cooperative societies knowledge is shared frequently. Was it in part this trait of working and living with others that perhaps made birds become so interested in us?

Among magpies, a bird that many of us encounter daily, personality shines through. While taking notes for John Gould, Mr George Bennett wrote of the magpie in his *Wanderings in New South Wales*: 'It is a bird of much importance in its own estimation. Struts about quite fearless of danger and evinces on many occasions great bravery. The bird was kept around homesteads to announce intruders where it provided in effect the warble of a canary and bark of a dog.' Bennett also remarked on how tame the bird could be, as David and Hilary found out.

MOST UNUSUAL OF MAGPIES

David and Hilary Ambler

In 1995 a most unusual magpie entered our lives. He arrived one eventful day and claimed us as his own. Saved by neighbours a year or so earlier as a seemingly orphaned fledgling, he soon made himself at home in three local households. He endeared himself to us all and was always free to come and go as he pleased. For many months he stayed with my wife and I and our Devon Rex cat and Staffie-cross dog. He soon ruled the roost!

He often slept in the house and would let us know he was awake by making his way into our bedroom. He would hop onto the bed and try to wake me. Sometimes I would resist his attention by pretending to be asleep. He would then try to open my eyes by grasping my eyelids with his beak. If that failed as it sometimes did (provided I clamped tightly enough), he would then thrust his beak up my nose and, grasping some nose hairs, would brace his feet on my bare chest and tug with all his strength. That always worked.

I enjoy doing crosswords in bed of a morning. He would grasp the end of my biro and then flop as if dead whilst still hanging on to the biro. I just ignored him. If he tired of being ignored he would let the biro go and then proceed to rip the newspaper into narrow quarter inch strips starting at the top. That got my attention.

The behaviour described above suggests the magpie was playing and getting into mischief! The magpie was displaying the behavioural traits of persistence and playfulness to see if it could get David's attention. As we talked about in the last chapter, interacting with others requires a mind that is flexible in its thinking and responses. Not just on some occasions but on a regular basis, and even over a lifetime. It benefits the bird to be an open-ended learner: to continue to learn from experiences throughout its life[1].

The key to group living is having a range of individual personality types with different experiences. This variation in behavioural types within a group (such as shy and dominant individuals) can be helpful in the group's response to novel challenges. This is because living in a group increases the chances that an individual will have experience and knowledge that other members don't possess[2]. Working together to solve problems as a group may be a survival trait for birds living in Australia.

Environmental factors are thought to influence how a bird behaves, suggesting climatic variables like temperature and rainfall may be related to patterns of sociability in groups of birds[3,4]. Australia's climate can be described as being the source of boom and bust resources such as water and food. Birds need to move quickly to find these resources before they disappear, often suddenly. Moving in a group means there are more eyes on the lookout for food and water. This would help explain why Australia has such a high number of bird species living in cooperative societies.

What enables birds to display such a range of behaviours when interacting with other individuals? Plasticity of the brain neurons is the key. Plasticity means having a flexible brain that is able to learn new skills and adapt to a new environment[1]. Brain neurons are the basic working units of the brain. They transmit information to other nerve cells, muscles or gland cells. The bird's brain can even replace the neurons that die. This means the brain is capable of learning new information from the environment and from other individuals[5].

A new type of neuron we knew nothing about was discovered which helped us further understand the importance of the bird brain. Mirror neurons were found in the human brain in 1992, and in the bird brain in 2007[6]. Mirror neurons have been described as the neurons that shaped civilisation[7]. It is widely assumed that mirror neurons were designed by evolution to enable understanding of action. That is, understanding what others are doing and how to copy what they are doing[8].

One of the remarkable features of mirror neurons is that they are active when we (birds and humans) are performing an action, but also when we are passively observing an action performed by another individual[9]. Mirror neurons enable us to reliably interpret the actions of others by comparing those actions against our own action repertoire. Such a process seems especially well suited to different aspects of communication[10]. This is because the matching capacity of mirror neurons could promote action understanding. In other words it recreates in the observer the same state as the observed. Mirror neurons have been shown to be an efficient mechanism of imitative learning because they are active and firing while watching the actions of another.

For the observer, this could provide a template for generating similar actions; mimicking the behaviour of another. For example, mirror neurons are activated when a bird is listening to another's song and firing most vigorously in response to sounds that are being imitated. Mirror neurons enable communication by establishing an equivalent neural representation of actions performed by the self and by others[11].

Juvenile songbirds learn to sing in a process that is strikingly similar to the development of speech learning in humans[12]. The reproduction of learned vocalisations is a primary component of human language that has evolved since we diverged from our last common ancestor, the chimpanzee[13]. In both humans and songbirds there is a phase early in development when auditor-vocal learning is accomplished, called the sensitive period. In the first few months of their lives, juvenile songbirds listen to and memorise one or more tutor songs. These memories can be stored for many weeks or even months before being recalled to guide imitative vocal motor learning[14]. Birds such as zebra finches tend to learn one song type as juveniles and stick to that song, while magpies show considerably greater variability in song, learning new songs as they grow[1].

A behavioural trait that allows individuals to successfully maintain important group relationships may become widespread throughout the population. You might, for example, find out about a predator because your mate has suddenly left the area, and you see your mate running. What are your actions? To start to run too! Not walking or hopping, but running, copying your mate's behaviour. One could speculate that the ability to behaviourally mimic another is evolutionarily advantageous.

Individuals who show the ability to cooperate successfully with others are desirable in a group. This is because such behaviour maintains harmonious relationships[15]. These individuals are more likely to continue to be included in the group and are therefore better able to survive. Research found that members of socially meaningful groups are mimicked to a greater extent than those belonging to other groups[16]. Individuals synchronise more readily with those with whom they share group membership. In addition, imitation can also serve as a means of reducing social distance when one has been excluded from a group[15].

The need for collective action raises the question of how individuals in social groups (i.e. fission–fusion societies) decide what to do and how and when to do it. Finding food, for instance, would require group members to decide on the location and timing of foraging activities[17], requiring a decision-making process. This can happen when one individual takes the initiative and provides direction. Others follow that direction, as in a leader-follower relationship. The leader-follower relationship is when one or a few individuals steer the behaviour of others in the group.

The key to those relationships is the need to coordinate movements[18]. The leader-follower relationship can be used for group activities such as mobbing predators and helping feed offspring. For instance, while in their night-time roost, birds exchange information about a resource such as food and the means to reach it.

When they fly out of this tree, in which direction will they go? Who will they follow? To produce the appropriate behaviour, the group members must exercise joint attention. Joint attention happens when two or more birds focus their attention on a single bird—the leader[19].

Is the leader always the first bird to leave the roost? What is this bird's motivation for leaving first? Those individuals most in need of a particular resource are more likely to be the leader because they are highly motivated[20]. Hunger can be a good motivator and other birds may interpret the bird as flying from the roost to locate food. Others from the roost follow this bird in the hope that they are correct. This is assuming that resources such as food can be acquired by individuals investing effort in searching for food or by exploiting knowledge by following the leader. For example, in ravens, individuals with superior information can guide groups to important resources such as food[21].

How important are personality differences in these roosts? For instance, do bold individuals always emerge as leaders while shy individuals are followers? Having unique knowledge or expertise increases the likelihood of an individual emerging as a leader and attracting followers. In species with dominance hierarchies (superb fairy-wrens, for example), the breeding individuals often take on leadership roles. What is interesting in many cases is that dominant individuals lead not because they enforce followership, but because they are better positioned to elicit followership since they hold a particularly strong influence and have an established importance within the group—such as the breeding male. The dominant fairy-wren is often the oldest and therefore has the knowledge to survive. Other birds want to learn this knowledge and pass it on to others in their group. By watching the actions of others, a bird can learn about predators, about prey and about potential mates[19].

Research on humans has shown that age correlates with leadership in domains that require considerable knowledge and training, but not in domains that require risk-taking and physical bravery[22]. Moreover, humans are extremely good at estimating the expertise of other individuals, even in newly formed groups, and knowledgeable individuals often emerge as group leader[23]. In the next story sent to me by Jill, a magpie appears to think he is very much part of a group that includes Jill's family.

OSCAR THE MAGGIE

Jill Favero

The bird I remember most is Oscar the magpie. My front yard was a fenced-in dry bit of lawn at a cottage attached to a large farm. One morning, after a big storm, a bedraggled magpie was shivering at our back door. He (or maybe she) stayed close by for the next weeks— and months— despite farm dogs and cats around the cottage. I don't remember why but I gave him the name of Oscar. I continued to feed him and after a few days all I had to do was call 'Oscar' and he'd swoop in. I was heavily pregnant at the time. In rare moments I'd take a rest on a banana lounge in the yard. Oscar would approach, hop up on my belly, and perch there until I got up. He used to cock his head and watch me—close up.

When the baby (my second) was born I'd wheel her in an old pram up the dirt road to the main farmhouse. Following the pram was my 18-month-old son, the pet dog and cat and, overhead, Oscar. My son came with me into the house, but the dog, cat and Oscar waited outside until I walked home again.

Did Oscar adopt himself into this family? Did he see himself as a pet as he waited with the dog and cat? Birds that live with others need the ability to recognise individuals and to remember who is in a relationship with whom. They need the ability to apply this information, to recognise and respond appropriately to others' emotional and mental states. Associating with known individuals should provide greater positive benefit than associating with unknown, random individuals[2].

A bird's behaviour is entirely down to its ability to learn how best to act at any given moment. Oscar's next behaviour is very interesting as he appeared to call out for Jill in the presence of a snake. Did Oscar know the snake was a threat to an important group member?

> Oscar's winning moment was when he saved my then-crawling baby from a snake. She'd crawled out the front door onto the front lawn. I heard Oscar's 'Kaw! Kaw! Kaw!' as I'd never heard it before. I ran out to find my daughter metres from a big brown snake. I snatched her up—and made sure the front door was snibbed after that.
>
> A few months later Oscar didn't appear every day. I took a portrait of him one day. The next day he flew off and didn't return. I'd like to think he made his own family and was busy protecting them. The baby that Oscar potentially saved will be 40 this year. The one-year-old that pulls my cat's tail is her daughter.

The ability to refer to external events was believed to be unique to humans, and therefore signals, such as when danger is present, may be a precursor of human language[8]. Signal perception happens when signals elicit an appropriate response from others in the group without the need for other cues, such as the sound or sight of a predator. Australian magpies perform a specific body signal in which the head and body are aligned and oriented towards perched predator birds in their territory.

A study into predator detection and responses by magpies towards wedge-tailed eagles showed a high level of group understanding[24]. It was discovered that when an individual saw the predator, it engaged in alarm calls and beak pointing towards the eagle. Other group members assembled and, after watching the first bird, adopted the same posture by pointing to the location of the intruder. This would suggest that onlooking magpies interpret the signal that a predator was present. They respond by altering their own behaviour appropriate to the original stimulus, not merely imitating the first signaller. The position is maintained until all the group members have indicated that they have seen the predator by giving calls or pointing towards it.

As we have discussed there are many benefits to group living. But there are social rules that must be followed to ensure harmonious living[25], rules that when broken can cause the breakdown of society—and then every bird in the group loses. In these cases, the group members would have to find a new group where they would need to establish themselves and even learn new rules. It is better to keep to the group rule to maintain your position within the group. Older birds usually end up as breeding individuals, so it can be worthwhile working with the current breeding pair.

When a bird behaves badly, others in the group may punish it or even kick the disruptive individual out. It is very important to behave in a socially acceptable manner by following established rules. So you might be wondering, how does a bird find out about these rules? By asking others, of course. By having a good network of other individuals they can trust and gain information from. For an Australian bird it is important to be a good networker!

Chapter 3
THE NETWORKING BIRD

We need to revisit fission–fusion societies, as this is the ultimate way of learning and sharing information with others. This is such an important trait that, among Australian birds, almost all social groups show some form of fission–fusion dynamic over their lifetime. This means birds are constantly interacting with and learning from other individuals. The inherent fluidity of fission–fusion social dynamics presents the bird with a unique set of challenges such as competition for resources. The ability to choose good group mates may be essential to reduce competition and aggression between members[1]. To identify which individuals will make good group mates may require the ability to communicate decisions. This information exchanged within vocal interaction between group members may decide whether or not to recruit an individual. This is because a bird's vocalisation can carry a variety of information about the individual including sex, age and relatedness. The ability of group members to recognise familiar individuals may allow for instant acceptance into a group[2,3].

In order to benefit from social cohesion, individuals in a group must be able to reach consensus decisions[1]. Fission happens when a full consensus is not reached and birds either leave groups individually or in pairs. Larger groups may divide into smaller subgroups when only a partial consensus occurs[2]. This could happen as a result of active decision-making processes but is more generally a result of individuals following social interaction rules.

You may be surprised to learn that partial consensus is particularly important in fission–fusion societies. For a partial consensus, and thus a fission event to occur, there needs to be variation in the costs and benefits of forming social associations with other group members. Although fission can occur stochastically, partial consensuses are typically driven by shared characteristics. In a group with mixed personality types, there might be a few birds that claim to have found food. But what if the food is in different locations? Instead of forming one large group, smaller groups form with each group flying to a different feeding location. Flocks return to the roosting tree that night and share their experience of the day's events. Was food found in all locations or did one group go on a fool's errand?

A prerequisite for establishing and maintaining a complex social system is that the interacting individuals can recognise each other[3]. This requires the ability to discriminate between familiar individuals on the basis of their particular characteristics. Family or group living supports social learning because living with others means memories are formed. The ability to associate previous experiences with the memory of those individuals may further increase the information available to a bird during a decision-making process[4].

It would be helpful if a bird could draw conclusions about relationships with others based on past experience. For example, a bird could draw conclusions about its probability of winning a fight with the same individual who beat him before[2]. Assessment of an opponent may be based on recall of losing in previous encounters with the individual. It may also be based on recalling the outcome of previous interactions with others with similar characteristics, such as body size. In the next story, a king parrot seems to make an assessment about two dogs, as Jane explains.

KING PARROTS

Jane Dow

Living in an area of the Royal National Park in Sydney we have king parrots visiting us. One time we had visitors from the UK on holiday. The first morning of their stay about eight to ten parrots arrived, bringing with them six babies. Well anyone who knows parrots knows how noisy baby parrots begging for food can be. The next thing the rellies were up seeing what was attacking us! They are used to the quiet English songbirds.

Later when I was in the shower, my husband appears and asked who let the parrot in? It seems we had come in and closed the door to our living room and had not seen the parrot sitting on the lounge waiting to be fed. It was unconcerned about our two dogs lying on the floor near him.

Did the parrot know the dogs would not be a threat? Was the parrot familiar with the dogs? Did the parrot have a memory that the dogs were not a threat? If so this would be an example of social memory.

Social learning, where birds learn from each other, enables novel behaviours to spread between individuals. This creates group-level behaviours which are termed 'cultural traditions'. Social transmission of a new trait occurs between interacting individuals. Could group dynamics and population structure determine the spread and persistence of traditions[5]? Experimentally quantifying cultural transmission in wild populations remains difficult. This is due to limitations associated with isolating and training individuals, tracking the spread of information across large numbers of birds, and eliminating individual trial-and-error learning[6].

Birds needs to recognise and categorise group mates by various characteristics: rank in the hierarchy, age, gender, reproductive status, and their position relative to each other. They can do this from monitoring social behaviour, coordinating foraging strategies, and then revising all social information as it changes. Birds need to manage all this social information, and they can do this by accurately reading the social signals of others, by responding appropriately to them, thereby predicting their behaviour, resulting in stability in a successful group.

Stability can result in informational conformity; that is, where individuals match their behaviour to the most common variant when first learning and then continuously update their information and behave accordingly. This strong effect of social conformity increases when individuals disproportionately adopt the most frequent local variants of behaviour. This behaviour suggests individuals in the group favour social over personal information by matching their behaviour to the majority[7].

Kin structure may be important in driving social interactions and patterns of fission–fusion. The indirect benefits obtained by interacting with related rather than unrelated individuals could increase the relative benefits of social cohesion, for instance reduced aggression or aiding social learning between group members[8]. High levels of kin structure were found in colonies of bell miners, with related individuals associating preferentially and being helped at the nest of related individuals. Colonies will come together to form flocks with other colony members in times of need, such as mobbing a predator[9].

Individuals are able to gather information about the relative strength or quality of neighbouring competitors through eavesdropping[10,11]. A bird eavesdrops when it is listening or watching for information between other individuals, avoiding the cost of personal experience and trial-and-error learning. An eavesdropping bird can combine its gathered information with its own direct experience of competitors, all of which provides additional information that can lead to more accurate understanding of the environment, such as where food is to be found.

Many birds have the choice of feeding either alone or with others, but individuals can gain benefits from social foraging. Firstly, group foragers avoid predation better than a solitary individual. Secondly, group foragers can watch the success of others and know where to forage. European starlings, for example, exploit hidden prey, probing repeatedly to estimate the current quality of a foraging patch. Other starlings were found to observe their flock mates' probing success and to use this information to decide when to leave one patch in search of another[12]. Could birds eavesdrop on us? Our next story, sent in by Cayleigh, tells of parrots watching her for cues about food and water.

OVERRUN WITH PARROTS

Cayleigh Mason

We have started every few days putting small amounts of wild bird seed out and made friends with a rather bossy king parrot. He is lovely and brings two females with him. A few weeks ago we had 21 king parrots, male and female, along with seven crimson rosellas waiting in a tree for the seed. It was magical hearing them talk, watching us while we were watching them.

We have lived in this house in Emerald, Victoria, for a year now and birdwatching is part of our daily routine. We are starting to get to know the regulars and are fascinated that within one species there are so many different personalities. We also feel that our daily visitors are comfortable with us being around and when we do the daily birdbath clean and fresh water is available, we hear the birds calling to each other and down from the treetops they come!

Eavesdropping females can gather information on the relative quality of males at little cost and/or risk to themselves. This is because evaluating potential mates might expose them to enhanced predation risk or sexual harassment. By observing the mate choice of another individual, the eavesdropper can gather even more information about potential males. For a young female it may be useful to learn what older females look for in their mate. This information can be used by the young female once she is ready to breed, reducing the need to spend time finding out who would make a good father.

While the individual who eavesdrops may gain information about the two interacting birds, its eavesdropping may influence the nature of the interaction if it is detected by the observed pair. The eavesdropper then becomes the audience, causing a bystander effect—a change in the behaviour of the observed individuals due to the observer's presence[13]. In other words, the audience is not taking part in the interaction, but its presence is recognised by the interacting individuals, causing a change in behaviour. Audience effects can be used to investigate an individual's ability to recognise others' social relationships and even monitor their social interactions.

Why should an individual that notices he is being observed alter his behaviour? So a female can see how committed he is to fatherhood. For example a female budgie can evaluate her mate's commitment to her at different stages during that season. Male parental care is likely to be an important variable in a female's choice of a mate. A male budgie, for example, delivers most of the food required for his mate and offspring throughout the breeding season. Females are primarily responsible for the early care of offspring during which time they allocate food provided to them by their mates. In male budgies, feeding of very young nestlings (less than eleven days) can be a good predictor of their propensity to feed their young when their nestlings are older (more than 25 days)[14].

The female budgie can assess her male's potential as a good provider by using the time he spends at the nest prior to egg laying. The male's attentiveness through mate-guarding his female from other males may be a good indication of his commitment to raising young. For the successful pursuit of extra-pair copulation, a male budgie needs time both to court and gain the cooperation of the female. A male who is courting other females is not as attentive to his mate as one who is not.

To test this, captive male budgies were given the opportunity to court an extra-pair female both when their mates were present as a potential audience and when no audience was present. Males were significantly more likely to court extra-pair females when their mates could not see them. The researchers suggested that female budgies may use mate fidelity in assessing male parental qualities[15]. Males that court extra-pair females only when their mates cannot see them may be trying to avoid weakening an existing pair bond.

Common ravens live in long-term monogamous relationships with their bonding partners and defend a large territory year-round when they become territorial breeders. Until then, ravens join fission–fusion societies that comprise non-breeding groups that can be structured by age, pair-bond status and kinship. Until ravens become territorial breeders, they aggregate in non-breeder groups with constantly changing group size and composition[16]. In a study, researchers found that ravens would modify communication during conflicts according to who was watching (audience composition). When being attacked by dominant birds, victims signalled their distress using defensive calls[17]. Victims were found to increase defensive call rates when their kin were in the bystander audience. In contrast, victims reduced call rates when the bystanders were mates of their attacker.

Another study found that ravens that had been separated for up to three years responded differently to calls of former group members than they did to familiar birds. The researchers concluded that ravens remember relationship qualities of former group members even after long periods of separation[18]. Interestingly, the study suggests that ravens will exaggerate the impression of body size when vocalising to unknown individuals compared with calls to familiar birds. This study confirms that ravens have sophisticated social knowledge as non-breeders that is remembered and even maintained into the territorial breeding stage.

The ravens' ability to differentiate between familiar and unfamiliar individuals in the experiments shows the importance of long-term memory to form relationships. These findings support other studies on songbirds, parrots and cockatoos remembering pair partners and territorial neighbours. It means they are memorising former group members according to nice (affiliates) and not nice (non-affiliates). This can even extend to us. When we share their territory, they will get to know us and then decide if we are nice, or not so nice. So make friends with the birds whose land you built your house on! We will talk more about how to do this later in the book.

Another study on ravens found that they will choose whom they want to cooperate with. This is because the birds already have a pre-established relationship resulting in reduced competition over access to food. Tolerance of another is a good predictor for cooperative success. The study also found that ravens were less likely to cooperate when they had been cheated out of food but it depended on who the cheater was. In contrast, the cheating bird remained motivated to cooperate and continue cheating by taking all the food[19]. The research suggested that ravens' choices to cooperate or to defect follow some sort of tit-for-tat rule. That is, the bird remembers the negative experience of being cheated and this leads the bird to not cooperate with the cheater. The study found that ravens who were paired with a friend resume cooperating earlier after being cheated on than those paired with a non-friend.

The researchers suggested a learning mechanism may be at play, in which birds learn that cheating is beneficial, as they always cheated whenever they got the opportunity[19]. While this is an interesting study, we need to remember the ravens were in captivity and may have changed their behaviour as a result. In the wild, ravens have been found to flexibly adjust their behaviour depending on their need for a cooperative partner in competition for food[20].

These studies on ravens show long-term memory could be particularly important in fission–fusion societies as it is common in many Australian birds. This is because individuals may meet regularly after long periods of separation. Similarly, memory load may increase when social relationships of group members need to be remembered, in addition to individual identities. Dealing with social relationships is often considered a critical driving force in selecting for long-term memory.

The question of whether cockatoos/parrots who learned human words can recall them once they are back in the wild is interesting. Even more interesting would be to know if they remember how to use words correctly. In our next story, we may have found the answer.

A COCKY LITTLE BIRD!

Carole Lawrence

One day I was hanging out the washing on the clothesline in the backyard when a flock of sulphur-crested cockatoos flew screeching overhead. Just to be cheeky I called out, 'Hello cocky!' in a loud voice. I got the shock of my life when one of the cockatoos from the flock dipped down and called out 'Hello cocky!' in return and then flew off with its mates.

No doubt it was an escapee from captivity and I was so happy to see that it had found a flock of cockatoos that had accepted it.

When a bird talks, it has something to say and others listen. It is not just mindless chatter or chipping or squawking. Instead they are actually talking to each other and sharing knowledge with group members who they have relationships with. This encourages cooperation of group members through sharing knowledge and working together. Why is mateship in birds so important? We need to go back 40 million years to help answer this question, as the history of Australia is important to help us understand what we are witnessing today. Working together as groups appears to be a winning trait for many Australian birds. A possible reason for this may stem from a common Gondwanan ancestor. Gondwanan Australia (40 million years ago) was covered in dense dark rainforest where birds kept track of each other through vocalisation.

Chapter 4

THE DINOSAUR BIRD

Australian birds are the descendants of the flexible few dinosaurs who survived the last mass extinction, and who, along with reptiles, evolved on the supercontinent Gondwana. More specifically Australia was part of Eastern Gondwana—and today's birds have a long claim to Australia, New Zealand and New Guinea as home[1]. These first avian dinosaurs who evolved alongside dinosaurs did not become extinct 65 million years ago, instead they adapted to the changing world and ruled the daylight hours. Our first ancestral mammal species was active at night, perhaps to stay out of the way of the dinosaurs.

The key to survival was adapting to the new habitat that earth formed. Birds did this brilliantly and today we can still see this. Today the last of Gondwanan rainforest is fragmented, and ancient rainforest dwelling birds are venturing out and adapting to the drier habitat. In our next story, Margaret tells an intriguing tale of a pair of catbirds.

PERFECTLY NAMED: CATBIRD

Margaret Warner

Three years ago I heard a catbird call and a pair of them was sitting on an Indian hawthorn bush at our front window. I chopped some grapes and banana and took it out and both birds showed their appreciation by eating it immediately. Later the same day I heard a noise as though someone was knocking on the front door. It was the catbirds back again. One was tapping the window with his strong beak.

Catbirds are bowerbirds, part of the corvid (crow) family. Along with others, including brush turkeys, lyrebirds, treecreepers and honeyeaters, they are the living outcomes of tens of millions of years of evolution. These birds moved out of the rainforests as Australia started to move north and become arid[2]. Birds had to adapt to a changing environment, from wet rainforest to fire-prone sclerophyllous vegetation, both woodland and shrubland. Sclerophyllous vegetation, including eucalypts, grevilleas, banksias and hakeas, evolved to cope with the hot and dry summers by developing leaves that are small, narrow and thick to reduce water loss.

The fossil records support the idea that rainforest habitat is the most ancient component of Australia. This ancient habitat declined with the expansion of the more dry-adapted sclerophyllous flora between 35 and 50 million years ago[3]. The shift appears to have been driven primarily by climate change as the Australian continent drifted north. Increasing aridity and warming, plus possibly deficient soil conditions—low levels of calcium and nitrogen—changed the flora, encouraging the diversification of sclerophyllous woodland[4].

Today we know Gondwana was a major source of flowering plant and perhaps bird evolution in response to this new niche[5]. Is this why Australia is the birthplace of birds? The expansion of flowering sclerophyllous woodlands offered new food resources to which birds were able to adapt. It has been suggested, for example, that the cockatoo ancestor appeared some 33 million years ago when open sclerophyllous vegetation dominated the Australian landscape. The vegetation changed into a mosaic of remnant fruit-driven rainforests and other broad-leaf forests to dry flowering sclerophyll communities that overflowed with nectar, while across the increasingly dry interior of Australia, open grassland and saltbush plains became dominant[6]. The landscape had changed from dense wet rainforest to dry fire-prone vegetation that favoured the thundery stormy climate of the time. For example, the plants adapted to the frequent lightning strikes to aid reproduction.

For a bird, did living in rainforest Australia require the same level of cooperation and learning? Let's go back to Margaret's catbird. Unlike other bowerbirds, catbirds are unique as they do not build a bower; instead, they are socially monogamous birds, staying with the one mate for years[7]. Two heads are better than one! Could these dinosaur birds be capable of learning from others? In the next part of Margaret's story, the catbirds try a new behaviour, copying the parrots to exploit a new food source.

> How did they know that I am to be found working in the office at my computer most afternoons, especially when they are very irregular visitors? They would come around for a few days then I wouldn't see them again for months although they were probably close by. They certainly didn't forget though that I work in my home office in the afternoons.
>
> I had no idea why these elusive birds would suddenly become so familiar. The only answer was that they had observed the king parrots who sometimes sat on that same bush calling for seed in the breeding season. They maybe figured, very correctly, that if they asked the food would come! I took a little more fruit out. The same routine followed for a few days and then I didn't see the catbirds again for

several months. In the interim we cut back the hawthorn fearing that the bird's strong beak might actually go through the glass.

Bowerbirds are a good example of birds' adaptation to the drying Australian environment. Satin bowerbirds, for example, have a wide distribution across a range of habitat types, from rainforest to open woodland. A study found that male satin bowerbirds adjust their calls to their environment type[8]. Calls given in denser habitats, such as tropical and subtropical rainforests, use low frequencies and have very little or no trills. In contrast, calls from the more open eucalypt habitats use higher frequencies and longer trills. As bowerbirds are ancestrally a rainforest-living group[9], call differences in the bird may reflect divergence in vocal characteristics following a move into more open and acoustically different habitat.

Bowers built by birds of eight species in three genera (*Sericulus*, *Chamydera* and *Ptilonorhynchus*) are found in habitats ranging from closed forest to open grasslands in New Guinea and Australia. Birdman John Gould reported that 'bowers were considered by some explorers to be the cradles of the infants of Aborigines and the mound of brush turkey to be ancient burial mounds', while many early Europeans thought they were nests made by the female. It was Gould who noted that they were sites for sexual display and mating[2].

Anthropologist Donald Thomson in 1935 reported that, 'Although the bowers of these birds are often built close to native camps, the birds are not molested. Bowerbirds are not eaten and Aboriginals do not destroy bird life wantonly.'[4] I would love to know why this was. Let's speculate. First of all, is there even much to eat on a bowerbird? Did Aboriginal people witness the hard work of the male as he prepares his mating area? Interestingly, Thomson said the bowers were built close to native camps. This would suggest that there was adaption to human changes before 1788. We have a serious lack of knowledge regarding bird–human interactions pre-1788. But we will talk more about this later in the book.

Back to bowerbirds! Bowerbirds are unique among animals in that males build and decorate elaborate structures. As we now know, bowers are only used for courting females, as females do not associate with males after mating.

Male bowerbirds build and decorate their bowers in different and possibly even unique ways. During sexual displays, the male will pick up and toss decorations about, or hold them in his bill to better expose them to visiting females[10]. It has long since been recognised that some aspects of bower-building go well beyond mere skill development into individual differences and preferences in the design of bowers. This suggests that bowerbirds have their own views on what is artistic, with their personalities invested in the design of their bower[11]. A story sent to me by Wayne tells of these preferences.

IN MY GARDEN: SATIN BOWERBIRD

Wayne Green

The owner of the bower was very popular with the ladies. Sometimes he would be busy dancing and doing his display repertoire and there would be two or three other female birds hopping around in the bushes nearby or peering down watching the displays and inspecting the bower. The bower was decorated with predominantly blue objects (plastic straws, pegs, milk bottle tops and the plastic rings which sit under the tops, crimson rosella tail feathers, toys and pieces of plastic). One day he decorated the entry and floor of the bower with fresh straw from a hay bale he must have found nearby where there were a couple of horses!

The bowerbird's bower is an extension of the bird himself, an artistic statement to show off who he is and how sexually virile he is, all to help reel in the ladies[11]. We need to consider that the sexual display of bowerbirds encompasses not only the construction of the bower, but also his dance. During a dance, males may bring their bower into the performance by grasping the end of the walls of the bower and shaking them during displays. As we will read about later, this is a behaviour shared with lyrebirds[12]. In both birds, the male is bringing together various natural elements of his environment in a coordinated manner, producing a construct that performs a function that his body alone cannot achieve. We will talk about dance in a later chapter also.

Part of the female bowerbird's choice of males is based on the quality of his dancing. As a result, males will put time into practising and improving their dance, even perfecting their own unique dance steps. They will even change their dance and behaviour in response to female signals during courtship, adjusting their displays[13].

Studies suggest that bower construction appears to demand high levels of learning and planning: bowers get better with experience, as the bird ages. Bowerbirds have a long childhood in green plumage when they can be seen hanging out in groups. What is going on in these groups? Learning! Bower-building skills appear to derive from learning by observation[14]. The ability to learn is integral when constructing and maintaining bowers.

Immature satin bowerbirds, for instance, build practice or rudimentary bowers. These bowers are very seldom, if ever, visited by females[12]. Unlike most bowers built by mature males, they are not the product of a single individual. Instead they are built, decorated, and even destroyed by a group of young males who do not yet maintain their own bowers. At these practice bowers, older immature males display to younger males, suggesting that these sites provide an opportunity for young males to practise building and decorating with their peers while learning from older (only slightly more experienced) individuals.

At times immature male satin bowerbirds will visit adult bowers[15].

Here they do not gain any reproductive success; in fact, they are generally only tolerated when females are absent. Young males may learn adult traits by observing adults at their bowers. This can be seen in Wayne's story about his bowerbirds.

> Sometimes I would observe a bird (either a mature male or a green bird) fly away with an object in its mouth. On inspection, it was noticeable that the bower had been vandalised and most of the decorations stolen. However, next day, the owner would have repaired and redecorated it again, ready for display!

There are several examples of behaviours of bowerbirds improving with age. This would suggest that practice over time can improve performance—just as in humans. The objects chosen for use in building the bower are also refined with age. For instance, young satin bowerbirds tried to use thick twigs of the wrong shape when building their first bower. They also chose objects to use as decorations in a much wider range of colours than those used by adults. A satin bowerbird typically takes between four and seven years to acquire an adult-style bower[16]. Over these years he is perfecting his own style, bringing his individuality to his bower.

As it is the female bowerbird's preferences which influence the quality of the bower[17], many females end up selecting the same male, while many underperforming males are left without mates for copulation. Females who mate with top-ranking males tend to return to the same male the next year and to spend less time searching. It is important to a female to know which males have the best bower as it means they save time in the breeding season. Indeed, research found that older females visited fewer males during a mating season, their search patterns suggesting that they built up knowledge of local males and their attractiveness over time. When an especially attractive male died, these older females visited a larger number of bowers in the following mating season[18].

Researchers have found that female assessment of bowers also changes with age. This would suggest learning capacity in female bowerbirds. Young female satin bowerbirds paid close attention to the number of blue items in a bower, while older females paid more attention to the dance of the courting males. The researchers suggested that young females relied heavily on rough cues; their discernment develops with age and experience[19].

Female bowerbirds often inspect a bower multiple times to see if the design meets their high standards. A study showed that when blue items in the bower were replaced with red ones, the bowerbird immediately picked up the offending item and carried it off, as far away as possible[20]! Such preferences vary between species: for example, female satin bowerbirds prefer large numbers of blue items[21], while female spotted bowerbirds prefer large numbers of green berries[22].

It was found that individuals building better quality bowers also demonstrate high quality mimicry[18]. These findings suggest that mimicry improves with age and this could provide females with a clue as to male age. Vocal mimicry provides an excellent opportunity to investigate patterns of learning, with differences in vocalisations apparent between populations.

Many bowerbirds are accomplished vocal mimics; it is likely that their vocalisations are the product of learning[12]. Vocal mimicry is, by definition, learned and is expected to vary between populations. Females prefer to mate with males that can accurately mimic many different species of birds—another way a female assesses the male's genetic quality through his prowess in vocal mimicry.

Could humans be influencing the bowerbird's evolution by providing durable blue items for them? One idea about their preference for blue items is that bowerbirds choose the colour that best accentuates their own colour[18]. In our next story, Julie describes what appears to be a female teaching another how to gather blue pegs.

BOWERBIRD

Julie Russell

We have many satin bowerbirds in our yard in Spingwood, New South Wales, and surrounds, and have had several lovely bowers constructed. One day I was going to the clothesline when I noticed a mature female perched on the wire next to our peg basket. She was accompanied by a younger female who she was very clearly showing how to toss the pegs out and look for the blue ones! They have trained us well as we now use a different style of basket.

If blue pegs and milk bottle rings are deemed more desirable by the female, then males would surely realise this. Remember the social brain, and learning from others? We might wonder whether males will begin to compete for man-made items in preference to flowers and feathers.

In regard to these very desirable colours in man-made items, I have had a few very sad stories sent to me about bowerbirds with blue milk bottle rings around their necks. Please do not provide these rings for your backyard bowerbird! Wayne's story shows the constant threats to birds of living alongside we humans.

I didn't realise how inherently dangerous displaying or decorating the bower could be for the birds until one morning I noticed a green-coloured bowerbird sitting on my (pedestal) birdbath, so I watched it, anticipating it was about to bathe or drink. But it didn't, it just sat there (for probably ten minutes), hardly moving. The bird was closing its eyes (half dozing), which worried me that it was sick. Then I noticed something blue in the corner of its mouth.

To my surprise, the poor thing had a blue plastic ring (those which sit under milk bottle tops) in its mouth and it had slipped over its head to form a gag! The bird couldn't open or fully close its mouth, preventing it from drinking or eating properly.

Unwittingly, we humans sometimes create materials that connect perfectly with the traditional ways in which certain bird courtships are conducted. As Wayne saw, the male bowerbird is especially taken by bright blue things such as those rings that snap off the caps of milk bottles when they are opened. Alas, as Wayne described, the ring can flip backwards and become trapped behind the nape of the bird's neck. This can permanently muzzle the male, then strangle him or ensure that he slowly starves. This is an example of a behavioural preference we don't want passed on, but perhaps females would eventually favour males that avoid getting the blue ring stuck!

I will leave you with the following story about a bowerbird finding a very interesting item for his bower.

AN URBAN BOWER

Carol Kerstholt

In May there were some new and surprising light-coloured objects in the bower in the garden. On closer inspection these items were condoms. They looked like they were found in a muddy puddle. He put three together and one was separate.

Many of the items he has brought look like they were found in dirt or mud. I asked the mechanic at the service station (who knows about the bird and the bower, with a collection of some of the bits of the service station dog's toys ending up in the bower) if people were leaving the 'items' in the large metal bin (accessible to the public). He suggested they could be from the nearby uni car park.

That's urban adaptation right there!

Chapter 5

THE 1788 BIRD

One of the most important considerations for the English in establishing themselves in Australia was that it could be a self-sufficient colony. That is, to establish free settlers who would farm the land using convict labour to provide food for its people. This would mean not relying on England to send food ships, so the need to establish agriculture was an urgent one. The parrots and their friends had other ideas, however. Would it surprise you to learn that 'The first grain grown in Australia was plundered by king parrots, rosellas, bowerbirds and currawongs'? This was observed by naturalist George Bennett who also reported that, 'Multitudes attack a field of corn or grain and are then so bold as to be with great difficulty frightened away.'

Bennett's report also shows that, in response to the advent of farming, parrots changed their feeding behaviour to exploit the new European farms:

> The parrot population being now divided in flocks about the different fields, when formerly they made their formidable attacks

> upon one or two only and then in such numbers that when left undisturbed for only a few hours, it would suffice to destroy the hope of the settler, at all events for that season. It was computed that thirty or forty thousand of these birds were about the field at one time; and from what I saw, I do not consider the numbers were exaggerated. It is not only ripe grain that suffers from them but when it commences to vegetate they assemble in immense flocks to root up and devour it.

What Bennett saw could be the first written record of Australian fission–fusion society! I find it amusing that perhaps one of the challenges to the establishment of England's undesirables and free settlers in Australia was the need to outwit these very smart birds. We will talk a lot about fission–fusion society throughout this book as it is the ultimate way to learn from others about food and water, as Dawn and Ralph found out.

BIRDS EAT OUR FRUIT

Dawn and Ralph Angus

The other raiders of the fruit and veggies, I can tolerate. Pale-headed rosellas at the guavas, currawongs stealing strawberries, crows at the tomatoes, cockies at the sweetcorn, fruitbats (not exactly birds, I guess) at the mandarins and, astonishingly, masked cuckoos at the chillies. (I have read that birds are not affected by chillies.) Still, there is enough to keep two old pensioners amused.

Might parrots and indeed other birds have outsmarted the early settlers by having a knowledge of the land that Europeans did not have? While parrots and cockatoos caused damage, they were not without their charms, as John Gould wrote of galahs 'enjoying perfect liberty and coming round the door to receive food in company with the pigeons and poultry amongst which it mingled on terms of intimate friendship'. Did the galahs learn how to exploit food by watching the success of the domestic chickens getting fed and deciding to try it for themselves? Was this a new behaviour learned from other birds? Was it an innovative way of obtaining food spread to others?

Cockatoos and parrots come from the same ancestor and they branched away from each other around 40 million years ago[1]. Today urban parrots and cockatoos occupy a wide range of habitats and feed on a variety of different food sources. It is speculated that the successful adaptation of cockatoos could have been driven in part by bill adaptation[2], as this may have allowed the birds to move into previously unoccupied niches. Some of those new food sources require manipulation (for example, large banksia seedpods) while others do not (small grass seeds and nectar).

Two types of bills evolved in cockatoos to gain access to the new food provided by the changed habitat[2]. The psittacid type is a Swiss army knife in its multi-functionality but highly specialised for shelling seeds intra-orally; this is the typical parrot-type bill. The calyptorhynchid type is also multi-functional but with reduced transverse mobility of the mandibles, requiring the assistance of the foot while eating. Larger-bodied cockatoos are a strongly lateralised species who eat large seeds extracted from seedpods; this requires manipulation with a limb. These cockatoos perch in a tree and extract seeds from seedpods by holding the pod in one foot and using a number of coordinated foot–beak actions[2]. Large black cockatoos (*Calyptorhynchus* species including the red-tailed, glossy black, yellow-tailed and carnaby black cockatoos) show a strong preference for arboreal habitat. They can be seen foraging, mainly for large seedpods, among branches at the top of trees, rarely foraging on the ground.

The foraging habits of black cockatoos, using their bills with their feet to extract seeds from hard-walled fruit, means they can make quite a mess while eating, as Kay reports.

YELLOW-TAILED BLACK COCKATOO

Kay Watson

Never was there a less appropriately named bird than the yellow-tailed black cockatoo, for I find the sound of these birds as they call above the treetops to be one of the most joyous sounds I know—black they may be but there is nothing funereal about them. The glint in their cheeky eyes communicates a sense of mischief. In fact, I was once told that these magnificent birds with their resounding, sonorous calls bring good luck.

There is, however, no such good luck involved should you find yourself walking beneath pine trees that bear the favoured food of these cockatoos. While they are not a common visitor to suburban gardens, if you are lucky enough to live near trees bearing hard-fruiting cones, you may well come into contact with a number of these birds. Summer brings pine cones, and half-eaten pine cones dropped from a great height can be rather disconcerting.

These messy eaters have no compunction about dropping debris on your head, as I found one January day when I was drawn to a spot beneath a neighbouring row of radiata pines by sounds of crunching, falling bits of vegetation and high-pitched snatches of avian 'conversation'. Given the number of falling missiles I dodged that day, I suppose we should be grateful that bunya pine cones are too large even for their powerful, heavy-duty beaks!

Approximately 22 million years ago, cockatiels were the first species of cockatoo to diverge from feeding in trees to feeding on the new open grass habitat that replaced rainforests[1]. The colonisation of open grassland with easy consumable seeds is believed to be the major factor in the loss of lateralisation of foot and beak when foraging. Cockatiels developed a new bill type (psittacid) to adapt to the physical characteristics of the new food sources[2]. Grass seeds are simply too small to handle, so these items are grazed on by the smaller-bodied species and shelled intra-orally rather than being manipulated by a limb in coordination with the beak.

Fourteen million years ago, other species of cockatoos including galahs and corellas, joined cockatiels in colonising the newly available open grasslands[1]. Corellas and galahs started to feed on seeds of grasses, tubers and roots. Although these birds can display lateralisation when eating hard-shelled fruit, this ability was not as important for the new food.

As in cockatiels, the parrot-type bill was used to eat softer and smaller seeds, but could also take tubers, large seeds and cones. Long-billed corellas possess a uniquely specialised and long upper mandible used to dig out a variety of storage organs from native plants, including tubers[3]. The diversification of cockatoos is believed to have been driven, in part, by this bill adaptation and specialisations that allowed it to move into the new niches.

What about parrot evolution—the Psittacoidea family? It is speculated that the modern parrots evolved about 23–25 million years ago[1]. The rainforest fig parrot was common in New Guinea as well as Australia and may even be the ancestor of today's parrots. Was it the parrot that took the risk and came out of the rainforest to say g'day to the new landscape? It is speculated that the fig parrots then broke into two different types: the lorikeets that went for the nectar, and the budgies that went for seeds. As few early fossil parrots have been found, it is still not known who a common ancestor of today's parrots may have been. But one thing is known for sure, and we can see this when we look at the parrot bill, the similar adaptation of the bill we see today in all species of parrots evolved to help them consume the abundance of grass seeds on offer in drying Australia. All parrots have the same type of bill; the sharply curved upper beak topped with a muscular prehensile tongue to help manipulate seeds.

Another thing we know is that many species of the families of parrots/cockatoos, corvids and artamidae had a few things in common to aid adaptation to new Australia, including forming year-round monogamous pairs which travel, roost and forage in temporary groups or societies. These groups/societies are formed by transient individuals coming together to learn about food and/or water in the area, or even further afield. When this happens, we refer to birds as being in fission–fusion societies. As these societies of birds are constantly changing, there is a need for a bird to be able to identify known individuals.

Let's recap. A fission–fusion society is one in which size and composition change throughout the day[4]. As birds move through their environment, they merge into a group (fusion) at certain times, such as when feeding or roosting at night. In the morning, these groups might split (fission) into smaller groups to go about their business. Birds in fission–fusion societies often interact with new individuals; the group can therefore be fluid. Fission–fusion societies enable linkages between birds across all levels of populations and are thought to facilitate behavioural plasticity[5]. As in these societies, it is vital for birds to understand what other individuals are saying in case it is something that is important!

As a bird needs information about the group it has just joined, it is helpful to know an individual already in the group. The bird needs a way to give a direct signal to specific individuals and not the whole group. One way a bird can do this is through vocally matching. Vocal matching happens through imitation in which the bird alters its vocalisation type to copy and match that of the bird with which it is communicating. Vocal imitation of individuals' distinct vocalisations allows birds to address specific individuals within fission–fusion societies.

What happens if the bird knows no-one in the society, but still wants to join? In these instances, rapid call convergence allows birds to mediate interactions with individuals that they have not previously encountered[6]. This can include individuals with whom they will rarely or never interact in the future. Rapid call convergence happens when the bird produces a close match to another call, and does this very quickly. The call can be the call of the dominant pair in the society, and the bird can do this without needing hours to learn this new call before it is produced[6]. The bird does this through imitation of the dominant call using those mirror neurons we talked about earlier[7].

The research suggests that these fission–fusion societies assemble for the purpose of social food and water finding. They serve principally as information centres from which knowledge about the location of good feeding and water areas may be obtained. The information learned during fusion could play a critical role in successful individual responses to finding patchy resources in a changing climate. The Australian climate is characterised by periods of drought followed by rain that can result in floods. Seeds germinate after the rains, leading to a boom in resources in certain areas.

These fission–fusion societies may have been key to the successful acquisition of knowledge about food and water distribution over the flat continent of Australia. There are no massive mountain ranges or vast bodies of water to stop birds crossing the country and sharing information about patchy food and water[8]. Many of our birds from fission–fusion societies learn what others know, whether it is about a predator in the area or how to find water in a drought.

Information about good feeding places is learned not only from other birds in the neighbourhood but also from birds who have come from further away and have knowledge of food and water in an unknown area. It is even more valuable if these distant birds are a different species in mixed flocks, such as we see among parrots and cockatoos, galahs and corellas, or king parrots and rosellas. It is these individuals who are especially desirable in one's society. Why, though, should a bird tell others of a feeding area, let alone a bird of another species?

It is possible this behaviour evolved in response to patches of food that were too large for one bird to consume[9]. One might speculate that food such as grain disappears quickly if not eaten promptly; otherwise the finder might benefit more by defending the food source than by tolerating other birds coming to share it.

Should the area be denuded of food by the birds, or the food source disappear for some reason, the birds can quickly determine the whereabouts of a new feeding area by taking advantage of the information available in the societies in which they have mixed regularly. Information can be gained by personal experience, from smaller flocks and from larger night flocks. While sharing this information birds can be very loud, as Sue reports in our next story.

LIVING IN AN AVIARY

Sue Woods

We often feel like we live in an aviary. Right at this moment I can hardly hear myself think for the flock of little corellas that are screeching around our house. We are located in a semi-rural area where there are quite a few large red gums growing, including on our one-hectare patch and, of course, all the parrot-type birds like these trees. We are extremely grateful that they decided to roost in a different location this summer and spared us the 4 am wake-up calls.

Imagine an individual flying out of the roost at dawn to a particular feeding area where it has fed successfully on previous days, only on this day to experience difficulty in finding enough food; the area no longer offers adequate food as it has done previously. The bird flies to a smaller day roost (a napping roost, for example) where it may spend time resting and drinking and trying to plan for finding lunch. The bird is hoping to follow a flock that knows of a good feeding area. However on this occasion the new area visited by the small flock is poor.

The small flock returns to the main roost that can consist of hundreds of individuals who have spent that day also looking for food. When the mood of the roost is good, this might be an indication that the majority of its members are behaving in the manner of successful feeders[9]. Other birds pick up on this mood, deciding between them that the site visited by birds in the afternoon is clearly worth returning to the next day.

While we can only speculate on the roost mood, we do believe chatter between roost members could allow the unsuccessful individuals to obtain information from others. We can speculate that there must be a marked behavioural difference between the successful individuals arriving at the roost from places where they found sufficient food and the unsuccessful birds which did not.

Roost mood is based on the excitement of planning a trip; it leads to vocalisations and interactions between members of the roost. For example, who will be followed, and whether food or water or, even better, both will be found? As we know this behaviour of continuous loud chatter, starting as the birds roost, can continue until after dark. The chattering begins again before departure at dawn: individuals need to find out which way they are heading once they leave the roost, and who is leading the group to the promised breakfast as Sue described.

It is possible that the choice of birds to follow is made before departure, provided the behaviour of the successful birds is distinctive. An indication of this could be the chatter occurring for some time before the departure. The individuals needing the information might hang back until other birds set off purposefully, and then follow these birds.

Might these fission–fusion societies among many of our birds have evolved in response to the conditions of post-rainforest habitat? Other birds which form these fission–fusion societies, and which we often hear before we see, are honeyeaters and lorikeets. These birds are the topic of our next chapter.

Chapter 6
THE NECTAR-LOVING BIRD

As we have discussed, the movement of the Eastern Gondwana continent resulted in rainforests giving way to a new vegetation type: sclerophyll vegetation. This vegetation was encouraged by the climate at the time that caused frequent fires resulting from thunderstorms. As we discussed in the last chapter, the new sclerophyllous vegetation was dominated by flowering plants[1,2]. One of the most readily recognisable characteristics of eucalyptus species is their distinctive flowers and fruits (gumnuts). Eucalyptus is a diverse genus of flowering trees and shrubs with more than 700 species native to Australia. Not surprisingly this is a very important plant as a mature eucalypt may take the form of a low shrub or a very large tree.

Eucalyptus trees and shrubs were favoured in evolutionary terms because they thrived on fire, infertile soils and year-round sunshine resulting in flowers producing huge amounts of nectar. The amount of rainfall is vital in nectar production; in periods of high rainfall the plant produces excess carbohydrates. This is why birds are often very active after rain and can suddenly arrive in huge numbers following the break in a drought. This rich, sugary, carbohydrate-laden nectar is found in flowers of trees such as wattles, eucalypts and paperbarks, and in a range of our native plants[3]. It is assumed that Australia's large size, erratic climate and boom and bust of resources make it beneficial to be able to fly to reach those resources as quickly as possible once they become available[4,5].

Did the flower favour birds over insects as a vehicle for pollination? In Australia, honeyeaters are major pollinators of many plant groups, including banksia, dryandra, melaleuca, hakea, and of course eucalyptus. In eucalyptus trees, the flowers evolve to make nectar accessible for as many bird species as possible. A specialised bill is not required, allowing birds who don't even favour nectar to take it. It is possible that birds may have been attracted to the insects feeding on flowers and casually started to discover nectar. This is supported by research that found honeyeaters will switch to insects under conditions of reduced nectar availability[6]. In unpredictable climates it is better to have two sources of food than one.

Parrots, of course, also wanted to consume this new food source, with today's swift parrots being thought to have evolved from granivorous (seed-eating) ancestors. Nectar-eating Australian parrots have slender beaks that are much weaker structurally than those of similar-sized granivorous parrots[7]. This is reflected in their reduced dependence on hard foodstuffs. Research suggests that swift parrots first evolved in the southeastern blue gum forests of Australia as there was an absence of lorikeets at this time[8]. Lorikeets spread into Australia from New Guinea, possibly through strong flight adaptation to enable island hopping, and were quick to respond to the new food. Rainbow lorikeets in particular are a native threat to swift parrots through competition, and today in addition to habitat loss, swift parrots only breed in Tasmania. After breeding, swift parrots migrate to mainland Australia, where they overwinter until returning to Tasmania in early spring. The parrot will feed on other flowers and invertebrates when flowers of their favourite blue gums are not in season[7].

The plumage of lorikeets and swift parrots tends to be tighter and glossier than that of parrots and cockatoos. This is thought to be an adaptation to prevent the soiling of feathers by nectar[9]. Australian honeyeaters usually do not share this adaptation, but the bare facial skin on species such as friarbirds and blue-faced honeyeaters may serve a similar function.

While the parrot family evolved the swift parrot to take advantage of the new flowering habitat, Australia also evolved honeyeaters. Research suggests that Australian chats are possibly the smallest living ancestor of today's honeyeaters. These arid-adapted species have a bill that is short and slender but also possesses a brush-tipped tongue. Spinebills are part of the honeyeater family that originally inhabited dry heathlands and woodlands and then spread into other areas and eventually into backyards[10]. This suggests that heathland-adapted spinebills were one of the earliest examples of honeyeaters adapting well to the drying of Australia and today can be common in urban areas.

Honeyeaters, who are part of the passerine (songbird) order in a family called meliphagidea (which also includes wattlebirds, miners, chats and friarbirds), diverged from songbirds approximately 45 million years ago[11]. At this time Australia was drying and eucalypts became the dominant vegetation alongside banksia and grevillea. Today, there are approximately 75 species of honeyeaters that feed on nectar but will take insects and fruit, with at least one species in every part of the continent[12]. How important the evolutionary relationship between the honeyeaters and the dominant eucalyptus species is is uncertain. We can speculate it must be a strong one as so many of these plants are fertilised by honeyeaters. While it is not completely clear why birds pollinate many of our plants, one possibility is that honeyeaters may be more reliable pollinators than insects.

Did these new, nectar-producing plants favour bird pollination over insect pollination? After all, the plants seem to want to attract birds by displaying their bright flowers overflowing with nectar. From the plant's viewpoint, perhaps birds could increase pollination between plants better than a bee[13]. Looking at this from the plant's perspective, longer-distance dispersal decreases the likelihood of inbreeding, suggesting that pollinators that travelled greater distances might be favoured. Birds are bigger than insects and can fly further between plants than insects. Being large, however, birds require more energy than insects. To adjust to this requirement, plants with bird-pollinated flowers tend to put more energy into nectar production.

Eucalyptus plants, for example, often produce large flowers to accommodate bird pollinators[6]. As honeyeaters are a highly mobile species, it could be a response to the patchy flowering eucalyptus landscape[14]. In addition, could they learn from others about where they found flowering plants?

Honeyeaters as a species are rarely territorial over a large area; rather they are territorial over a flower or a plant, even a tree[15]. Just as we saw in the last chapter with parrots and cockatoos, honeyeaters will also form fission–fusion societies where information can be gained. As a result, there can be a local abundance of birds in areas where there is copious nectar production. As a result honeyeaters display ownership of flowers to keep other individuals away. Plants appear to encourage this behaviour as they need to ensure fertilisation with a distant plant. Studies have found that while nectar-giving flowers are defended by larger honeyeaters like wattlebirds, smaller honeyeaters can still access them. As a result, there can be many different sizes of birds feeding on one tree, and they are constantly interacting, as Allan found out in our next story.

DEATH OF A DUSKY

Allan Pratt

We have taken delight in watching more than ten of the species that are regulars on the property. These include the Lewin's, duskies, scarlets, white-throated, white-naped, yellow-faced, eastern spinebills, blue-faced, browns and New Hollands. We adore them. Their colours and antics are the stuff of Walt Disney.

And, in keeping with the Disney theme, they dance and sing and mischievously chase each other around. All is sweetness and light . . . or so we thought.

But then something sinister happened, more in keeping with a Stephen King novel than Walt Disney. Two New Hollands actually *caught* a fleeing dusky and savaged it.

The New Hollands flew off but the distressed little chocolate creature was prone, clinging on to life. Sadly, the bird expired some time later.

While Allan's story is an extreme example of interaction between two species, honeyeaters can interact in mixed flocks while feeding on nectar. The defence behaviour of honeyeaters suggests that the plant is getting a greater pollen carryover from a wider diversity of honeyeaters.

This goes back to the high level of interaction of the fission–fusion society. This is in contrast to insects and flightless mammals which are less social and less likely to spread pollen[13]. Relentless feuds of birds over flowers ensure that pollen-dusted birds are always coming and going as birds interact with each other. In birds, pollen is usually found on the forehead, face and chin feathers, or on its beak. High mobility and social behaviour among honeyeaters when interacting with others helps pollen transfer and promotes diversity in plants that they pollinate. A honeyeater engages in a variety of social activities throughout the day. These can include participating in breeding tasks, foraging, bathing, and maintaining and defending territory.

The patchy nature of nectar, as a result of patchy rainfall, results in mass movement of nectarivorous birds in search of flowering plants[15]. Being a nomad in an environment such as Australia's may provide advantages over other foraging strategies. Nomads may be better able to persist in a landscape under severe conditions than resident specialists who stay in the same place. This is because they can move and switch between different food sources. For example, red wattlebirds and noisy friarbirds can forage singly, in pairs, or in small groups[16]. They can also form foraging flocks, sometimes numbering in excess of 100 individuals.

Noisy friarbirds and red wattlebirds are both common and highly mobile honeyeaters with complex movement related to flowering patterns. They are able to utilise a wide diversity of food resources and are thus considered to be nomadic generalists as examples of honeyeaters that follow the flower. Both friarbirds and red wattlebirds have similar habitat preferences, meeting and chatting, engaging in social and foraging behaviours where there is overlap in food distribution[17].

Nomadic foragers may be able to build up knowledge of resource-rich areas throughout their range or may wander randomly, taking advantage of local food sources as they become available[18]. They may combine both strategies in dealing with unpredictable food resources in the landscape. It is likely that the patchiness in food resources rather than competition between species is what shapes the niche and foraging behaviours of nomadic generalists. This suggests the importance of social skills and cooperative behaviour in honeyeaters for finding food and water. We are back to fission–fusion societies!

Information learned during fission–fusion could allow a honeyeater to know who to follow to find nectar. With many eyes over a flat landscape, a bird is more likely to find patches of nectar. Fission–fusion provides nomadic honeyeaters with the ability to make decisions by listening to others. What do they know that I don't? In doing so, the uncertainties arising from environmental or social conditions are vastly reduced. This could include sharing knowledge about predators, to more complex problem-solving associated with accessing new food sources[18].

As nectar is low in protein, honeyeaters need to acquire proteins from other sources in their diet, such as insects[5]. This was noticed early on by George Bennett who reported about New Holland honeyeaters: 'Although sweet juices of flowers form part of their food, yet insects are probably the principal object of search; in absence of either, they take the sweet juices of fruits.' Many honeyeaters can thrive on nectar because they eat insects as well to provide missing nutrients, as Lusi saw in the wattlebirds visiting her garden.

WATTLEBIRDS IN MY GARDEN

Lusi Perrin

There always seem to be yellow and red wattlebirds in the garden at any time of the day. They gorge themselves on the grevilleas (especially the *Grevillea* 'Superb'), bottlebrushes (callistemon), correas and anything else that takes their fancy. They don't confine themselves to just natives, I've found. They love the tubular flowers of salvias and red hot pokers, and sip from roses and camellias too.

Insects also form part of their diet. I sometimes see a yellow wattlebird hopping through the nasturtiums looking for caterpillars of the cabbage butterfly. They work their way along the spouting, where cobwebs indicate the likelihood of a spider or two. When conditions are just right at dusk, you can often see them dive straight up into the sky, homing in on insects. This display often includes some acrobatic twists and turns.

Let's have a closer look at the main two food sources of honeyeaters: nectar and invertebrates. Invertebrate prey can be hard to find and are mobile and therefore can be at any location. From a honeyeater's perspective, once the invertebrate has been eaten it has gone. Telling another honeyeater about where it found the invertebrate is therefore of little use. Unlike insects which are gone once the bird consumes it, nectar production is depleted only for a short time. To illustrate, research found that noisy miners plan their search path when foraging for nectar, but not when foraging for invertebrates[19].

To be a good forager, a bird needs to remember what flowers it fed on and which of them still have nectar. This is because the flowers produce more nectar after the bird has visited, perhaps several hours later or the next day. Nectar is depleted and replenished on a predictable schedule that a bird can learn[20]. The bird needs to rely on memory to know which flowers have and have not been visited. In doing so, the bird avoids making unprofitable revisits when searching within a tree[21]. We would expect honeyeaters to remember not only the flowers visited but also to be able to plan for the order of future visits. Route planning may be energy-efficient if it allows search paths to be minimised[22]. It would mean a bird does not actually have to remember each individual flower it has visited. Instead, the honeyeater simply needs to remember its planned route and where along that planned route it currently is.

John Gould reported in his work on birds that 'The call of the little wattlebird is like a person vomiting, lorikeets roar like sporting crowds when they swing into trees in screeching hordes, their whisper a shout.' One reason for this is that bird–plant interactions reward loudness, especially in the large, open canopies of trees. It is smarter to shout warning threats from a distance than for the bird to wait until it arrives. A study of red wattlebirds and noisy friarbirds found a relationship between the proportion of time they spent foraging at flowers and the time they spent in defending flowers[23]. This suggests that nectar is an important resource worth defending. You can see how plants work with birds in the large, open canopies of wattles and eucalypts. The small, narrow leaves of these trees allow better visibility, so an intruder can be seen coming. Birds therefore start calling from a distance, using harsh cries as an assertion of ownership over the flowers. Honeyeaters in general tend to have loud, relatively low-pitched aerial alarm calls, as Cheryl found out.

HONEYEATER CALL

Cheryl Howell

'Four-o-clock four-o-clock four-o-clock.' The sun is just below the horizon and it's actually five o'clock but noisy friarbirds are not ruled by digital devices, their clamorous calls initiate the dawn chorus with salutations.

In the courtyard the flowering native *Callistemon* 'Harkness' attracts dusky, Lewin's and yellow honeyeaters; however, the noisy friarbirds totally dominate the tree, announcing their arrival via a precise route, bare black skin heads probing the red blossoms on the outer canopy, often hanging upside down, defending their feeding branch with noisy, harsh and discordant, deep honking sounds, 'look-back look-back' or a sharp 'owk owk' while scattering and chasing off competitors.

Common urban and garden native plants often include hybrid types of eucalyptus, banksia and grevillea. Plants such as these are widely available, chosen for their prolific flowering and long flowering season. These have gained recognition as genera that are an important resource for native nectarivores and insectivores in suburban areas[24]. There is a downside to this as urban plants often have either a prolonged period of nectar availability or a continuous supply of nectar at times when nectar would normally be scarce, forcing birds to move on[25]. This often results in birds reaching population densities far in excess of those in more natural settings.

Due to the relatively consistent supply of nectar in suburban and urban areas from winter-flowering banksia, seasonal eucalyptus, and year-round flowering hybrid grevilleas, the same large-scale tracking of nectar resources is not required, thus favouring more constant suburban/urban nectarivore communities. There appears to be a trend towards larger, dominant, nectarivorous species being more common and smaller species less abundant in suburban areas[26]. This is possibly a consequence of a constant supply of nectar. It suggests that the provision of nectar-rich plantings will attract larger and more aggressive honeyeaters and cause a reduction in smaller species. Grevilleas, for example, are of significant value as continual nectar sources. As soon as nectar is removed it is replaced, so that birds can return to the same flower and obtain further rewards. Grevilleas can attract birds to gardens with a large floral display, providing sufficient food to enable them to become residents.

If you want to encourage more birds into your garden, consider planting a range of different native plants instead of just one species. You might want to have vegetation in the form of trees, bush and grass layers with lots of cover and at different levels, to allow smaller birds to hide. Grass seed heads are an important resource for many parrots as well as insects, so don't be too quick to cut back the weeds or mow the grass. In fact, get rid of your lawn and replace it with native grasses and flowers! If you don't want a garden entirely of native plants, you could create a small indigenous zone and see if there is any difference in the birds that visit. For an idea of what is native to your area, visit your local park or other national area. Water of course is vital for any bird and should be supplied. We are going to talk more about this in our next chapter.

Chapter 7

THE BATHING BIRD

Let's go back to 1788 and this time look at the weather, the likes of which had never been experienced by the British before. Just as the first European settlement was being established, there was an El Niño event that brought a drought. In December 1790, a Mr Watkin Tench reported in *A Complete Account of Settlement at Port Jackson* the event: 'Nor did the perroquettes though tropical birds bear it better. The ground was strewn with them in the same condition as the bats.' The drought continued into April 1791 when Tench reported that 'In several parts of the harbour the ground was covered with different sorts of small birds, some dead and others gasping for water.'

By 1848 John Gould noticed the effect of drought on native birds, writing: 'There are also periods when some species of birds appear to entirely forsake the part of the country in which they have been accustomed to dwell, and to betake themselves to some distant locality where they remain for 5 or ten years or even for a longer period and whence they as suddenly disappear as they had arrived.' This must have really frightened the colonists; not even the native birds could survive the weather! Drought was not a common occurrence in rainy old England.

As we discussed in the last chapter, the climate across the flat continent is characterised by extremely high rainfall variability between years. This is largely driven by the natural cycle known as the Pacific El Niño-Southern Oscillation (ENSO) cycle associated with a sustained period of warming (El Niño) or cooling (La Niña) in the central and eastern topical Pacific. The ENSO cycle loosely operates over timescales from one to eight years.

Australian birds have had to adapt to irregularly occurring periods of drought and flood that resulted in fluctuations in resource availability associated with plant growth such as time of flowering, fruiting and even insect abundance[1]. Birds adapted to the unpredictable rainfall that resulted from the continent moving northward and growing more arid. Mass movement of birds can vary from 1 kilometre to more than 100 kilometres (local nomads such as honeyeaters), to much longer distances, with continental scale nomadism even seen in some ducks, parrots and pigeons[2]. Bird density seems to be directly influenced by the presence of water. Species attracted to or staying close to water will be those that need to drink regularly, such as granivorous pigeons, cockatoos and finches as well as honeyeaters[3].

A bird needs to be able to respond and adapt in order to be able to locate and use food which is there one year and gone the next. As discussed, they do this by finding out information from other individuals through fission–fusion societies. A bird may find water sources by monitoring the activities of others in its group, allowing the bird to acquire information about potential new sources of water, even if they are artificial.

A major change for native birds was driven by irrigation schemes which arrived in the late 1800s, and by the artificial water sources in the form of dams, tanks or troughs that appeared over the last 150 years. This means that there are fewer places more than 10 kilometres from water across approximately 70 per cent of the continent. Despite the negative effects of agricultural land-use, artificial water bodies such as dammed lakes do represent key spots for bird diversity. Artificial lakes are valuable habitat that can greatly enhance the richness of local bird species. These new sources of permanent water have resulted in a number of bird species increasing in abundance and even expanding their geographic range. These birds include crested pigeons, galahs and zebra finches. Artificial lakes feature larger arrays of bird species compared to those at natural waterholes, especially of water birds. This is likely to be a function of size as artificial reservoirs are, on average, 20 per cent larger than natural waterholes[4].

Although birds are highly mobile, the short timeframe in which dehydration can occur makes it unlikely that they will escape all drought events[5]. Birds need to evaporate water to maintain body temperature while at the same time conserving water and avoiding dehydration[6]. One adaptation is apparent on very hot days when birds forage and drink less, sitting in the foliage of trees and staying out of the sun. On these days, a bird can lose up to 5 per cent of its body mass per hour and rapidly reach dehydration point[5]. Chris sent me a story about a hot day in the bush, capturing the heat beautifully.

HOT DAY IN THE BUSH!

Chris McCracken

The bush around the house was dry, but today it was a tinderbox. There was a constant crackling as the eucalypts shed leaves and small branches in their response to the constant dry conditions. It was eerily like the sound of flames. And there was no humidity. The air was so dry it hurt my nose and my eyes squinted and smarted as I looked through the haze of heat that shimmered from the earth. I can see right through the trees as there is no undergrowth this year: no hibbertias, no hops bush, even no St John's wort! I had the feeling

> that if I shuffled my feet, or snapped my fingers, I could spark a fire. The birds were still also—under bushes in the garden, with their beaks open in a permanent gasp. Two crimson rosellas spent the day on the floor of the fernery in the one spot they could find moisture and coolness. They squatted, with their beaks open, ignoring the bowerbird that similarly sat, just above them. There was no hissing from the bowerbird at any bird that joined them over the day . . . too hot for a pecking order! I stepped quietly past the fernery as I went to refill the birdbaths many, many times on this relentlessly hot day.

We are all familiar with those very dry, hot days. Chris writes about birds with their beaks open, a practice that helps them cool down. The moisture from their mouths evaporates, absorbing heat from the body, so that each time the bird breathes out some of this heat is carried outside, leaving the bird feeling cooler. Birds can also lift their feathers and hold their wings out so that air can reach their skin and carry away some of their body heat.

Birds can use specific cooling behaviours in order to prevent their body temperatures from rising to lethal levels, including wing-venting, panting, and gular fluttering. Birds wing-vent by dropping their wings away from their bodies, allowing convection to cool the torso and facilitate convective heat loss from the blood vessels located on the underside of the wings[7]. Panting by breathing quickly moves air across the moist surfaces of its lungs, throat and mouth[8]. Gular fluttering is similar to a dog panting. The bird opens its mouth and flutters its upper throat muscles to promote heat loss.

Smaller birds are in increased danger of heat stress as they have less water storage in the body for evaporative cooling. They also gain heat more rapidly when the ambient temperature is higher than their body temperature[9]. It may therefore be important for smaller birds to conserve water by wing-venting rather than panting.

One bird very good at surviving the hot, arid climate is the budgie. Gould reported that, 'The beautiful little warbling grass parakeet [the budgie] which prior to 1838 was so rare in the southern parts of Australia, arrived in that year in such countless multitudes on the Liverpool plains that I could have procured any number of specimens and more than once their delicate bodies formed an excellent article of food for myself and party.' Aboriginals used birds such as budgies and zebra finches to find desert water, noting that 'as thoroughly reliable guides to water in very dry regions the birds have no rivals. They also help us tell the weather to find water.'[2] The Indigenous people of the Liverpool Plains in New South Wales used the term *betcherrgh* when talking about budgies, translating as 'good food'.

Budgies are nomadic, moving frequently in different sized groups in response to rainfall and the consequent appearance of food. Daily activity begins at sunrise and ends at dusk. Most feeding takes place in the morning and afternoon, with drinking sporadic, occurring at any time of day. During the midday heat, they tend to rest and preen in the branches of trees[10].

Budgies can form small flocks or large flocks depending on rainfall and food availability—fission–fusion societies again! This fission behaviour provides individuals with the opportunity to learn socially about the location and quality of water and about novel water sources. We have mateship here again with important relationships maintained; parent–offspring and sibling–sibling interactions. Individuals within a flock form pair bonds outside of the breeding season that remain together throughout the year[11]. Budgies are capable of breeding from the age of three to four months, doing so following rainy periods when food is temporarily abundant. While budgies can be seen in smaller more stable family flocks, try to find a waterhole where you can watch them come together in bigger flocks to drink and bathe. You will hear them constantly chattering about the wonderfulness of the change in weather and how they must let others know water is back!

At the other end of the Australian bird spectrum, but equally well adapted to the challenging climate, is the emu. I was amazed to get a story from Helen about emus moving into urban areas during a particularly bad drought.

THE DAY EMUS CAME TO TOWN

Helen Day

I lived in Longreach, Queensland, for three years and during that time there was the worst drought in living memory. Residents of Longreach put water out for the birds, and the most striking visiting birds were the emus. Usually emus could be seen off in the distance and rarely came close to humans or their homes. Thirst forced them into the town of Longreach. They were never aggressive and it seemed to be the most natural thing in the world for them to be wandering around the neighbourhood stopping to have a drink of water where residents left water out for them. I think leaving water out for them saved this particular population of emus from certain death. They even wandered down the main street with a large group of tourists following them snapping photographs. It was a wonderful experience to get up so close to them without them showing any fear. Once the drought broke, we never saw the emus again.

What is going on here? Did the emus always know there was water in urban areas but chose not to visit? Did the emus have previous experience with urban areas? The emus did visit the area in groups and there is safety in numbers. Research has found that prior to the breeding season, female emus move in pairs, while the surplus of unpaired males either forage solitarily, join other unpaired males, or join larger groups. The composition of groups is highly changeable. The emus that came to Longreach during the drought were smart enough and brave enough to take a risk, remembering that urban areas pose a real threat to them—from people, dogs and cars, for instance. Emus being big birds probably helps their confidence!

Today, water, often in the form of birdbaths, is an important resource in urban areas. Water is also provided through dams, swimming pools and ponds. Because urbanisation provides reliable water throughout the year, breeding periods can be extended. This could potentially result in increased recruitment of birds to urban environments[12]. This may result in birds missing their cues to leave to resume their previously nomadic lives and becoming urban residents instead.

Watching other groups could provide birds with knowledge about where to find water and drink safely, as Lou saw when he had a family of thornbills visit his birdbath. Thornbill flocks are highly vocal which suggests that group vigilance allows individuals to relax the need to be alert[13]. In this case, being familiar with the caller benefits the receiver[12]. This is because they can assess the reliability of the signal when deciding how to react to it[13].

BATHING YELLOW THORNBILLS

Lou Citroen

One very hot day I was attracted (or distracted, more to the point!) by a lot of (tiny) bird chatter at my birdbath. Thinking at first it was coming from superb fairy-wrens, I should have recognised these little guys. To my amazement, it was a group of a dozen or so yellow-rumped thornbills chattering to each other with much excitement about the spectacle of our two birdbaths! Although the thornbills are around in nearby paddocks at this time of year, I don't remember having seen any in our backyard before. Then followed the comedy show. While they are, as most will know, ground grazers of seed, when they noticed our birdbaths—as though for the first time—one

> by one they popped up on the rim of one, chattering like there was no tomorrow. This was clearly a novelty to them and offered much to discuss amongst themselves.
>
> Then, one mustered up the courage to take a dip but then flew up in the air as quickly as it went in, clearly getting a fright from its own reflection. It and a few others tried several times. While it appeared that there was nothing too nefarious in that water, their attempts were very cautious. The excited chattering amongst the lot of them just continued until it seemed as though one of them called out 'Come on guys, let's go home now' . . . and the whole chattering party took off over the fence together.

Was this group of thornbills out on a recce to find out whether the birdbath was safe? Birds that live in groups are constantly interacting with each other. The yellow thornbills may have watched the superb fairy-wrens use the bath before.

> The next day, at about the same time, it seemed the entire party had decided to return, again heralded by much chattering, to check out the birdbaths once more. Emboldened, their reflections this time did not seem to bother them (at all!) as they plunged in confidently, happy to splash and share with a few sparrows.

I think you are right, Lou! The birds seemed to remember their experience from the previous day. I would just like to say here, if you don't provide water for birds, consider doing so. You will get so much enjoyment out of watching what is going on. As Lou saw, baths can be situated where birds socialise as keeping clean is important for a bird. Consider putting a range of baths at different levels around your garden. You don't need a fancy bath, a pot/or saucer on the ground will do nicely. It can take time for birds to discover your birdbaths, but once they know it is an established water source and frequently refreshed, they will come to rely upon it.

As cats are a big risk for birds while bathing, consider elevated or pedestal baths near plants where smaller birds can go for refuge if disturbed. Stones or rocks in the centre of the bath can give smaller birds such as wrens and thornbills a place to perch while bathing. As birds need to clean their feathers daily, don't assume water is only important on summer days. Birds need to bath on cold, wet windy days as well. I have even had stories sent to me about birds breaking the ice over a bath to get at the water for a cold wash.

Like all bathrooms, birdbaths need to be cleaned regularly as a dirty bath can spread disease. Birds can become susceptible to infection where individuals congregated at these communal baths. To clean your bath, scrub it well with disinfectant soap and wash it out well to ensure there is no residue from the soap. Then, top it up with clean water and if possible keep the bath in direct sunlight. Even though this will increase evaporation of water, sunlight is nature's disinfectant. But do keep your baths filled, your birds will expect you to!

Chapter 8
THE TALKING BIRD

In the last few chapters, we have talked about the challenges for a bird living in Australia, a land where having relationships with other birds is so important for finding out where food and water are located. As we have discussed, this is done through fission–fusion societies where birds can source information from each other. An Aussie bird needs to think and plan ahead, ensuring it is in a good flock that has the knowledge and his mates won't hold back on him.

We know why birds need to communicate with each other, but exactly *how* do birds communicate with each other? We return to mirror neurons from Chapter 2. Mirror neurons allow birds, as well as humans, to understand and copy the behaviours of another. The primary role of mirror neurons is in action understanding[1]. That is, in understanding actions performed by others, and in knowing what a given action means.

Social learning and in particular imitation in birds has received considerable attention in recent years as we find evidence of similarities with humans. In fact using information provided by others to guide your behaviour (mirror neurons firing to allow imitation) is thought to be the foundation of language and speech learning[2]. In birds as in children, juveniles learn their song through a process of vocal imitation also known as mimicry. Infants acquire speech by imitating the sounds they hear performed by their mum, dad and even siblings. Many of our parrots and cockatoos are well known for being able to learn human words, as Tony reports in our next story.

HARVEY THE COCKATOO

Tony Healy

We dreamt of getting him to say 'Aye me hearties' or 'how much for cash?' but all we managed in the early stage was 'Hello Harvey' which is what we said to him all the time. We loved this bird—he was a supreme character with loads of personality. The other cockatoos would come around and talk to him and he would return their chatter, punctuated with 'Hello Harvey' every other sentence. I wonder what they made of our multi-lingual cockie who could speak dog and English as well as cockatoo.

Adopting a behaviour displayed by another instead of learning by individual experience is considered a key advantage of sociality[3]. Social group-living birds often synchronise their behaviours with others in their groups. Research found that behaving similarly is, in essence, the glue that holds groups together[4]. For example, in birds, stretching and yawning often precedes a change in activity, from resting to flight. These behaviours appear to be contagious among other group members[5]. Such contagion provides a means of preparing the group for flight and synchronising the group's change of activity.

Zebra finches learn their song by imitating the adult 'tutor', usually the father. Research has found that there is a delay of up to 48 hours in reproducing any learned song or vocalisation, but thereafter it is replicated in its entirety[6,7]. Birds such as juvenile magpies spend months intensively and repeatedly practising their tutor's song before successfully producing an imitation of it.

Both songbirds and our own infants learn through listening and imitative learning. Just as in infants, songbirds can go through a babbling stage while learning adult song. Vocalisation during the babbling phase is known as subsong[6]. It is followed by plastic song when the young individual's vocalisation gradually comes to resemble the adult form or the song is crystallised. Like speech, learning is a demanding task for the firing mirror neurons, so birds need to rest and sleep.

While the functions of sleep are not fully understood, what we do know is that sleep makes an important contribution to learning and memory processing[8]. Birds experience the same cycles of slow-wave sleep and rapid-eye-movement sleep that we do. These patterns of activity during sleep are believed to play a crucial role in the growth of bird and human brains[9]. Young zebra finches first exposed to the singing of an adult tutor tended to fall asleep quickly after exposure[10].

Birds are the only non-mammalian group to exhibit high amplitude slow wave EEG activity during slow-wave sleep[9]. This is fascinating, as it suggests that when a bird is sleeping—as in humans and other mammals—memories are formed! Both reptiles and amphibians lack distinct forms of slow-wave sleep, and the rapid-eye-movement sleep stage that is only found in mammals.

Compared to our own sleep, birds' sleep is fragmented, thought to occur in short bouts of one- to four-minute durations. For example, a bird could be remembering part of a song during slow-wave sleep through memory consolidation[11]. That is, the memory continues to evolve as the bird practises to sing while awake and the memory is recalled while sleeping through a process of consolidation[12]. Memories of who's who in a group is very important. A bird needs to be aware of the social context of its group. Could we speculate that slow-wave sleep, as a way to form memories, co-evolved in birds as a way to cope with a social life, by forming social memories that can be recalled?

A hallmark of social memory is the differential display of behaviour towards familiar and unfamiliar individuals. Individual vocalisations may contain a 'signature', which is unique to the caller[13,14]. Indeed, many species that live in stable social groups learn to recognise unique variations in unlearned calls (signature calls) to distinguish between familiar individuals. For instance, vocal sharing occurs with the warble vocalisations within groups of magpies. Magpies in the same group share more warble syllables than magpies from different groups[15].

Vocal learning can permit flexibility in social situations that would not be possible with non-learned signals. Vocal learning of contact calls, for example, is unique to a social group; these are group-specific calls, in other words, using a call that is recognised and used by individuals to stay in touch while flying or foraging. It is important for many social birds to have the ability to learn new contact calls throughout adulthood. This would be vital for a bird changing groups and needing to establish new relationships. One way to achieve this is to match the call of others within the group to aid social bonding and recognition[16].

Duets represent an advanced form of vocal synchronisation in which partners adjust timing and type of vocalisation to match their mate. It is thought to be important in intra-pair communication; that is, for sharing information about food or nesting places, and for maintaining pair bonds. Duetting is a specific form of communication in which one bird initiates a call and another one answers. It is useful when visual contact is lost or is at risk of being lost.

Neighbouring magpies can synchronise territorial defence calls[14]. This occurs among prolonged monogamous pair bonds and between magpies that are neighbours. Magpies produce some of the most complex songs and have one of the largest ranges of vocalisation of any songbird. They have tremendously large song repertoires. The magpie song, not specific to the breeding season, is performed by both males and females.

Magpies position themselves, adopting a distinct body posture before carolling[15]. The bird widens its chest, splaying the breast feathers, tilts the head backwards, and inclines its entire body backwards a little. Magpies are known for their mimicry ability in their song, as Judy describes.

OUR MAGPIES SINGING

Judy Margolis

Let me introduce you to our magpies. They are a gracious pair who kindly let us share their domain. The male is eloquent in his melodious chortling with an extended repertoire including electronic warbles reminiscent of R2D2 and a very convincing imitation of our neighbour's whinnying pony.

Budgies will form large flocks of hundreds of birds. In such large flocks, how does a budgie recognise its mate? It uses a shared short distinct call which has the potential to allow for rapid identification of companions. It is the male who shows his commitment to the female by taking on his mate's call. The male will drum up a perfect imitation of her contact call. The female judges his suitability as a mate by how well he can imitate her call. This special call is used by the female to keep in touch with her male as she flies, feeds and mingles with others.

Budgies share another type of call that aids recognition of other flock individuals, even if they are only temporary members. Having a call recognised by others in the group can aid group membership and permit the recognition of social alliances[17]. A shared vocalisation facilitates recognition of other group members, which is especially important in large or fluid social groups. Learning to produce a shared call would be more efficient than learning and remembering many individual calls[18], much like it is for people; it is easier for us to address a crowd of people by saying, 'Okay people, listen to me,' than call for attention using each member's name.

It has been suggested that birds could learn song-dance coordination as an extension of the process of learning songs[19]. Male palm cockatoos from northern Australia, for example, use a modified stick or seedpod to strike a hollow tree limb repeatedly during their vocal and visual display. This behaviour is remarkable because the palm cockatoos use their tools only to make sound, not for foraging[20].

In male palm cockatoos, drumming occurs alongside other aspects of display, such as darkening of red cheek patches (blushing?) and crest erection to attract a mate. In addition, it was found that males drum for long periods without accompanying vocalisations or visual displays. Palm cockatoos would rarely have the chance to learn a beat from others as drumming sounds travel only short distances (less than 100 metres). Male palm cockatoos thus appear to be more like solo musical artists who internalise notation of a regular pulse and then generate the motor patterns that create the beat. It was found that individual male palm cockatoos have their own consistent drumming patterns (or signatures).

The addition of individually recognisable rhythmic signatures in palm cockatoos to their complex vocal displays may perform a similar function. It is also possible that drumming displays encode further information about the bird, indicated perhaps by the age-related beat rates in this long-lived bird. Palm cockatoos are the only species known to fashion specific tools to amplify the sound made by using a limb alone, and then using the tool to drum in a regular rhythm[21].

Dance has been reported in at least nine species of birds, including several types of parrot, all of which are vocal imitators and several of which show motor imitation[22]. One of the best-known species for mimicry in the wild is the lyrebird, where the male's dancing ability is judged by females[23]. In dance, the male impresses a female by dazzling her with his lyre, the two special tail feathers that get shaken while he dances and sings. The males perform a dance display on circular mounds they have built on the forest floor. Similar to bowerbirds mentioned earlier, they add a rhythmic pattern to the display by shaking nearby vines as if to accentuate the performance at rhythmically emphasised moments[24]. However, things don't always go to plan, as Leon found out when a lyrebird visited him.

DANCING LYREBIRD

Leon Trembath

It must have been September when this senior lyrebird saw his reflection in the glass window of the back door of our home in the eastern end of the Strzelecki Ranges as he strode purposefully past the kitchen door. Even though it was the end of their breeding season, the urge to mate was ever-present and most powerful.

There is nothing odder than to see a senior lyrebird in full moult of his tail, as they have nothing but the vestige of tail remaining, a mere stub, with their rear end looking more like a plucked turkey ready for roasting.

Now this bewildered, ever-wishing-to-breed lyrebird could well see his frontal appearance reflected in the glass of the back door which, from his perspective, looked for all the world like a female in waiting as there was no male plumage array to be seen. With a closer look, one could see the stub of his tail slowly beginning to lift. This is the most natural happening for any male lyrebird. With this female waiting on his every movement and watching him intently

> from the window, it was utterly impossible for this entrapped male to know that he was trying to court himself, hence his imaginary tail was performing as it should, despite it being at the very end of their breeding season.
>
> With his stub now sticking up in the air, in his attempt to display his maleness over this willing female, he went into his ever-so-soft rapid tap tap tap, imitating the sounds of a portable typewriter (which we had). At the same time he was doing his ever-so-soft rapid drumming from foot to foot which under normal circumstances would have swept the female off her feet by this ever-attentive, courting, bald, senior male lyrebird.
>
> In time he simply gave up. Frustrated that his normally impressive breeding behaviour didn't succeed, he sauntered off into the regenerating rainforest. His plumage would in time return enabling this grand bird of the eastern rainforests of Oz to meet another and hopefully willing participatory female.

This lyrebird was not planning on meeting his reflection. You might think the lyrebird was stupid not to recognise his own reflection, but think of it from the bird's point of view: in the lyrebird's natural habitat it would only see its reflection while drinking or bathing[25]. Is it therefore any surprise that the lyrebird thought he was confronting another bird? This behaviour may have been a spontaneous response to seeing a potential mate. The reaction to seeing his reflection was to interpret it as female due to his missing tail. The reflected bird would have copied his dance moves but not his vocal sounds.

Is exhibiting motor imitation an indication that the bird knows the message it is trying to convey—that is, what it is trying to say? Motor patterns such as in dance moves can be learned socially or individually, which would suggest a bird can increase its message by rearranging pre-existing moves or notes into new sequences. We refer to this as contextual learning. This form of learning occurs in both the calling/dancing bird and the listening/watching bird, who both understand the message. When a bird uses its knowledge of the watching birds to use different notes or moves in new contexts, we refer to this as production learning[26]. In human language learning, this is the ability to acquire and apply rules to understanding and producing the sequences of words that make up meaningful sentences. Like humans but much less so primates, many bird species produce vocalisation in which acoustically different elements are produced in rapid succession in structured sequences.

For instance, could a bird be an inventor of a new call, or a new meaning behind a call? Invention in this case refers to new notes that are not modifications of any of the bird vocalisations or similar to those heard. Instead, they are sufficiently different to be classified as a new type of call[26]. However, to be successful this new call would need to have an adaptive value. For example, if a female prefers novelty in her mate's call, a new call might result in a mating opportunity. In contrast, if a female is more interested in a particular known and established call type, a novel call can be ignored.

One bird species that has become a highly successful model of vocal production learning is budgies[27]. As we touched on earlier, budgies are capable of acquiring new vocalisation as juveniles and adults. This ability suggests social interactions, including visual and physical contact, might be particularly important in vocal behaviour[28]. Budgies may need motivation in order to be able to vocalise what they hear; they will not mimic mindlessly. We see this in other birds when it comes to territorial protection which may play an important role for vocal imitation (for example, duetting magpies). This highlights the complexity of vocal learning and mimicry in birds such as budgies and arguably even humans[27].

When we learn languages we acquire the ability to apply rules to understanding and produce sequences of words that make up meaningful sentences. Can a bird do this? As we have discussed, like humans, birds are taught how to vocalise. An interesting study found pigeons were able to memorise and recognise hundreds of pictures individually. Not only that, they were able to form categories based on shared physical features, such as male and female faces[29]. This suggests that pigeons can acquire more abstract concepts like 'same' and 'different'! Remember that pigeons don't have a reputation for being particularly smart, so could we suggest that having pattern recognition is a common cognitive ability in all birds?

What about facial-recognition capabilities? Let's talk about swooping magpies here. Magpies swoop during breeding season as it's a nest-defence strategy. Swooping magpies are nearly always male because the female is busy attending to the nest. The males' warnings that you are getting closer to the nest come in a number of stages[14]. These warnings include carolling, beak-clapping and swooping towards an object or intruder, but not near it. When these warnings are ignored, the magpie will start to swoop, this time closer to the target. If the swooping is still ignored, the magpie will actually set out to attack with his mighty beak. If you think about it from the magpie's viewpoint, he has given you warnings and you ignored them. So maybe it's your own fault you got swooped?

Magpies have been found to remember and recognise human faces and will remember them for years. When we share our backyard with magpies, they come to know us and even recognise and remember our movements. We all have our routines, and magpies can get to know them, especially in terms of when food is provided. Magpies living close to humans are less likely to swoop, as trust has been built[14]. They will remember someone who was good to them; equally, they will remember negative encounters.

Mistaken identity can occur, however, when the magpie gets it wrong. A magpie who had a bad experience with a young boy in a school uniform with a hat on might swoop any boy fitting this description. It is just a case of mistaken identity on behalf of the bird. This might help to explain why magpies often swoop people in uniforms!

What should you do if you get swooped by a magpie? One suggestion is to take a stick or branch and wave it above your head to keep the magpie away. Cyclists should descend and walk slowly onwards, using anything they might have to wave behind their heads[15], or just avoid the area for a while. It might also be worthwhile showing the magpie respect. Look it in the eye when you are walking by and nod your head to it. Even say, 'g-day maggies'. Let the male know that you know it's there by acknowledging it. Show the bird respect—it is facing the same challenges we are: keeping his home safe, his wife happy and his kids well fed.

Chapter 9

THE PERSONALITY BIRD

Do birds have a personality? I think by this stage in the book we can say a resounding 'Yes! They sure do!' Indeed, individual differences in terms of how they behave may be expected to evolve in social species. This is supported by research on personalities in social birds that found isolated individuals behave differently in group settings. In a study monitoring movement decisions in wild English great tit birds, evidence was obtained that personality is related to individual differences when making group decisions[1]. Great tits were given a choice of four identical feeders, and it was found that all individuals tended to move towards more highly populated feeders. This resulted in highly synchronous flocking behaviour with differences in where individuals fed. That is, more bold/exploring personalities fed in higher-density areas, while shyer individuals tended to feed at the periphery of the flock. It is important to consider personality differences of members of social species within and across different social contexts[2].

Birds engage with us in such unique ways, appearing to show individuality by changing their behaviour (behavioural plasticity). A shy individual, for example, may respond to a bold individual by behaving more boldly[3]. But what will be the behavioural consequences if this shy individual is paired with an even shyer bird, thus making the shy individual the relatively bolder partner? Judy sent me a story in which she describes the personality types in her visiting magpies.

WATCHING MAGPIES

Judy Szekeres

The most wonderful thing about this group is the moment we see each other for the first time each afternoon. I am suddenly aware of them under the verandah at the window, chortling away to catch my attention.

Each one has a distinct personality—there is the forever young one who is bottom of the pecking order and still hasn't figured out a strategy for getting food ahead of the others. There is one magpie that stands almost on my foot, getting every morsel that might drop out of my hand. There are three older birds who are silent (except for the occasional warble) and patient, and stand on the periphery watching intently and waiting their turn. There is the one who rushes about trying to catch everything that gets thrown, tumbling into the others and squawking incessantly. And there are two that wander in and out nonchalantly, often taking one or two morsels before disappearing again.

Magpies have a dynamic system rather than a stable one. This social complexity of magpie groups means they need to learn about other individuals in the groups. Many adult magpies remain mobile and continue to disperse to other areas, so there are constant changes of boundaries and affiliation between magpies. Unlike choughs, fairy-wrens and many other cooperative breeders, magpies are not always cooperative. However, their social system is flexible enough for rearrangement, such as in variability of group sizes. While the word 'stable' best describes the ideal life condition of adult magpies, as territories are hard to come by there is considerable mobility for the rest of the adult population who can't breed.

It would help if the magpie could adopt behaviourial flexibility[4]. That is, if it could change its behaviour to meet the needs of the other individuals in the group. But what behaviour should the magpie change? The magpie phenotype comes into play here. Just like in humans, differences in experience and genetic make-up give rise to differences between individuals in behavioural flexibility. Birds such as magpies, bowerbirds and fairy-wrens are relatively long-lived with personalities forming from a mixture of genes and personal experience as they grow[5]. Early experiences in a bird's life can affect the development of personality structures, with such effects temporary or permanent. A bird's phenotype, its genetic make-up and past experiences interact with each other, leading to individual differences in how birds react to a situation[6]. Just like us, no two birds have the same personality.

Flexibility in their behaviour allows individuals to efficiently respond to common environmental challenges, such as finding food after rain. It allows the bird to change between behaviours according to the bird's current needs, instead of consistently producing the same behavioural response on the basis of its previous experience[7]. A personality that can change in response to others in the group during fission–fusion events is essential when a bird needs to join a flock to find food.

As we have discussed, living in Australia frequently offers a high abundance of clumped food resources (such as nectar). Such increases in density of a food source can lead to a greater expression of one behaviour: aggression. All individuals have the capacity to behave aggressively, even if the behaviour has never been expressed before or expressed only in lower frequency[8]. An example of this could be found in urban birds where they need to act more boldly when interacting with others for access to nectar. The winning trait is to act more boldly so a bird can defend what is theirs, therefore all individuals act aggressively. Variations in food density thus substantially increases the behavioural repertoire of bird populations.

Whether or not the population can persist in the face of a changing climate depends on whether or not the population has individuals that can show the appropriate behavioural responses for adjustment. Groups that exhibit differences in personalities are more likely to contain these individuals who are able to cope with novel conditions. This is due to the diversity of responses from different individuals in a group[2].

Of course, not every bird is brave, and not every bird is shy. Having a group of mixed personality types is key. Individuals from the same population often vary substantially in their level of behavioural plasticity[9]. Personality differences between individuals would also be expected to influence their social decision-making or rule-following[10]. Perhaps groups need different personality types to aid learning. If a bird is good at exploring, it may find new food sources, but it might also die in the attempt. An exploring bird may investigate its territory and surrounding area. The shy bird would have learned a lot if it had been watching the exploring bird. It would have benefitted if food was found, but it survived by not following the exploring bird. Is it possible that some birds are born explorers, while others are shy and learn from experience?

Could a shy bird become an explorer if it had positive experiences from exploring while playing? Less exploratory individuals may be more responsive to their social environment and pay more attention to how others communicate with one another[11]. By contrast, more exploratory individuals may not tend to be as aware of others in social situations. As we know, behaviour is flexible and we may expect that less exploratory individuals could adapt their behaviour once they gain confidence to match that of their more exploratory mates.

The 'pool of competence' hypothesis suggests that larger groups contain more individuals, and so have a higher chance of containing individuals competent at solving novel tasks[12]. Individuals living in larger groups may demonstrate greater individual problem-solving success by monitoring and maintaining social relationships[13]. The next story sent to me by Susan tells of a magpie displaying juvenile behaviour that the adults were determined to change!

TWO-TONE MAGGIE

Susan Radamanthos

This is about a young magpie who was nicknamed Two-tone. While his brothers and sisters had learned to feed themselves, Two-tone still wanted to be fed by mum. One day he arrived without his mother but still screeching for food. To my amazement Two-tone started to screech and follow the adult birds around. As they continued to ignore him and feed themselves he started flapping his wings, a bit like shivering. While they continued to ignore his pleas for food, he flopped down and tried to look very small while still flapping his wings and screeching. The adults had obviously experienced this behaviour before and ignored him, letting him fend for himself.

As we have discussed, behavioural flexibility can play a large role in determining the success of an individual[14]. You might be the boss of your small group but once you join a bigger flock, you have to listen to others. We could speculate that living in a large group requires different cognitive abilities from those required for living in smaller groups. A bolder individual now needs to act more submissive when in a larger flock. We would expect a bird that is in tune and responsive to the moods of others to be especially important for long-term partners. Being in a socially monogamous relationship means paying attention to your partner, including seeing the world through their eyes by observing them (responsive). As with humans, information can be gathered by following the direction of another's gaze (head and eye direction) and being able to read your partner from across the room by looking at their eyes.

This tendency to follow the gaze of another suggests the bird is curious about what another individual is thinking or seeing. Gaze provides others with a means of evaluating an individual's interest in their environment. Eye gaze can be used to attract the attention of another, encouraging them to look in the same direction. The eyes provide very subtle signals to others. In this instance eye gazing involves not so much reading the behaviour of another as interpreting what the other might think it sees as important[4,5]. The simple question is, what are you looking at?

Hand-raised common ravens were tested to see whether they could follow the direction of a human's gaze. The researchers found that not only did the raven look up when a human looked up but also looked up when the human was looking at something hidden from the raven's immediate view by a barrier. The raven went over to the barrier and peered around it[15]. If the raven were responding only to simple cues, we would expect the bird to do no more than stay where it was: look at the barrier, find it uninteresting, and go on with whatever it was doing before. Instead, the raven behaved as if it were aware that something interesting was located behind the barrier.

Body movements can also serve as an important means of communication that requires another to interpret an intention. Pointing behaviour occurs with head-turning or whole body turning, and even with eye gaze and eye-gaze following[5].

Another aspect of behaviour which has been studied is the matching of vocalisation to increase social bonding. As we talked about in the previous chapter, this occurs when one individual makes its vocalisation more similar to that of its mate[16]. This behaviour is aided by vocal learning as it allows the bird to change the vocalisation to add a new one[17]. Raven pairs match their calls by copying each other's sounds to enhance their social bond[16]. When the ravens were further away from each other, their call was found to be very similar compared to the short calls used when the birds were closer together. When together, the ravens displayed soft calls, beak interaction and feather grooming to show commitment between strongly bonded individuals. It is not as important to keep to a specific call when you are together! Birds with strong bonds can share unique, shorter, more random calls to communicate. Our next story supports this use of soft calls to communicate about a task, as Jeanette reports.

BELLA AND THE CROWS

Jeanette Pump

One morning while eating my breakfast I was startled by the sound of a crow. It was sitting on the back of an outdoor setting chair on our verandah about 2 metres from where I was sitting.

I watched the crow for a minute. It was curiously looking down onto where our 14-year-old labrador Bella was sleeping. I might mention here that Bella was not only old but she was deaf and blind and spent most of her days sleeping.

The crow called a couple of times then I heard a second crow call back, it was perched on an arbour about 4 metres away. They seemed to be communicating.

After a few back and forward calls, the crow on the back of the chair hopped down and stood at the edge of our dog's bed about 30 centimetres from the dog.

I watched as the crow then hopped onto the dog's bed and after another call from the other crow it grabbed a tuft of fur from the rear end of my dog!

> I couldn't believe what I was seeing. My dog sat up with such a start and the look on the dog's face was much the same as when the vet takes her temperature: her eyes nearly popped out of her head. The crow then with its beak full of fur jumped back onto the back of the chair, it then after a short time did it again.
>
> I believe the crows knew our dog was old and possibly deaf and it seemed like the crow on the arbour was egging on the crow on the chair, saying 'Go on, I dare you.'

The crows in Jeanette's story showed different behaviours, one watching and encouraging while the other was carrying out the brave action. The birds could be using the fur to line a nest to keep chicks warm, so the dog's hair could be an important resource. Was this the first time the crows tried this behaviour? Had the crows been watching Bella and assessing if she was a threat or not? The crow succeeded this time in its brave act of robbing fur from Bella's behind, but will it ever try this again? Would the crows try it with a younger or more energetic dog?

In recent years there have been an increasing number of studies demonstrating the existence of consistent individual differences in behaviour. Notably there is a growing body of evidence showing that individuals differ in their propensity for risk-taking or reacting to stressful situations. A study into the temperament of rooks provided evidence for an effect of individual temperament on the success of cooperative actions[18].

The study tested rooks individually to measure a number of behavioural traits related to boldness and found this to strongly influence their performance in a cooperation task. When at least one partner was more risk-prone (bold), the couple performed well. A reason for this finding may be explained by the behaviour of the shy bird, which waited for its bolder partner to go first before joining it. The study showed that shy rooks only take part in a cooperation tasks when their partner is bold enough to approach first. The percentage of successful cooperation in a pair of shy birds was very low. This finding could be explained by the fact that each individual was waiting for its partner to make the first move.

As suggested, bold individuals differ from shy ones by their inclination to take risks. The more risk-prone individuals appeared to function as catalysers, making it possible for shyer individuals to cooperate under circumstances that they perceive as risky[19]. The shyer bird thus profited from a dilution of perceived risk thanks to the presence of the bolder bird; assuming that bolder birds will take shyer ones along with them. Could an older sibling take a younger sibling with them while exploring the territory? Cooperation may succeed because bolder birds can encourage more fearful individuals to engage in tasks in which the latter would otherwise not have participated.

The question of whether birds have similar personalities to humans is difficult to answer in science as we can be reluctant to use labels common in humans. Anecdotal evidence, such as the stories used in this book, suggest the existence of personalist behaviour in birds. While the question of whether birds show differences in personalities is the topic of our next chapter, it is still up for debate in biological research.

The study of understanding individual differences is important as it can demonstrate the value of a more holistic approach over studying certain behaviours in isolation from others[20]. It is important for the interpretation and design of bird experiments as individuals with different personalities may react differently to the same experiment[19]. Different animal personalities may show variations in vulnerability to stress and artificial housing conditions, leading to welfare concerns. We might even find that a better understanding of bird personalities may help to provide a better understanding of the evolution of our own personalities when interacting with others.

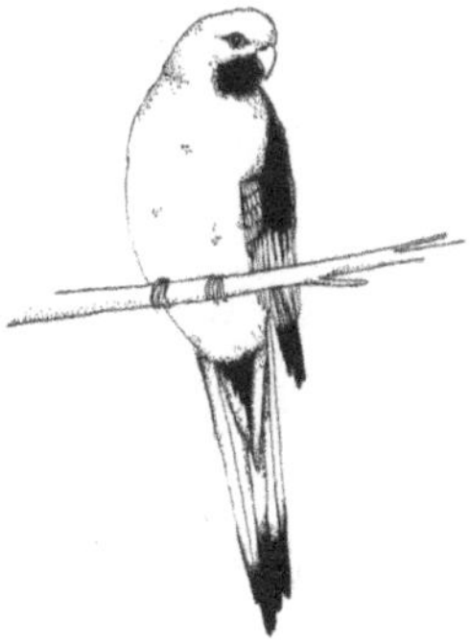

Chapter 10
THE SELF-AWARE BIRD

It is important to have a sense of who you are. What is your personality type? The perception of self may be an important issue during encounters with other individuals, such as during mate choice. A bird needs to be sufficiently self-aware to understand how it looks from another's perspective[1]. Am I a handsome bird? Do others think I am a handsome bird? Or am I a just-pretty bird because I only have one eye? Will I still find a mate even if I am half blind? A bird might ask itself these questions.

For example, what is the point of going after a higher-quality mate when the risk of divorce is high, or if acceptance by this higher-quality mate in the first place is unlikely? Why waste the time and energy chasing a bird that is just out of your league? Just as with people, research is starting to show evidence that high-quality males are not always the most attractive mates for all females when it comes to birds[2]. Instead, attractiveness of another might be influenced by the chooser's own state. Beauty is in the eye of the beholder!

A male may be able to influence particular selection pressures by choosing who they are being compared to. For example, males with poor sexual condition, only one eye, a weak wing or a broken leg, for example, may associate with other poor-quality males, with their own weaknesses. This may enable them to increase their relative quality compared to the other males in the group; the best of a bad lot. The bird might be the best looking in a group compared to the other individuals. In addition there might be better opportunities for these lower-quality males to find a mate in large flocks where they might meet a female who will bond with them (fission–fusion societies).

A study on English blue tits found that although groups were highly unstable over short periods of times, the interactions between different individuals in the population were not so. The researchers suggested that the patterns of group membership arose through association preferences of individuals. They chose who to hang out with; possibly based on their own self-awareness in addition to the existing composition of the group. Interestingly, the researchers also found individuals sorted according to their status as immigrant or locally born birds.

This appeared to be driven by spatial sorting rather than social decisions in the flocks. There was a strong relationship between residence and dominance, with birds that held or previously held a territory having a higher dominance than non-residents[3]. This may lead to spatial partitioning if resident birds exclude immigrants from important resources, pushing these immigrants to marginal or bordering areas. This effect may even include resident juveniles being dominant over non-resident, recently arrived adults[4].

In science, we can investigate self-perception through exposing a bird to a mirror. Does the bird recognise itself? John Gould was sent a dead brush turkey with a letter detailing how it died: 'The creature had mistaken its reflection in a well for another brush turkey, like a young Narcissus gazing at his own image. But rather than falling in love, the turkey had interpreted the blurry form as a rival and thrust forward in a diving attack. Unfortunately the silly creature drowned.'

Okay, before we term the bird silly, let's think about this from the bird's viewpoint. It is more natural for a bird to see its reflection in water while drinking or bathing, so that the bird sees its image horizontally. What happens when the bird sees its reflection in a vertical mirror? Research has found that upright mirrors, such as car wing mirrors, can evoke socially aggressive behaviour[5]. Let's look at magpie larks. Firstly, they appear to have, inherently, a bold temperament. Many of us have watched as they attack their own mirror image, as Garry describes in our next story.

'YOU TALKING TO ME?'

Garry Knight

Our resident pair of magpie larks (or mudlarks as we refer to them) just love a mirror or glass window/door that is at times reflective. In true Robert de Niro brashness as portrayed in the movie *Taxi Driver*, where he stares into a mirror to practise his most aggressive verbal assaults, the larks are obsessed with challenging the 'other' bird they see.

With a jumping flutter they fly at the reflection, usually pulling up in flight just before impact, retreat and repeat this 20 or 30 times. Eventually the lark decides itself to be the winner and takes off to strut around the lawn to catch some insects. Somehow though the victory must feel hollow as it returns to repeat the process again and again throughout the day, at wherever a reflection presents the intruder.

Before we declare the bird dumb, we need to remember that the magpie lark had no cues indicating that the bird was a reflection. A bird knows its own smell and what it sounds like. The bird in the mirror has neither a smell nor a vocal response to let the bird know it is seeing itself. Remember the story of the male lyrebird without a tail who met his reflection in the window in Chapter 8?

Mirrors or mirror-related toys are often provided to budgerigars and cockatiels. Most of us might believe the bird makes friends with the bird in the mirror as a substitute for social interaction. However despite their widespread use, exactly how mirrors relate to social behaviour remains a mystery. Does the budgie really think its reflection is another bird? Research has found that mirror use can be beneficial for birds in captivity. Those birds accustomed to a strong pair-bond may use mirrors because they give the illusion of a stable partner, providing the budgie/cockatiel with social interaction.

Social birds appear to show a stronger interest in their mirror image when they have been socially deprived[6]. A study on captive starlings found they reacted differently to the presence of a mirror according to sex and social experiences. In captive starling groups, it was found the birds form same-sex social affinities and groups[7]. It was posited that being with only one other bird (the bird in the mirror) could be comforting, especially as that bird in the mirror is mimicking behaviour. The study went on to show that a male's reaction to the mirror depended on his social experience. A bird used to living in groups will be more social than a single-raised isolated bird.

Another study found that age can affect a bird's capacity to know what it looks like. In this study, newly hatched domestic chicks were dyed red or green, or left their natural yellow colour. Results showed that newly hatched chicks had no preference for red, yellow or green mates. When they learn the colour of their companions by eight days of age, however, they approach them selectively. This led the researchers to suggest that colour of other birds is learned[8].

Sexual selection theory posits that females should choose mates in a way that maximises their reproductive success. We assume that females seek a male of the highest possible quality in terms of the genes or resources he can provide. As we touched on earlier, male birds can show their good genes through ornamentation, such as the peacock tail. Females that prefer males with the most elaborate ornamentation (tail) or display (bower or dance) will profit by obtaining genes that will enhance their offspring's chances of finding mates[9].

A study on zebra finches found that some females consistently preferred red-beaked males whereas others preferred orange-beaked males. In addition, some females preferred high song rates and others low song rates. Some female finches were even found to show a preference for aggressive males, while others preferred less aggressive males. This shows there are many different traits that make a suitable mate for an individual and we cannot always predict what a female or male will choose. We also have to remember that captive birds may alter naturally occurring behaviour in mate-choice processes due to artificial conditions[10]. The unpredictability of environmental and nutritional conditions of Australian fission–fusion societies means there are opportunities to mix in larger groups and meet more potential mates. Similar to budgies and cockatiels, zebra finches need to breed quickly as they need to take advantage of rainfall to provide the correct conditions. It is better to have formed a strong bond with another so you can start breeding immediately.

Could the female's own quality bias her judgement of male attractiveness, such that male quality and attractiveness do not always coincide? Female condition may lead to divergent female preferences, with low-quality females actively preferring low-quality males over high-quality males. Another study on zebra finches found that females reared in poor conditions develop acoustic preferences for songs of males reared in similar conditions; low-quality females unanimously preferred the songs of low-quality males. Further research found that female zebra finches reduced their choosiness when their body condition was compromised and therefore weak[2]. Possibly similar to us, females preferred males whose quality matched their own. This implies the existence of mechanisms that alter females' mating decisions in relation to their own phenotypic quality[11]. Findings of female phenotypic quality affecting mate preferences have so far only been reported in humans. For example, women with self-perceived low attractiveness preferred to date men of lower attractiveness when compared with women with self-perceived higher attractiveness[12,13].

Being aware of one's own quality or attractiveness may be useful, at least in species with mutual choice, in deciding which mates are unattainable and therefore not worth courting. The bird cannot risk being deserted by the mate, or may not be accepted by them in the first place[14]. If pursuing these mates is likely to waste time or energy, it may pay to avoid high-quality mates altogether and target low-quality partners instead[15]. I am going to use a story sent to me by Elizabeth about two sulphur-crested cockatoos, Monte and Pat, to discuss this further:

MONTE AND PAT

Elizabeth Gossell

Monte was a raggedy-looking white cockatoo with a hanging-down wing from some previous injury. He flew well enough on it, but we always wondered how it impacted his feeding ability and defensive practices. When his wife, Pat, turned up with him eventually, we realised the strength they had was in their bond. She was not perfect either, having a damaged blind eye, as she was very tentative at first and would swing her head around so that the good eye was always keeping watch, even on us.

Pat and Monte would sit together on our verandah railing, patiently waiting for the food we provided. They would sit closely, him with his good wing outbound, and she with her good eye also

> outbound. That meant that both handicaps were between them, and what faced the world was a normal wing and eye!
>
> We assumed they developed this strategy on their own for protection. Monte was a cranky chap and would challenge most other cockatoos who came near. She, likewise, would raise her comb, open her beak to screech at any who dared steal their food. They were a formidable pair.

Is beauty in the eye of the beholder? I would like to believe so. Were Monte and Pat aware that they were matched in terms of mate choice? Could there be subconscious mechanisms at work? Is there an internal physiological monitoring informing individuals about their body conditions? This could lead the bird to adjust its preferences[16]. Individuals may gain information about their quality relative to others from previous social experiences. If so we would then expect the bird to be sensitive to the level of interest it receives from the opposite sex. An individual may therefore change its preferences in response to physiological and social feedback without directly perceiving its own attractiveness[17].

In cockatoos there is considerable parental investment by males as well as females as they are a long-term monogamous species. The male and female need to cooperate in raising their offspring to ensure their survival. Having a stable mate through the years may gain an advantage. Perhaps this is why we have so many strongly bonded birds compared to Europe where conditions are more predictable, like rainfall, resulting in short-term bonds between short-lived birds during short breeding seasons.

The time and energy costs of searching for a mate are typically high, but mate-choice decisions can strongly affect reproductive success. Individuals who are too choosy may fail to find a mate and be forced to forego reproduction altogether, while those who are unselective may end up with a mismatched partner[18]. This may result in low parental investment and a high risk of desertion or divorce.

When discussing attractiveness, we should be aware that this is a measure of how much a particular individual is preferred by another. As we have discussed, this is related to the quality of both individuals. High-quality males are not always the most attractive but if they breed successfully, it is worth staying together. Successful breeding is a sign of winning! Monte and Pat raised young together, as the next part of Elizabeth's story tells.

> They had many nestlings over the years and would usually introduce one or more at some point in the summer when the babies were leaving the nest to enter flight school. It was a joy to meet the young. At high summer their flock would usually disappear to forage elsewhere for a month or two. They always came back though.
>
> In September one year, the local bushfire brigade burned off a river reserve at the end of our road. Sadly, the chicks were still in the nests, not yet ready to fly. Pat went missing the last week of the burn-off/put-out activity and we were very worried as we knew they nested in that reserve in the hollows of the big eucalypts there.

Attractiveness is not an inherent property of a particular male phenotype. Rather it is a combined outcome of the male's phenotype and the female's response to the male[15]. Females may vary in their responses, in which case the same male is attractive to one female but unattractive to another[18]. Despite this, females may still agree on which male has the highest quality. For example, female zebra finches consistently laid bigger eggs when mated to high-quality males, despite preferring males of their own quality in choice testing[19].

So what happens when one of the partners dies? How will the widowed bird adapt? The end of Monte and Pat's story is not a happy one.

> We knew the worst had happened when Monte finally showed up without Pat and desperately hungry. After a quick feed, he took up sitting in the top of our giant forest red gum tree which was 225 feet tall. He sat there for days and keened and called for his mate. It broke our hearts to hear it. She never came back, and we have every reason to believe that she may have been killed in the burn-off as she would not have left her chicks, and the tree we believed was their breeding tree was severely burned, not once, but three times. Monte lasted a few months more and took up roosting in a tree very near us. Finally, he too disappeared, never having got over the loss of his lovely Pat.

What are the chances of Monte getting another mate as good as Pat? Will Monte now join other unpaired males and spend his days as a bachelor? I suspect this is what happened. Monte joined other single males in the hopes that he might just be lucky enough to find another Pat. Either way Monte and Pat formed a great partnership that displayed working together to raise their young. Not wanting to leave you on a sad note, I would like to share a happier story, sent by Bev. This story shows similar mateship in a pair of healthier rosellas. It's about sticking together through the good and bad times.

IN-LOVE ROSELLAS

Bev McKay

> Our previous house had a wall of glass which gave a perfect reflection of our garden. Unfortunately from time to time birds flew into the windows, very often injuring themselves. One day a pale-headed rosella crashed, and I rushed to rescue it. After it came to, and obviously couldn't fly, I put it in a small bird cage which I used to hang in a garden tree during the day. During that time its mate would come to visit, crawling around the outside of the cage and keeping it

> company. After two weeks the injured bird was ready to fly away and the pair flew off together. How sweet is that!

These rosellas stayed together; the mate did not desert its injured partner. Why do you think this is? Perhaps the rosellas had been together for years and the time already invested in the relationship meant a strong bond.

Chapter 11
THE CUCKOOED BIRD

Did you know that Australia is home to more than 20 per cent of the world's cuckoo species[1]? Not only this, our cuckoo–host interactions are different from other countries. Australian cuckoo–host interactions are characterised by lower rates of cuckoo egg rejection by host birds in comparison to European counterparts[2]. Why is this? Researchers suggest our milder environmental conditions provide host birds with longer breeding seasons, allowing for multiple clutches and more opportunities for cuckoos to lay compared to the short breeding seasons found in Europe

Previous studies have proposed that cooperatively breeding species are more likely to be hosts of cuckoos than are non-cooperative species. Why is this? One thought is that cuckoos can acquire superior care for their usually larger young by targeting cooperative breeding birds. Cooperative breeding occurs when three or more individuals (breeding pair and another) contribute to the care of young in the nest. Host defence against cuckoos may be strengthened by helpers at the nest[3]. This may be because group living reduces rates of parasitism as the female can spend more time at the nest. In this way, helpers can act as community guards with vigilance increasing with group size.

Superb fairy-wrens are particularly well-known cooperative breeders. While Horsfield's bronze cuckoos parasitise a range of host species, superb fairy-wrens are the primary hosts throughout their range. Superb fairy-wren groups comprise a breeding female, a dominant male, and up to five male helpers. A nine-year study on superb fairy-wrens found that 72 per cent of males spent their entire life on their natal territory—that is, the territory into which they were born—with the oldest helper often inheriting the dominant position. Of those males that dispersed, 95 per cent settled in a territory immediately neighbouring their natal territory[4]. In contrast, the natal dispersal distances of females are longer than males with breeding females leaving the local area. While looking for a territory, these small females suffer high mortality. This is thought to result in the strongly male-favoured sex ratio that characterises superb fairy-wren populations[5].

Parasitism usually takes place the morning after the host bird lays her own egg, with the bronze cuckoo removing one host egg before laying her own[6]. Parasitism of a nest by more than one bronze cuckoo is rare. The eggs of bronze cuckoos usually hatch one or two days before the young of the host. The cuckoo chick evicts all eggs and nestlings of the host from the nest within two days of hatching[7]. The fairy-wren hosts lose all their own offspring and go on to invest around 50 days in rearing the bronze cuckoo, from the start of the incubation period.

So the female needs to learn about techniques that may help in defence against cuckoos. Female superb fairy-wrens have come up with ingenious ways of helping them detect cuckoo eggs. A study found that superb fairy-wrens were more likely to abandon a single chick in years when adult Horsfield's bronze cuckoos had been seen or heard in breeding areas[8,9]. In addition, females teach their young a password call while they are still in the egg! Mum starts calling to her eggs around four or five days before hatching. While in the egg, the cuckoo chick does not learn this song, only the fairy-wren chicks. The female repeats the password call to her eggs approximately sixteen times an hour when she is alone and incubating her eggs. This is known as embryonic call learning[10]. It shows us that chicks start learning while still in the egg.

The parents can detect intruder nestlings as they have not learned the password—they can correctly conclude the chick is a cuckoo[9]. The female shares the password with her mate as, once hatched, the nestlings use this call when begging for food.

Host birds and cuckoos are constantly trying to outsmart each other in an 'evolutionary arms race'. For example the eastern koel is a migratory species that arrived in Australia from southeast Asia to breed in spring. Although rarely seen, the koel is known for its loud, repetitive calls. The same female lays eggs in the nest of numerous hosts and these may be within the same male's or a different male's home range[11]. Cuckoo trickery involves adaptation to counter successive lines of host defence, including tricks for gaining access to host nests, egg trickers and chick trickery[12]. This has resulted in the evolution of host-bird strategies to prevent cuckoo parasitism. In turn, selection for counter-adaptations in cuckoos circumvent host defences[13]. Host birds try to outsmart the cuckoo as the cuckoo adapts to the host birds' techniques. As the cuckoo's chick hatches, it usually evicts all the other eggs of its foster parents. This comes at a great cost to the host parents who spend time and energy feeding a cuckoo chick, as Di describes in our next story.

CHANNEL-BILLED CUCKOO CHAOS

Di Robinson

My friend and I were doing her monthly bird count in her large wild garden of several hectares. It has huge natural trees scattered through it, an understorey of banksias with many honeyeaters darting to and fro, and a lower storey of small shrubs for wrens and spinebills.

> As we walked towards the rear of the garden where we knew Torresian crows were nesting, we heard the raucous calls of a channel-billed cuckoo as it swooped overhead. The calls soon ceased and were replaced by muffled, hoarse 'squarks'.
>
> We rushed towards the origin of the calls and looking upwards with our binoculars through the branches of a tall tree we saw the crow's nest with a crow sitting. On top of it was a huge channel-billed cuckoo apparently attempting to lay its egg.
>
> The crow was protesting the intrusion of the heavy bird. The cuckoo sat there for several minutes and then lifted off and flew away. The poor crow stood up, ruffled its feathers and finally settled back down on the nest again.
>
> The outcome of this encounter was evident weeks later as two ragged-looking crows worked hard to provide food for the ever-increasing appetite of the 'cuckoo in their nest'.

As host parents are often relatively small compared to cuckoo chicks, the hosts have to work hard to ensure a sufficient feeding rate. Cuckoo chicks often exploit this by making extravagant begging calls that increase in frequency as they grow larger, in combination with a conspicuous begging display[13]. Research found that bronze cuckoo nestlings are striking visual mimics of their host parent with the accuracy of their mimicry varying according to the diversity of hosts they exploit[14].

Recognition of cuckoos by the host birds is not innate. This means the ability to identify a cuckoo needs to be learned. Host birds might learn to increase their defences against adult cuckoos from personal experience, but opportunities for individual learning can be limited. This is because cuckoos are very secretive when surveying prospective hosts and their laying visits are extremely short, so can easily be missed. In addition, a number of cuckoos resemble birds of prey, so individual learning may also entail a predation risk to the prospective host bird[15].

Let's look at other ways birds can learn about cuckoos. Learning by an individual bird can occur through an associative process, known as associative learning. It occurs when an individual learns an association between two stimuli, for instance when a host bird learns to associate a cuckoo at the nest with the subsequent appearance of an odd egg in its clutch. Another type of learning is relational learning which occurs when an individual develops the ability to categorise one stimulus as distinct from another, for instance when a host bird learns to differentiate the odd egg in its clutch.

Then there is perceptual learning[16]. This occurs when an individual's ability to visually learn improves with experience, such as when a host expands its internal template with the appearance of its own egg. Perceptual learning can be risky if a host bird forms a chick-recognition template based on its first breeding attempt. What happens if the host nest happens to have a cuckoo egg during this first breeding attempt? Perhaps an outcome is the host rejecting its own chicks in all subsequent breeding attempts[17].

Research found experienced female superb fairy-wrens were more likely than inexperienced breeders to reject a single chick[18]. This suggests that females refine their nestling recognition template following exposure to their own young, or improve their ability to recognise adult cuckoos through experience. Chick rejection in superb fairy-wrens could be based on the breeding experience of the female combined with whether adult cuckoos are present in the area.

Naive female fairy-wrens were found to make more recognition errors and fewer accurate rejection decisions than experienced females[19]. This may be the result of a lack of recognition of adult cuckoos and therefore a reduced ability to reject an egg according to the presence or absence of cuckoos. It may even be simply a lack of experience with their own nestlings. Either way, misimprinting of a cuckoo nestling can happen, as Isabel reports.

SCRUBWRENS AND PALLID CUCKOO

Isabel Temple

I heard a different sound—a different bird call. Further along the verandah sitting low on a small tree was a bird I hadn't seen before—it was constantly calling and fluttering, attracting attention. I went to my field guide book and identified it as a pallid cuckoo. I called my husband and we watched over the days as those poor little scrubwrens darted and disappeared and returned to feed this oversized chick.

They were wonderful parents and their 'baby' flourished and disappeared after a while. The wrens went back to their normal life and enjoyed another year of happy life together.

Well you can imagine my surprise when the next spring brought the very same event—they rebuilt their nest in the same planter and the cuckoo returned, and obviously knowing those little birds would re-nest there, it did the same dirty trick on them again. Once again they were incredibly busy feeding this cuckoo chick to maturity. They never faltered or gave up. I felt so sorry for them but they were single-minded.

These little birds had three seasons of rearing a cuckoo chick. I often wonder how many times this would have happened for this dedicated pair if they had not been lost to the fire of 2009 in Churchill.

While individual learning is important, it may be more beneficial to learn about the risk of parasitism from others[16]. A host bird could obtain information about how to identify and respond to cuckoos through watching and learning from others. As we have discussed, individual learning can be costly and error-prone. It may be better for individuals instead to learn socially. That is, using public information to guide their responses[20].

It is possible that hosts increase their repertoire of defences through social learning as there are always more tricks to learn. This information could be socially transmitted, enabling individuals to modify their behaviour by observing others. Social learning could lead to rapid cultural transmission of defence strategies in local host populations. This can occur when naive birds learn to mob a cuckoo by observing another individual mobbing it. The bird could use this information itself, then communicate its success to others.

Host species may attempt to prevent parasitism physically by mobbing the female brood parasite. One of the most ubiquitous host defences is the mobbing of cuckoos. Collective mobbing by multiple individuals can provide a more effective defence than solitary or pair mobbing, and represent a selective force for cooperative action. Mobbing behaviour has been well studied in some cooperative breeders such as superb fairy-wrens. It was found that large groups of fairy-wrens mob cuckoos more aggressively, and go on to experience low rates of parasitism[9].

One way social learners can learn is by eavesdropping on other birds to find out what they know[21]. This would suggest that discrimination against cuckoos at the nest may also be learned through eavesdropping on what others know, learning the cues around the likelihood of brood parasitism. This type of learning avoids many of the trial-and-error costs that come with learning from personal experience. Some host birds, for example, possess special alarm calls that are elicited almost exclusively when they see a cuckoo. In superb fairy-wrens a graded alarm call means a brooding cuckoo closer to the nest and therefore more of a threat[15]. In both instances, however, such calls and associated behaviours may allow other individuals to learn about the parasitism threat that comes with seeing a cuckoo in the area. This suggests superb fairy-wrens recognise other alarm calls and can modify their responses to cuckoos based on learned cues.

It is generally assumed that public information is used for enhancing nest defences against cuckoos. This is because host birds can use direct cues, such as the sight of brood parasite adults, eggs or chicks. They can also use indirect cues, such as the start of breeding season, that increase parasite encounters. All information is used to modify defences to reduce the risk of parasitism. Prevention of parasitism carries the lowest cost because the host's own reproductive attempt can continue undisturbed. In our next story, Janet describes two exhausted magpie larks acting as hosts.

CUCKOO STORY

Janet Spinaze

My local magpie lark couple have raised a koel! They nest in a forest red gum right next to our house. Once fully feathered and left the nest, the koel is constantly calling out, awkwardly moving from shrub to shrub in our garden while waiting to be fed. The peewees always look absolutely exhausted, constantly collecting food for the 'little one' to satisfy its insatiable hunger. This is the second year they have raised a koel. Both years we observed the frantic feeding of the koel and the daily goings-on, but then one day, the koel was gone. I know koels are migratory birds, but I find it fascinating how a koel raised by peewees can instinctively know when to leave and where to fly to. I would truly love a baby peewee next year though . . .

Learning appears to be important for a bird to respond to alarm calls of a different species. However, learning might not be required if a bird can identify alarm calls based solely on their acoustic structure. For instance, apostlebirds responded to the mobbing call of a North American Carolina wren despite having no opportunity to learn it[22]. This study implied the importance of acoustic similarity for prompting a response to unfamiliar alarm calls. Recognising another species' alarm calls might occur because the calls of different species converge on broadly similar acoustic structures.

Alarm calls have two common designs, depending on their function. Mobbing alarm calls attract others to join the caller in harassing a predator. Flee alarm calls, such as aerial alarm calls, are produced in response to predators in flight. While fleeing alarm calls can be cryptic and prompt escape, mobbing calls are conspectus and incite others to approach and harass. In a study on superb fairy-wrens who were in the same area as white-browed scrubwrens, the fairy-wrens responded to scrubwren aerial alarm calls by immediately fleeing to cover[23]. However, a population of fairy-wrens living in the absence of scrubwrens did not respond to scrubwren calls. This study suggested that fairy-wrens are capable of high levels of acoustic discrimination. In addition, the acoustic similarity between those calls cannot be detected without experience.

An example of this was found in a study on the fleeing response of superb fairy-wrens to the very acoustically dissimilar alarm calls of New Holland honeyeaters. The study found that call similarity was not essential for response. The fairy-wrens learned the meaning of the honeyeaters' alarm call was that a cuckoo had been detected in the area[24]. Furthermore, fairy-wrens usually did not respond to the honeyeater calls when the researchers played a recording of the call backwards. This was despite the reversed calls having almost all of the same acoustic properties as the more familiar normal calls. The study implied that the fairy-wrens learn to respond to the very specific acoustic structure of normal New Holland honeyeater calls.

Learning and working together for a common goal helps reaffirm bonds between neighbouring birds and helps keep harmony between groups[25]. The neighbour bird and his mates will help in times of need, such as ariels mobbing a predator. In these times, strength in numbers fighting a common enemy helps birds to bond. But life is not always that simple. What happens when an individual decides not to work with other birds—to cheat instead of cooperating?

Chapter 12
THE CHEATING BIRD

The problem in explaining the evolution of cooperative behaviour is the need to explain the selective forces that resist cheating. Let's think about it from our point for view. Why work if you can get away with living on benefits? Why be sexually monogamous if you can cheat? From a male's view, if he gets the neighbouring breeding female pregnant, it has no strings attached. Her socially monogamous male will raise them as his own. So what might be the mechanisms that prevent an individual or partners from cheating while engaging in cooperative interactions? A possible mechanism for enforcing cooperation could include rewarding cooperative birds and punishing cheaters. In ecology there is currently a lack of agreement on what a 'cheat' actually is because it is not always clear, nor is it clear whether a cheat is always a cheat. The science is still uncertain regarding the means by which selection favours individuals that cheat, or how we expect others to respond to cheating. In this chapter, cheaters are individuals who do not cooperate, or cooperate less than their fair share. The cheaters are potentially able to gain benefits from others who *are* cooperating.

Birds such as superb fairy-wrens are well-known birds that often pop up in gardens. These birds can give us an excellent opportunity to investigate the interplay of cheating and cooperation in social groups. Our next story, sent in by James, describes helpers feeding offspring.

FAMILY LIFE OF MY FAIRY-WRENS

James Jones

I am always amused while watching a family of superb fairy-wrens chattering to each other. The dominant male with his bright colours seems to hold court while the youngest hop around him. I often wonder, what is he talking about? It appears to be very important!

I often watch the youngest fly in and out of the nest, I think they are feeding the nestlings but who knows! At breeding times they can be so quiet compared to other times of the year.

As we have discussed, superb fairy-wrens live in groups comprising a single female paired to a dominant male, with one to five male helpers[1]. Superb fairy-wren males are constrained from dispersal primarily by a lack of available territory and non-related females. Male fairy-wrens rarely disperse from their natal territory, but when they do it is over very short distances[2].

Although male fairy-wrens can start breeding in their first year, they can also remain as helpers for up to seven years. Male superb fairy-wrens need to be at least four years of age before they start showing their bright blue colours. As many males don't attain a territory they have to stay in their home territory. This restriction of dispersal by young males could be that dominant males are able to exploit the contributions of helpers. Females only mate with males as they become bright blue and are thus considered attractive by breeding females.

Although socially monogamous, superb fairy-wrens have one of the highest known rates of extra-group fertilisation. In other words, a male or female mates with an individual from a different group but doesn't help raise the young that come from their affair. Extra-group fertilisation is a fancy way of saying, 'I cheated on you and I am now pregnant.' Not that a bird would share that information with its mate! Instead it is a term used to understand the high rate of cheating males and females in fairy-wrens. In fact more than 60 per cent of offspring are sired by males outside of the social group, and the male does not appear to provide care for these offspring[3]. This is the difference between being sexually monogamous compared to socially monogamous.

During the breeding season, helpers contribute to the feeding of nestlings and dependent fledglings, and help with territory defence. Helpers do not appear to have responsibilities during the non-breeding season when territory boundaries are relaxed, with groups frequently coalescing to form foraging flocks. In these temporary groups, birds communicate and learn from each other; fission–fusion at work again.

Does a helper benefit only if it is known they have helped? Indeed helping may be seen as an indicator of quality. This would enhance an individual's reputation within the group and increase its chances of future breeding, for example. In other words, they may gain social prestige!

As far as the research shows there are two main types of helpers: those who are related to the dominant breeding pair and therefore the chicks they are feeding, and those who are not related. When the helper is related to the dominant breeding pair there is motivation for the helper as there is a direct genetic relationship to the young.

Could we speculate that the relatedness of breeders and helpers may influence the likelihood of cooperative helping? Related helpers, such as non-breeding aunties and uncles, helping to feed their nieces and nephews. Such indirect benefits limit conflict of interest between breeders and helpers, and also increase the likelihood of voluntary helper contributions to offspring care[4].

In cases where helpers are not related to the breeding pair, what are the benefits of helping? To pay rent! Similar to parents who have kids still living with them at home; if you want to live here you have to pull your weight and help around the house. One way in which the helper bird can assist is to provide care to the young through 'alloparenting'. Alloparenting is a term used for parental care provided by helpers to non-descendent young. A possible reason for helpers providing alloparenting is that it constitutes rent for their continued residence within the territory[5].

Like our own *older* children who are yet to leave the nest, helpers pay 'rent' in order to enjoy the benefits of living in a familiar social group. Conflicts of interest can nevertheless arise between breeders and helpers. For example, alloparenting care is beneficial for breeders but comes at a cost to helpers. It also costs the breeding pair to have helpers at the nest, because the helpers must compete with the breeders for food and may attract predators, or even harm the breeders' eggs or offspring[6]. In our next story, Brigid tells of helpers following the lead of the dominant male.

BULLY FAIRY-WRENS

Brigid Krohn

Why are fairy-wrens such bullies? With his constant chatter and pushy personality, he rules my garden. The others follow him around the garden as he searches for food. I feed the wrens meal worms and the male always seems to have first choice of the food. He has become so accustomed to me, he will sit on my knee and take the food from my hand. The others wait nearby and hop around my feet hoping the male will drop some more food down to them. He never has!

I hear the wrens jostling and squeaking grumpily at each other for being disturbed. During the day if a wren spots a snake or a blue-tongue on the ground, the whole family gathers in the bushes above it, peering down and hopping from twig to twig, all the while chattering furiously in their 'look, look, danger, danger' voices!

It has been suggested that 'The original paradox of cooperative breeding largely disappeared with the widespread confirmation that helpers frequently do improve their chances to become breeders and they frequently do obtain large indirect genetic benefits by helping to rear collateral kin'[7]. However, some important questions still remain unanswered. In particular, our understanding of the varying level of helpers' contributions within and between species remains poor[8].

Mixed groups of helpers result in mixed personality types with different motivations for helping. A helper has different inclinations; some will actually help, while others will not. In some species, younger individuals may not be as good at providing parental care as older individuals[9]. Helpers in white-winged choughs, for instance, have a long period (four years) before reaching sexual maturity. Once fully mature, breeders must have at least two helpers to breed successfully[10]. Having helpers means there are more individuals to feed the young. This increased productivity compared to smaller groups with fewer helpers reduces nestling starvation. Helpers appear to get better at providing food, as younger helpers show inferior foraging ability and do not supply the same amount of food to the nest as older birds[9]. Younger helpers still have much to learn as they do not yet have the experience in effective foraging that older helpers do. They may spend more time following older birds to learn foraging tricks.

Family groups arise over time as young birds grow older and have nowhere to go because of the lack of free territories. For instance, in white-winged choughs who are members of a group, size increases slowly as they usually recruit new members through reproduction. This shows fledglings are extremely valuable as they act as helpers. An unusual observation is of groups raiding their neighbours and kidnapping their recently fledged young[11]. These young are unrelated to their kidnappers yet receive normal levels of parental care to foraging independence. They eventually become helpers in their new groups. In addition, if one of the dominant pair dies, there are unrelated young in the group to breed with and take over the territory.

If helpers are beneficial to the dominant breeding birds, we could expect the latter to be choosy in allowing the most helpful individuals to stay in the group and evict the lazy ones. We could expect this to happen in birds where the number of potential helpers available in the group is large, such as superb fairy-wrens[12]. This can occur where ecological constraints such as available territories hinder dispersal, resulting in many available helpers to choose from[13]. Thus through eviction and/or punishment of group members who aren't cooperating (lazy helpers) and tolerance towards efficient helpers, the dominant pair can ensure good workers. It is important to consider that failure to cooperate does not always represent being lazy, as a helper may be in poor body condition and unable to feed the young at a high rate.

Another reason for describing a bird as a lazy helper is because helping may not increase the brood's fitness. For example, if the number of helpers at the nest and the level of care provided increases, and a sufficiently high level of provisioning is reached, what is the point of continuing to feed the sated chicks? There would be no motivation for the helper to continue this task. An example of this is found in the cooperatively breeding carrion crow, where helping effort varies greatly within groups, with a gradient that ranges from individuals that work as much as the breeders to others that completely refrain from visiting the nest[14]. A study asked whether lazy helpers could act as 'insurance helpers'[15]. In other words, an insurance workforce that fully compensates for a reduction in the provisioning effort of another group member, avoiding a decrease in reproductive success. The study on carrion crows also found that the laziest non-breeder increased their feeding rate and individuals that initially refrained from visiting the nest started helping. In contrast, breeders did not increase chick provisioning. This study showed that lazy non-breeders can act as a buffer and will start working when that group's success relies on the potential contribution of mixed personality group members.

One way a helper can cheat is through false-feeding. False-feeding happens when helpers bring food to the brood but then consume the food themselves rather than delivering it. This type of cheating, reported in several species, is often interpreted as a strategy of deception. The existence of false-feeding provides us with evidence that helpers believe they may benefit from being known to have contributed. A study found that young, white-winged chough helpers frequently brought food to the nest and even placed it into the bill of a nestling, but they then removed it, consuming the food themselves[9]. It is interesting to note that helpers were most likely to false-feed when they were alone at the nest. There were no other group members to witness the deception. Dominant breeders sometimes aggressively chased helpers that arrived without food. The study also found that helpers engaged in false-feeding were more likely to be young, inexperienced or in poor condition.

Another method of cheating is to steal another bird's food. Birds from the corvid family are examples of food-catching birds. Ravens will transport food to areas where potential raiders are scarce and scatter their caches there[16]. A number of studies have shown that ravens can remember the exact locations of numerous caches. The chance of another bird finding caches would increase if they could learn through observation and remember the location of caches they have seen others make[17].

A study on ravens found caching birds responded to the presence of other individuals by hiding their caches behind structures, obstructing the view of potential thieves[18]. In addition, the presence of potential raiders led to caching birds changing cache sites frequently. The study suggests ravens are capable of withholding information about their intentions, as raiding caches of others is a tactic ravens regularly use to scrounge food.

What happens when helpers are caught cheating? Can dominant individuals punish or coerce them into cooperating? Can the cheater learn from being punished and not repeat the cheating action again? Could cheating have led to the evolution of punishment in animal societies? Could uncooperative individuals have low fitness levels because other members of their social group punish them?

One way cheating could be prevented or discouraged in a group is by rewarding more cooperative helpers (that is, positive reciprocity). Punishment occurs when an individual reduces its own current payoffs: for example, stops feeding to harass or attack a cheating helper (negative reciprocity). Providing punishment should reduce the benefits of cheating and thereby promote cooperative behaviour from the cheater. Our next story, sent in by Sarah, tells of a magpie that appears to be punished by others.

MY FAMILY OF MAGPIES

Sarah Homes

I have a family of magpies that visit me daily and I have come to think of them as family. The way the family interacts with each other keeps me entertained for hours. There is one magpie that has a balding head and the others will sometimes peck it and it seems to be in bad condition compared to the others.

I wonder what this magpie did wrong and why it gets picked on?

If birds can learn, punishment may cause individuals to cooperate through changing their behaviour. Was the magpie Sarah describes punished for a behaviour not witnessed? Punishment is most likely to be meted out where cheating is a discrete event, rather than a regular behaviour. We would expect helpers to increase their contributions to care if this avoids punishment, reduces the harm caused by subsequent attacks, or prevents eviction from the group.

It is suggested that enforced cooperation could occur when individuals in groups differ in their competitive abilities. This is often seen when the breeding male dominates helpers. Because the birds know who is boss, we would expect aggressive encounters to be resolved quickly and without the fighting escalating, thus ultimately reducing the cost to the dominant individual of aggressive behaviour.

Could dominant breeders tolerate extra-group individuals that showed submissive behaviours or provided help, and attack or evict those that did not? Effective punishment requires some aggressive behaviour by the punishers that would cause the cheater to behave more cooperatively in future. Otherwise what is the point of punishment? This is supported by a study on superb fairy-wrens which found that dominant individuals harassed apparent defector individuals when they were experimentally prevented from helping[19].

It is worth considering the cognitive mechanism that might favour investment in punishment. A punisher who is constantly monitoring and evaluating others is doing it at a cost[20]. Punishment therefore involves an immediate cost to the punisher, one not paid if the cheat is left alone. In addition, a cheating bird needs to understand the link between its behaviour and the punishment. Just like in our own children, punishment is most effective when it occurs very shortly after the cheating behaviour. This is logical, as long-time delays between cheating behaviour and punishment are not conducive to associative learning.

Is having a 'conflict of interest' with another bird deemed punishable, for example when two individuals attack or threaten each other until one of them retreats while the other establishes dominance? Or what about when another individual in a group challenges the dominant bird? The dominant bird will attack the challenger, and usually wins. The losing bird will still remain in the group but as a subordinate to the dominate male.

You might be wondering about theft at bowers? As we found out earlier, males are known to steal objects and destroy neighbouring bowers. If the male catches the bird in the act and attacks the thief, is this punishment?

The Machiavelli intelligence hypothesis predicts that social complexity includes being able to detect cheats and may help to drive the evolution of intelligence. If you think about it, group living puts direct pressure on birds to compete for mates and resources such as food or nesting sites. Could group living have evolved to facilitate cheating detection and reinforce co-operation?

I will leave you with a quote from the man credited with this term, Italian diplomat and political theorist Niccolo Machiavelli (1469–1527). It is taken from *The Prince*: 'It is much safer to be feared than loved because . . . love is preserved by the link of obligation which, owing to the baseness of men, is broken at every opportunity for their advantage; but fear preserves you by a dread of punishment which never fails'[21].

Chapter 13
THE GRIEVING BIRD

As we have discussed, many of our birds have bonds with others that last years, so what happens when one of them dies? Do birds grieve for their mate? If birds are in long-term relationships and one dies, will a bird mourn the loss or just move on to another partner?

One of the first written reports of a grieving bird in Australia comes from John Gould in relation to a regent bowerbird who was shot by one of Gould's party. What Gould reports could be easily interpreted as grief on behalf of the female: 'The female bird came down and uttered her peculiar note. She continued flitting over the place and calling for her mate. On visiting the scrub on the following and several successive days, the female bird was seen in the location of the bower and by her constant calling was apparently lamenting the loss of what might seem to her the inconstancy of her mate.'

Regent bowerbirds, as with all bowerbirds, are part of the family of crow (corvidae) and birds of this family have been seen by many people having 'funerals'.

A funeral can be defined as birds gathering around the dead of one of their own[1]. But why do they do this? Is it possible that the birds are revisiting their memories in order to find new social opportunities? Are they saddened by the loss of an individual in their group? The female regent bowerbird reported by Gould may have been calling for a new mate, or even having a hard time trying to connect the sound of a gun with the disappearance of her male. Guns were a new predator that Australian birds had to learn about.

As death is final, it is important for a bird to learn about threats. Indeed, research suggests that a dead individual can be used as a source of public information. In other words, information about a risk is shared with others. While we don't know for sure if the birds are indeed gaining any information from the carcass, we can suspect that information about potential risk may be learned using cues from the body, for example cues from seeing the dead body when a predator was also seen in the area.

Birds may well depend on cues in the environment to assess and minimise the risk of death or injury[2]. As a result, birds may increase vigilance or minimise time spent in the area. We call this 'landscape of fear' and this landscape can change when new information is encountered. For instance, a previously safe location is considered less safe if predator cues (dead body) are encountered. Information about potential risk can come from tracking evidence of the predator's prey left behind. Some predators do not swallow their whole prey but leave behind remnants of their meal, with feathers and various body parts, in the place where the prey was attacked or consumed, offering evidence of the attack[2]. Encountering evidence of death through finding a body part may influence a bird's perception of which areas are now dangerous.

Birds gathered around the dead body have a common interest—to find out how this bird died[3]. Information gathered could include: Did a predator kill this bird? Do we know what kind of predator? And importantly, is the area now unsafe and so we need to move? These funerals are good opportunities to decide on how to act next. If it was a predator, the birds can form a group to mob the predator[4]. Mobbing is more effective when the group of attacking birds is larger[5]. Since there are many birds gathered around the dead individual, it's a good opportunity for alliances. For example, territory owners may benefit from tolerating unrelated individuals, allowing them to join in the mob after finding a dead bird. A larger group may also dilute the threat of attack on any one individual[6]. Mobbing may also function to warn others of danger[7]. Mobbing occurs when territorial neighbours benefit by responding to mobbing calls if it reduces predation risk on their adjacent territories. Many of us will be familiar with noisy miners mobbing birds bigger than themselves. In this case it is power in numbers that is the winning trait. Many birds from different groups have the same goal: intimidate the undesirable bird into leaving.

A study found that when American crows learned that a dead individual was the result of predation by a sparrowhawk, mobs of crows formed[8]. These mobs contained crows recruited from outside the territory of the breeding pair. Moreover, these mobs tended to be larger and more persistent in looking for a predator (sparrowhawk) in order to drive it away. The researchers found that the crows appeared capable of assigning guilt by association. More amazing is that the memory of these associations can potentially persist for months or longer, just as they can remember the call of old friends during a fission–fusion event.

Death of any group member is a cause for concern, especially if that member is similar in size to the others, making them all vulnerable to similar deaths through predation. Was the death of this crow caused by a predator larger than the living birds in the group? While inspecting the dead body, crows were found to rarely touch it, suggesting they respect their dead, as crows are known to feed on the dead of other species[1]. There may be another reason birds do not touch the body, such as fear of disease contagion which may actually be less likely than transmission between aggregating individuals[8]. We don't know if they are paying some sort of emotional respect, or simply using this event as an opportunity for discussion. Watch out for the anthropomorphic trap—that is, the tendency to automatically project human thoughts and feelings onto the bird—as you read our next story sent in by Sneska.

THE DEATH OF A CROW

Sneska Saliba

One cold morning, we heard the sad, mournful sound of a crow in the tree. Puzzled by this persistent wail, we had a look out of the window overlooking our verge. On it was a dead crow. It was very sad to see and hear its partner in life who was so distressed by this death that it remained by its side the whole time. We were worried that, by staying on the ground near the road, the mate could also meet a cruel end.

We took steps to do the kindest thing possible so we buried the dead bird underneath the tree. It was only then that the other crow eventually flew away.

It was a very sad day that day. Birds are just like people when they lose their loved one. They feel emotion and loss. Grief.

The birds continue to mass in the tree. The squawk, chirp and the caw caw of the crows goes on all day long. They are like a musical cacophony. They will again have young ones in nests to feed. And the whole cycle will begin again.

The loss of an individual from a group has many consequences for the remaining birds. They may benefit from the death by improved chances of survival or reproduction due to reduced competition. However, the immediate consequences of losing a member of a group are likely to depend on how the remaining individuals interact with one another. When a dominant male bird dies, for example, other males in the group need to find out who is going to replace him. Another reason for funerals is possibly as a place for learning of opportunity. Perhaps similar to us when attending a funeral, we talk about the dead person. We come together with family and friends to pay our respects, but perhaps also to find out information about what happened. How did he die? But he was so young and healthy! Who is taking over the territory? Who is the widowed bird? Are there offspring that need raising?

The loss of a female in the partnership differs from that of the loss of a male. In the case of Australian ravens, for instance, the loss of a female from an established pair is often followed quickly by replacement of the female by the widower. The new female will sometimes help raise her predecessor's nestlings. This would suggest that the male generally has no difficulty in defending his territory and attracting a new mate at the same time.

If the male raven dies, however, the surviving female appears unable to remate and to defend territory. This is because any new male on the scene would have no idea about territory boundaries or neighbouring birds. The tension between courting the widow and learning the boundaries of the territory appears too much for potential suitors. Widowed females often join a flock of unmated birds where they can forge a new pair bond and may even achieve territorial status again[9].

As we know, birds must always contend with the risk of injury or death. Many birds reduce this danger by assessing environmental cues to avoid areas of elevated risk. A dying or dead bird can be a relevant source of information regarding potential risk in an area. Could behaviour have evolved to warn others of nearby danger? The bird who finds the dead body will often produce alarm signals to bring other birds over, forming a gathering of 'mourners', as Dennis witnessed in the next story.

COCKIE FUNERAL

Dennis Johnston

While encouraging native birds into our garden over the 40 years we've lived in Ferntree Gully, we have always regarded the sulphur-crested cockatoo as a most intelligent bird.

One day I observed from my back garden a row of ten or so cockies sitting together on the power line opposite our house.

To my amazement they were taking turns to drop down off the line and fly up again. When I investigated from the street, I found that there was a dead cockie lying in the street gutter directly under the line of cockies. I watched in awe as each bird descended from the wire and individually walked around the dead cockie and silently stood beside what I assumed had been a fellow member of their group. I watched this ritual for about ten minutes until all the birds had completed what I believed was their farewell process. After all the cockies on the wire had completed their individual 'rites', the group flew off.

I feel that I was most honoured to have witnessed such a unique avian event. I have related this story to several of my friends, some who are birdwatchers. They have not had the privilege of observing similar bird behaviour.

What might they be talking about? Do you think the birds were saying farewell or was something else going on? This was a social gathering of the group, so it presented an opportunity for learning and passing on information to each other; it was a chance for them to share ideas about what might have happened.

Let's look at it from a bird's point of view. Failing to recognise a predator can have serious consequences, as in the death of the bird, so it is important to find out if the bird died because of previously unfamiliar or unrecognised threats. Consider the following story, sent to me by Jane.

CALL OF THE WILD

Jane Noyes

Three magpies are reasonably new visitors to my lawn. For years they have teased me and carolled from the top of my flame tree but until recently never ventured to the ground. Having now discovered the grass is kept moist and holds some tasty morsels, they do land and trust me as I sit and watch them feed. Last evening their trust in me escalated to an urgent level. As dusk was slowly closing a lovely still day, the quiet was interrupted by abrupt, guttural cries which made me race out to the street.

Did the magpies call Jane or are we falling into an anthropomorphic trap in suggesting this? Were the magpies calling to other magpies in the area to let them know something strange was going on? Once predators are detected, many birds use specific vocalisations that communicate the type of risk or level of danger and which elicit an appropriate response by receivers. Or did the magpies see Jane as part of the group and want to share the strange event confronting them? Jane's story continues.

There from the power line hanging almost motionless opposite them was a large brush-tail possum. Was it the gentle breeze swaying it or was it alive?

Instantly the birds seemed to sense I was trying to help and they settled and watched as I raced to get a ladder and blanket, hoping to coax the poor creature, if still conscious, to fall into the outstretched blanket. A long five minutes passed as the three pairs of eyes supervised my attempts and gently sang sounds of encouragement.

The possum rallied and did let go, but not into my blanket. Instead it had a long fall to the ground and, although stunned, it scampered across to the magpies' tree. The ending was not a happy

> one but it was inspiring that my black and white army cared and stayed until the possum was out of danger. With a soft chorus of thanks, they then flew off into the night. It is wonderful to think that compassion is not just a human trait.

The magpies certainly do appear to be watching and quietly talking to each other. It is possible that the magpies see this as a learning opportunity, a chance to exchange information about danger and a possible enemy. Possums can take a magpie's eggs and their young. Or were they just interested in what was going on in their environment? For birds, it is important to have good information in human-altered environments where changes can occur rapidly and frequently, potentially introducing new threats. The bird must be able to recognise and respond appropriately to predator threats, so it would be important to understand what was going on. Anti-predator behaviour needs to be flexible in an urban environment, because predation risk can change as the predator moves around[3]. Different types of predator defence can develop in a group. Did Jane's magpies learn anything from watching her interact with a nocturnal enemy? Learning allows novel cues to become associated with predators. This is important in both the acquisition of anti-predator responses and in the adjustment of pre-existing ones.

Magpies are an excellent example of birds that notice when things are amiss. Read below about magpies Archie and Missy who endear themselves to Elf and Mary on the death of their dog.

ARCHIE AND MISSY THE MAGPIES

Elf and Mary Stella

My interaction with birds started with the death of my dog. He had been diagnosed with cancer and was unwell for some time. I had been vaguely aware of some magpies hanging around and finishing any biscuits he didn't eat.

> The day after he died, there were still some biscuits in the bowl and I noticed the birds approach. They did not go straight to the food but instead went to his nearby kennel. They both peered inside, saw he wasn't there and looked at each other as if to say, 'It looks as if he's gone.' Only then did they start eating.
>
> Their apparent concern touched my heart and I have been feeding them ever since, for the last five and a half years. My grandchildren named them Archie and Missy.

What do you think is going on in the minds of Archie and Missy? Were the magpies attracted to Elf and Mary's garden because they noticed the dog had not eaten his biscuits? Did the magpies come down to determine why this was? Once they checked the kennel and saw no dog, did Archie and Missy only then decide to eat the biscuits? From the birds' point of view, was there now a new food resource with no competition from the dog? While further research is needed to answer such questions, one thing is certain: navigating a risky environment is a necessary part of staying alive. The need to use the most relevant information available to assess and manage risk exposure may help survival, as will sharing that information with others.

Chapter 14
THE PLAYFUL BIRD

Do you think birds play? Conventional wisdom suggests that animals play to practise skills needed for success later in life. A criteria for recognising play excludes behaviour in which the player is stressed as a result of play. Play, fun and even exploring appear to be important adaptive behaviours that provide birds with the opportunity to learn and practise behaviour that could be used later in life[1]. Indeed, lack of play can be an indicator of psychological and physical wellbeing, as it is usually the first activity to disappear if the bird is stressed, anxious, hungry or ill.

Natural selection may favour playful young because play offers opportunities for the bird to learn and to develop behaviours that will help their survival and their chances of reproduction. The intrinsically rewarding nature of play motivates birds to engage in behaviours that to us serve no purpose but are repeatedly performed. The complex and stimulating nature of play helps the brain develop flexible thinking, leading to flexibility in behaviour[2]. Birds can hone their skills for problem-solving later in life, as play builds memories that allow an older bird to live and breed better than a bird that does not play[3].

As we have discussed, many of our birds are long-lived and have a long developmental period or childhood. As many of our birds live in social groups, the young play with one another to promote social skills and bonds in the group. A juvenile bird that plays is engaged in the acquisition of social skills and the training of cognitive abilities, ensuring enhanced performance in future real-life situations[2]. This would lead us to wonder if play could be a means of training for the unexpected.

Difference in personalities could help explain the degree of playfulness of birds and thus differences in future behaviour. For example, an individual who gained experience while playing may be better with the challenges of adulthood than a less playful juvenile. However, this idea is just speculation as it has rarely been tested.

Could the bird's personality influence its propensity to play? Would a shy bird be more keen to play than a confident bird? Whether playfulness is indeed a personality dimension in birds and how it is related to other behavioural traits still needs to be addressed; however, on the assumption that play enables individuals to cope physically and emotionally with novelty, we could expect playful birds to be less anxious and more explorative than less playful birds. It may enhance an individual's resourcefulness and flexibility, helping it adjust to novel conditions. Play may also enhance the bird's ability to cooperate with others and to coexist with older members through interacting with them.

Let's look at this in more detail. It has been suggested that play enables birds to develop flexible emotional responses to unexpected or stressful events. In particular, it has been hypothesised that, by playing, birds learn to deal with the emotional aspects of surprise or unpredictably that come from a changing environment. Play promotes the ability to deal with unexpected events and to cope emotionally with stressful situations[4]. This implies both physical and psychological advantages as play can vary considerably within a given population, with individuals of the same age and sex differing in their propensity to play. While playing individuals may develop social skills and cement their social relationship, play may also serve to improve the ability of a bird to both compete and cooperate with other members of a group[2].

As juveniles are protected and looked after by parents and helpers, they are safe to explore their environment and experiment with a variety of objects that they find [5]. Juveniles can learn from their mistakes while in relative safety. To us, play-fighting may resemble serious fighting, but the fights are not serious. Participating birds generally don't aim to hurt each other. During play-fighting, pairs will often alternate between playing the aggressor and playing the victim[6].

The birds most commonly reported at play are those in our parrot/ cockatoo, corvid and magpie families, but George Bennett describes in his *Wanderings in New South Wales* the curious play behaviour in finches:

> Among themselves these birds are eminently sociable, assembling and building in company. When several are kept together and allowed their liberty in a dwelling room, they are up to all sorts of frolics, and there is hardly anything that they like better than to join a companion at opposite ends of a strand of cotton and to pull for dear life one against the other in a veritable 'tug-of-war'. One bird would even address himself so vigorously to this game of cotton-pulling as to allow himself to be lifted off the ground by one end of the fabric, while he held on with his beak to the other, and so hung suspended in the air for several seconds. With their owners, whom they speedily grow to know, Firetails place themselves upon the most familiar terms, exploring his pockets, penetrating up his coat sleeves and taking no end of liberties.

For a young bird, the days are long so it has lots of energy and time to explore and interact with others. How do they communicate their desires to play or even continue to play? Play in birds can involve particular play signals that differentiate play behaviour from 'real' behaviour[7]. The birds understand that playtime is generally a safe time when both are relaxed. Individuals need to cooperate with one another when playing. For instance parrots that play-fight usually fence with their bills or push with their feet, or bite the feet or feathers of the play partner. There is no apparent resolution, no winners and no losers in the contest. It is just for the fun of it!

As discussed in the last chapter, death, an everyday threat for a bird, must cause them stress. Having a brain that deals better with stress would seem a very plausible adaptation learned through play. Remember, a bird's brain does not develop in isolation but alongside other brains. Play could be a valuable way for birds to hone their stress response, such as when interacting with others. For instance, through encounters with others in its group such as mates, offspring, adversaries and unfamiliar strangers, this could result in more flexible adults.

As with funerals in the last chapter, it is hard to assess play, and the examples used in the literature are too limited and anecdotal to categorise confidently. Play seems to be a behavioural domain of remarkable complexity and variability, both within and between species, and is far from fully understood. Just because we cannot categorise play, however, doesn't mean it is not happening, as observed by David in our next story.

TENNIS BALLS AND GALAHS

David Mclean

The galahs, being prone to investigating their surroundings, soon began to arrive on the table ahead of the normal feeding time and engage in what seemed to be 'play'. I added a tennis ball to

> the mix one day, which was quickly adopted as a play item which over time became a favourite. I then added a tightrope to the table along with some other items that hung from it. The galahs quickly became quite adroit at quite distinct games with each of the items. I supplied more tennis balls, the preferred type of ball, which were often fought over, and were used to balance upon, roll over on, and the pièce de résistance, hold above their bodies whilst lying on their backs.
>
> It appeared as though those less familiar would spend some time watching a bird run through its repertoire and then attempt to do the same. Similarly, playing on the tightrope, swinging upside down, chasing each other up, down and all around the table and its adornments became the norm with others.

Individuals seem to fine-tune ongoing play sequences to maintain a play mood between the pair and to prevent play from escalating into fighting. In David's story, could the galahs have used subtle and fleeting movements and even rapid exchanges of eye contact to exchange information from moment to moment to make sure all is right? There appear to be numerous mechanisms at work, including play invitation signals such as when a magpie rolls onto its back or its bouncy walk. These signals help to facilitate the initiation and maintenance of social play. In other words, signs between the playing birds constantly reassure each other that they are having fun, and let's keep playing! Mirror neurons may be in use here again. As we discussed earlier, these neurons are active and firing when watching and understanding others' mental states.

Play, fun and exploring your surroundings seem to provide birds with the opportunity to learn and practise ecologically relevant behaviour. Researchers have found that birds such as common ravens engage in three types of play: locomotor, object and social play.

Locomotor play includes all forms of flight-related play, such as aerial acrobatics, hanging and flying upside down. This is when cockies show off their aerial skills, as Brett reports.

COCKIE DEMONSTRATES HIS AERIAL SKILL AND DARING

Brett Hart

Amongst the rowdy racket I studied one cockie sitting on an upper branch of a massive eucalyptus. Mimicking a gymnast on a horizontal bar, 'he' allowed himself to fall forward . . . his talons holding on loosely to the horizontal branch.

He used his mighty beak to right himself, albeit rather awkwardly, wings flailing, to an upright stance, completing the loop. He tried another forward roll, and this time righted himself with more style, due to an increase in speed.

No doubt this was fun. So much so, he continued. He accelerated these rolls till he was doing two or three per second. When he stopped, he shook his head, crest out and flapped his wings erratically, maybe to relieve the dizziness.

After washing off virtually all the speed he 'pulled back' and gently landed, luckily quite close, chucked his crest out, squawked a bit and probably laughed. I know I did. I was mesmerised—I never realised any bird had so much personality!

Object play occurs when the bird is exploring and curious, and involves object manipulation. This type of play includes the close inspection of objects, allowing the bird to learn about the object, whether it is edible and how it works[8]. In object play, birds may learn to use sticks as tools.

Corvids such as young ravens exhibit especially pronounced social and object play behaviour. During their first years of life, young ravens were found to manipulate objects such as sticks and stones over long periods[9]. This interest in non-edible objects declines rapidly with age[10]. One game that was favoured by the ravens was a catch-and-retrieve inedible object game. This behaviour may help their learning about dealing with potential competitors for food caches. In our next story, Julie describes play with a stick in grey currawongs.

GREY CURRAWONG AND STICK

Julie Constable

When we moved from the hills to the flatter coastal country, we left behind the seasonal chorus of flocks of pied currawongs for a sedentary pair of grey currawongs. Quiet most of the time, they occasionally raise the alarm with their loud kling-kling call.

One day my partner Kim saw one of the grey currawongs playing with a stick, lying down and holding the stick with its claws, stretching and rolling about in the adjacent paddock.

This year another grey currawong appeared to lie down on the driveway. I moved closer, saw the stick, and realised I was seeing similar behaviour to what Kim had witnessed a couple of years before! The currawong lay on its back, gripping the stick by the claws almost as if the bird were lifting weights. This was followed by holding one end in the beak and stretching out, then rolling from side to side. We don't know if this was the same bird playing with the stick, or whether both times it was the young progeny of the resident pair.

As we touched on earlier, social play is all about playful engagement with other individuals in a safe space. To play together, partners need to recognise each other's playful intentions and anticipate each other's movements. Birds adjust the timing and nature of individual acts, adapting their moves to the strength and age of their partner[10].

Social play can sometimes be confused with fighting and courtship as it involves a lot of chasing, tussling and rough-and-tumble. Social play frequently involves objects, where favoured objects are stolen or fought over, as well as interacting with and responding to others, and exchanging information, as Mal describes in our next story.

CROW AND CARPET SNAKE

Mal Jones

The two birds worked together to confront the snake. One came from the front, causing the snake to rear up and show its open mouth in a threatening manner. Meanwhile the other crow came from the rear, pecking at its tail. Together with their loud calls, they intimidated the snake, ensuring that it would get no rest. It squirmed around but had nowhere to go.

The crows had another trick to try as well. The bird at the danger end of the snake danced in and out of range, enticing the snake to unwind and lunge. Waiting at the tail, the other crow started jumping up and down on the branch to unsettle the snake, making it lose its grip and drop out of the tree. The snake held on. The snake got no rest that day as the crows never let their attention waver. The next day it was gone, having retreated under cover of darkness. I wonder if the crows felt like a nap.

Could the crows' behaviour in this story have evolved from playing, perhaps a mix of social play and object play? After all, these types of play are not mutually exclusive. Juvenile magpies have been reported spending large proportions of time playing with social partners as well as objects. Increased play behaviour is exhibited shortly before fledging and during the fourth and eighth weeks post-fledging[11]. The post-fledging peak in such behaviours has been associated with the transition from provisioning by the parents to self-feeding. Time to pay rent!

Playing together seems to require a particular kind of focused attention to one's partner. This has led some researchers to use social play as a lens through which to study complex cognitive abilities such as the evolution of shared intentionality that results in joint action[2]. This is because birds typically exchange communicative signals during play, possibly including signals that flag their ongoing commitment to the action. The two birds learn to understand what each other is thinking, while playing and forming a bond that can be maintained for years.

A study on juvenile magpies looked for a difference in exploration, play with objects and play with social partners[12]. The study found that on a daily basis, exploration and play with objects were related to the skills needed for foraging. However, there was no such relationship found for exploring surroundings and playing with social partners. A possible explanation for the difference is that exploring and play with objects appeared to be involved in two important behavioural changes: leaving the nest to explore and learning to feed by picking up and inspecting objects. The transition from dependent to independent feeding by juveniles primarily results from changes in the relationship between parents and offspring. With increasing age of juveniles, adults become increasingly reluctant to feed them. The researchers concluded that juveniles attempted to solicit more food from adults but as this became increasingly difficult, they switched to self-feeding. A bird can still make mistakes, as our next story tells.

KOOK AND FAKE SNAKE

Lowana Chapman

My country cousin was regularly woken early in the morning by a bird attacking itself in the reflection on her bedroom window. Next time I visited her I took a fake snake bought from Binns shop in Chatswood and that seemed to deter the bird for a while. One day

> soon after, my cousin was in the garden and a kookaburra swooped down and flew off with the snake in its beak.

Ground rules of group living can be tested while playing to find out what is acceptable to others. How hard can I bite? How roughly can I interact with another before I hurt it? There is an importance to playing fairly and trusting others to do so as well. Is there a social code of conduct that regulates? What is permissible and what is not? There are few penalties for rule breaking when you are playing. Could we say the existence of such codes might have something to do with the need for social morality? In fact, behaving fairly during play could help younger birds to acquire social skills needed as they mature.

Although it is suggested that birds are experiencing pleasure when playing—that is, they are having fun—there is little research done in this area. We can speculate as to the adaptive nature of having fun, but a major obstacle is the idea that studying animal emotions is unscientific: the fear of falling into the anthropomorphic trap of applying human emotional or mental states.

Chapter 15
THE URBAN BIRD

In a little over 200 years, Australia has undergone rapid urbanisation and birds have had to respond to a changing landscape. For a bird, the urban landscape has a number of important environmental features to which it must adapt. Although some birds thrive in urban areas, no single defining trait predicts a species' urban success. Instead, success in urban environments may depend on a species' ability to adjust to the demands of the new habitat. As we have discussed, birds do this by modifying behaviour and taking risks. Three effects of urbanisation have been identified: the loss of natural vegetation as it is replaced by built structures or fragmented by buildings and roads; the tendency of food sources to become artificial and often spatially concentrated; and the presence of direct disturbance from cat predation pressures or night-time lights and noises.

Being flexible in behaviour is believed to be the main mechanism through which birds adapt to our urban environment. This is because urban environmental alterations are often drastic and rapid, and can demand behavioural adjustments from birds to ensure they can continue to live in the artificial habitat, in other words by being flexible in their behaviour by changing it to suit the current state. This type of behavioural adjustment would facilitate population persistence where there is a sudden change in the environment. The bird's behaviour can often be rapidly modified to solve new ecological problems, that is, by contributing to reducing the uncertainties and adaptive mismatches in behaviour that arise when environmental conditions change[1]. If other members of the group are starting to pair up to breed, I should really do the same as the weather is warming up.

One way we can measure behavioural flexibility to urban areas is through comparisons of urbanised and non-urbanised populations of the same species[2], to examine if they behave differently to the same resource such as food. One study that did this was on the introduced common mynas[3]. The study found individuals from highly urbanised areas were more opportunistic when foraging and less fearful of predators than suburban mynas. Interestingly, the study found that this behaviour was not a result of personality but instead an overall population adaptation to urban life. The study suggests that urban birds with a long history of living with us (such as the house sparrow) are continuously having to change their behaviour to adapt to the constant challenge of living in built-up areas[3].

Another study with urban house sparrows found foraging problem-solving (opening a lid to get access to food) was solved quicker and more effectively in larger groups (six birds) than in smaller groups (two birds). The research suggests that an individual will learn from others' efforts in the group, with success coming from having innovative group mates. As we have discussed, these bolder individuals are explorers and more likely to investigate and have a go[4].

Crested pigeons moved into urban areas during the mid-1900s[5]. John Gould considered the crested pigeon to be one of the 'loveliest in its tribe, not surpassed in beauty by any other form from any other part of the world'. Due to their bossy ways, these birds have adapted well to urban areas, as our next story sent in by Gilbert tells.

BULLY CRESTED PIGEONS

Gilbert Porter

The ones that are a pest on the seed tray are the crested pigeons. There is always at least one male that wants to display and chase others. Not satisfied with doing that on the ground or in the tree, he must also use the seed tray then gets into a scuffle and seed goes flying everywhere. So I chase them off for a while. Now I don't know if the male magpie knows that I keep a watch on the crested pigeons and chase them off every now and again. Also, does he copy me? What happens every now and again is that the male magpie will come swooping in to the seed tray area and 'shoos off' and scatters the crested pigeons away from the seed tray!

One way we measure how well a bird has adapted to urban areas is through how they respond to heavy human traffic. Humans are an important source of disturbance for birds, but it has been shown that successful urban birds can respond to direct human disturbance by changing their behaviour[6], for example by walking away from you instead of flying away. And how close can you get to the bird before it flies away? We call this measurement the 'flight initiation distance' (FID).

Watch out for this behaviour the next time you come across a crested pigeon, magpie, lark or the even the common city pigeon. See how close you can get to the bird before it flies away. Will it have a short flight initiation distance? This means you can get really close before the bird takes flight. We use this as an indication of how well the bird has adapted to humans. I would not recommend trying this with a magpie. You might well end up in a standoff with the bird which will end with the mighty beak making contact!

What is going on in the mind of the bird as it walks away from you? We assume cognition is involved in such decisions[7]. In fact there is evidence that fear of humans can diminish. This is when individual birds are exposed to human presence for long periods of time and know there is no real threat[8]. Instead they may feel more of an annoyance at having scientists follow them and making them fly!

Research was carried out in Melbourne on FID in rock doves and spotted doves, both introduced into Melbourne in the mid-1800s, and on native crested pigeons who are more recent colonisers, arriving in the last fifteen to twenty years. Not too surprisingly, researchers found that rock doves had the shortest FID from an approaching observer, meaning the observer was nearly touching the rock dove before it flew away! Interestingly, crested pigeons had a similar FID to the spotted dove.

This is surprising as crested pigeons have only recently become urban dwellers. You would think that urban bird species (rock doves and spotted doves) that have lived with humans and adapted to cities would have a shorter FID than recent urban colonists[9]. But by this stage of the book, are you really surprised? Crested pigeons are an arid adapted bird, currently moving into more urban areas. These birds are seed-eaters, live in social groups and have adapted well to towns and cities. There is not much research into these birds but I am willing to suggest that they are very smart. As many of you will know, they have bossy personalities: when they arrive at feeding tables in backyards, other birds scatter!

As discussed, social learning in a group can increase the spread of behavioural change with fewer costs than that of individual learning[10]. Social learning can benefit birds where it helps them adjust to human-induced change. Social learning can also prove detrimental where it spreads behaviours that lead to human–bird conflict.

For a bird, the colonisation of urban environments happens in three main ecological stages: arrival, establishment, and increase/spread[11]. Not all birds are able to reach or to settle in urbanised environments. The arrival stage is a first filter that contributes to eventual differences in biodiversity between urban and surrounding habitats[12].

Arrival is essentially a combination of two processes: dispersal and habitat selection. Both processes may lead to non-random arrival of individuals or species as a function of their behavioural plasticity and variations in their personality types. Dispersal behaviour is generally regarded as highly flexible, but habitat selection may not be[13].

Let's look at the arrival stage in more detail. We would expect an individual to be a better fit in habitats similar to those in which it was raised. This may be because they are already adapted or because they have previous experience (habitat training). As urban environments are so different from natural environments, the expectation for many species is that they will simply avoid settling in such habitats.

There are reasons to think that birds that spend their lives learning new behaviours and new adaptations would be more likely to change their habitat than less adaptable birds. The adaptable birds would show a stronger tendency to explore and to take advantage of novel ecological opportunities; that is, to develop a generalist-opportunistic lifestyle. Indeed, many urban dwellers are regarded as highly opportunistic in their ecology[14]. In contrast, less behaviourally flexible bird species would avoid novel situations, making them less prone to changing their habitat.

In the establishment stage, a bird's choosing to settle in an urbanised environment is no guarantee that a self-sustaining population will result, even when individuals are able to survive and reproduce. The probability of establishment is driven by population dynamics in the context of small populations and novel environments. Increase and spread can be determined by how many birds established themselves in the new environment in the first place. In small populations, some species may have failed to establish in urbanised environments because they arrived in low numbers and were therefore vulnerable to extinction. How flexibility and personality types may influence small populations remains controversial. Behavioural flexibility associated with learning can be considered one of the main mechanisms by which birds can avoid extinction. Indeed it is considered key to their establishment in urban environments.

From a bird's viewpoint, one key to successful urban living is the ability to tolerate high levels of disturbance, such as traffic, cats and dogs and, of course, us! A bird needs to learn and remember if a disturbance is a threat or not. For example, humans could be seen as a harmless disturbance as we walk past them. However, the dog on the leash with the human makes this human a threat. One way a bird could find out more about us is to watch us as we go about our lives.

Tawny frogmouths have been described as 'having a charming disposition, very similar to that of parrots. They are avid communicators with strong individual personalities, have a long lifespan and form permanent partnerships'[15]. Once established, a pair will usually stay in the same territory for a decade or longer unless it has been subject to some unfortunate event.

These birds appear to be doing well in the urban environment, suggesting a degree of adaptation[16]. Part of the adaptations could include tawny frogmouths showing flexible behavioural traits and generalist habitat requirements such as nesting; that is, they do not rely on hollows for nesting, for example. Pairs construct very basic nests from small woody twigs, locating them in the forks of trees, branches, or trunk/branch junctions, or occasionally utilising an abandoned bird's nest[15]. Theresa shared a wonderful story about her encounter with a tawny frogmouth.

TORNEAU, THE VERY FRIENDLY TAWNY FROGMOUTH

Theresa Bint

I live with my partner Col in the Sunshine Coast hinterland. Our acre and a half is well-treed and somewhat overgrown—we have a lot of resident and visiting birds.

We met Torneau one Friday night a few years ago. A bunch of us were in our bar/shed, having drinks and singing and playing guitars. He swooped in through the doorway, landing on a cushion on a low seat. We were all a bit stunned and then talked to him (could've been a her, really) and it seemed he intended to stay for a bit. He didn't seem to be after food.

We started to play and sing again, and he just stayed there. Then we tried some frogmouth-friendly songs, just to make him feel welcome. '*Who* Are You', '*Who*'s that coming round the corner' ('5:10 Man'), and so on. After about half an hour, he flew off.

One of my friends said, 'Well, that's something that doesn't happen every day,' and just as she said it Torneau flew back in again. He stayed for an hour or so then took off.

Over the next few months he was a regular visitor—sometimes we'd find him in the house (the back of the couch got a bit messy, but what can you do?), sometimes in the shed, sometimes on the verandah. We did offer him food from time to time, just to be polite, and occasionally he'd take it, but generally he just seemed to enjoy our company. He'd even fly to me if I called and held out a bit of meat—he enjoyed sitting on my head and pecking my ear. His beak was leathery, not sharp, so it didn't hurt. Much. Interestingly my partner Col could hear his deep 'oom oom' calls easily while I rarely registered them.

We feel totally privileged to have had this experience and it gave me faith that some animals think that humans are okay.

It's always good to know your feathered and human neighbours. Many urban birds do not shy away from us, instead exploiting us to get what they need. Behavioural flexibility may be important in allowing birds to minimise costly and unnecessary fear responses or to maximise those responses to deal with new dangers. In the case of birds such as Tourneau, he reduced costly and unnecessary anti-predator responses by selectively responding to specific humans. In fact, many territorial birds respond less defensively to neighbours than to strangers—we call this the 'dear enemy phenomenon'[17].

The dear enemy phenomenon represents neighbour–stranger interaction. It was first described in 1954 to explain neighbour–stranger interactions characterised by reduced aggression from territory owners towards familiar individuals (a neighbour bird)[18]. This allows the birds to be established in neighbouring territories, compared to their interactions with *unfamiliar* individuals—strangers.

A resident bird responds less strongly to the intrusion of familiar or trusted individuals than to strangers. In other words, stranger equals danger! So put more energy into fighting the stranger than into fighting your neighbour whom you see every day. Yes, the neighbour represents a threat to you, but the devil you know is better than the devil you don't know! Having a good relationship with your neighbour is important as you may need their help at times, such as mobbing a predator.

The dear-enemy relationship is not a stable relationship and may be influenced by changes in the social situation. For example, when there are changes in boundaries due to some human disturbance, or when a vacant area appears between two territories, or by the arrival of a new bird to claim a territory after death of the neighbour. Accepting neighbours as dear enemies is a tit-for-tat conditional strategy. It ends if neighbours fail to respect mutual territorial boundaries, and is stabilised in part by retaliation against cheating birds. Both neighbours have to recognise and respect the boundary line. If one bird breaks these rules and tries to slyly alter this invisible line in his favour, full on war can take place.

Sometimes when a new individual takes over a territory, this new bird may try to bully the neighbour over where the boundary line is. This can lead to direct fighting as the established bird tries to hold on to his full territory. One of the main advantages of maintaining the same territory for a long period of time is the maintenance of a network of known neighbours, a community if you will[17]. Information gathering might be expected during interactions with neighbours. Residents may lose both their territory and their mate because of interactions with strangers, whereas they may lose only their mate from interactions with neighbours already in possession of a suitable territory.

How is a stranger recognised? Successful discrimination between neighbours and strangers requires the existence of reliable indicators of identity. Intruder neighbour or stranger identity could be discerned through a range of factors, including sound, sight and smell[19]. The stranger might even be acting strange in its behaviour and this draws the attention of others in the group.

Among many social birds, group members participate in vocal choruses which can have distinctive group-specific signatures—it is the song of their group. While individual intruders may challenge the breeding success of certain group members, the threat posed is not the same for all members of the territory-holding group[20]. There could be various incentives for participating in defensive actions. The identity of the intruder may influence the nature and level of threat, and thus the resulting responses. For instance, the greater the threat the more likely it is there will be rewards for individuals who assist in defence, or punishment for those who do not help sufficiently. Lesley sent a story about magpies assisting a younger individual who was in trouble.

DAD AND HIS KIDS

Lesley Westbrook

I call my male magpie 'Dad', the juvenile is 'Bubby', and the three females are 'The Girls'. I feel a bit of a connection with 'Dad'. He sits down next to me, and there's almost a sense of trust between us . . . I'd like to think we have a bit of a bond going on? Anthropomorphising perhaps?

One day I was observing a large predatory black raven harassing the young magpie chick when all of a sudden the whole magpie family chased the predator off in no uncertain terms, he'd certainly met his match there!

How can we best live with the urban bird? By making friends to establish ourselves cooperatively—to live in harmony. I feel respect is important. If we don't respect these birds and instead see them as dumb annoying creatures, then you deserve to be swooped! Common urban birds—magpies, sulphur-crested cockatoos, red wattlebirds and even noisy miners—are the birds that survived European arrival, the loss of habitat they evolved to live in. They did this in less than 300 years!

But just because seeing and hearing these birds is commonplace, are they any less special? If a bird is common, do we undervalue it? They seem to flourish despite us, and we can see them because they are always there watching us, perhaps even following us from our cars to meet up at the kitchen window, waiting for us to provide them with their expected treats. I feel we need to celebrate these birds, and as we will talk about in the next chapter, these are the innovative birds that survive and even thrive next to us.

What else is important to live with the urban bird? From the bird's viewpoint, he might consider the following: is there food and water? A place to hide and shelter from the weather? A place to roost safely while sleeping? Can I raise young in this garden? As we have discussed, providing resources such as a range of plant species at different heights and density will help increase diversity of birds. If you only have a small yard or a balcony, consider a mixture of potted plants and a water source. Even if you just get spotted doves, they will still thank you for making their life a little bit easier.

Chapter 16

THE INNOVATIVE BIRD

A bird's responses to novel stimuli may influence its survival in urban areas. The extent to which a bird responds fearfully to novelty may help or hinder its success depending on the danger and benefits associated with novelty. For example, having high levels of fear may help a bird avoid danger should the novel objects of its fear harbour predators or toxins. On the other hand, having reduced fear allows a bird to approach and exploit potentially advantageous novel resources[1]. This is important as urban areas offer combinations of food, danger and new habitat types, all of which often differ substantially from more natural habitats in less disturbed environments. Understanding how birds respond behaviourally to novelty is important in understanding how they adjust to the urban environment. For instance, a shy bird with a specialist diet and/or nesting requirements is less likely to adjust as well.

An old English proverb states that 'Necessity is the mother of invention'. In other words, the primary driving force for most new inventions is a need for them. Of course, to be innovative you need to be behaviourally flexible[2]. Innovative problem-solving is a key feature of intelligence; it has played a major role in adaptation to urbanisation. Behavioural flexibility is key to innovation as it is the ability of an individual to create a new behaviour or to adjust an existing one to a new context. The behaviours that yield desired outcomes increase in frequency, and those that do not decrease in frequency. Innovation propensity is also influenced by persistence of the behaviour in the environment. Do other birds copy this behaviour and then it spreads among the population?

What is innovation in birds and when do we see it? We could define innovation as a new or modified learned behaviour that has not been found previously in a population[3]. What is clear is innovation introduces novel behaviour that works and is adapted by others in the group.

George Bennett wrote that welcome swallows 'always seem to prefer the society or protection of the human race'. Bennett went on to say 'Numerous birds were now busily engaged in constructing their nests under eaves of houses. When these little birds are not in the vicinity of dwelling of man, they construct their nests in the hollow trunks of trees and under over-hanging rocks.' This would suggest that welcome swallows adapted quickly to the new habitat that developed after 1788.

Could we expect urbanised populations to be different in terms of innovative behaviours when compared to rural birds? Take the next story from Raymond on welcome swallows working together to free a pair of parrots.

SWALLOWS TEACH PARROTS

Raymond Eshman

Early days, circa 1983, our first structure was taking shape and at the time we were what was known as absentee landholders, and some years before there was a birdbath.

> During our long absences the welcome swallows had taken up residence in our less-than-secure building and there were three or four breeding pairs. During one of our visits to our then country hideaway, we had opened the roll-a-door for human access to the building, thus allowing the entry of a pair of startled red-rumped grass parrots.
>
> Well! These poor parrots had NO idea of how to escape from a building and repeatedly crashed into the translucent polycarbonate sheeting of the gable infill at each end of the building. They flew, crashed and landed several times before Mr and Mrs Welcome Swallow actually sat beside them.
>
> With every further attempt at escape by the red rumps, the swallows actually flew at their side in order to guide them out. After several attempts their mission was successful and the swallows had 'their' shed back.
>
> Obviously the swallows' intent was less than honourable but instead a means by which to rid themselves of invaders. What a remarkable event to witness AND the thought process and planning that went on in those tiny heads.

When breeding, welcome swallows often form small, loose groups to protect their nest and territory, especially against predatory birds. These birds, living in groups or pairs, can learn from each other and work together, as Raymond's story tells. This has helped the birds adapt well to man-made clearing for both farms and urban areas. Raymond's story illustrates how the swallows worked together to get the confused parrots out—surely a sample of innovative behaviour. Among the factors predicted to influence innovation is necessity. Being innovative, birds are more likely to survive in harsh and changing environments like Australia.

Innovative behaviour in urban areas allows a group-living bird to learn problem-solving skills from others in the group. In theory, social learning should be favoured over individual learning as less risky to the individual. Indeed birds have been found to match their behaviour to the common behaviour in their group: this is how others are behaving, so it must work[4].

Through social learning we expect a novel behaviour to spread between individuals to create group-level behaviours, termed 'cultural traditions'. Cultural traditions result in social transmission of information occurring between interacting individuals. It is the group dynamics and population structure that determine the spread and even the persistence of traditions. A study of wild great tits in the United Kingdom found that the tits used social learning to acquire novel behaviour. Foraging techniques introduced by a few birds could spread rapidly to the majority of the population. This appears to be a result of informational conformity. That is, individuals match their behaviour to the most common technique when first learning. Then through life they will continuously update their personal information through interacting with others[5].

Trying to quantify cultural transmission in wild populations remains difficult. The ability to invent new behaviours and/or use pre-existing ones in new contexts means birds can adjust to novel environments like backyards. The next story, sent by Julie, shows just how smart and innovative pardalotes can be. While reading this story, remember that pardalotes like tunnels, their nests usually being at the end of a narrow tunnel excavated into an earth bank.

PARDALOTES IN THE NEST BOX

Julie Stevens

We love being surrounded by trees and watching the birdlife come and go. Our most exciting spring yet involved watching a family of pardalotes. We have a parrot nesting box on our back deck which gets used every spring, but one year we noticed a small bird attacking his reflection in our decorative mirror and investigating a small ornamental bird house. A quick internet search revealed that this small bird was a striated pardalote. Our local national park sells bird boxes, so we popped out and purchased the correct-sized nesting box. My partner had the idea of adding a toilet roll tube and extra stick to the nesting box as we had read that these birds like a tunnel. Success, the birds started using the box within hours! There appeared to be three birds in the group with one bird constantly attacking his reflection in the mirror, so we decided to remove it. We spent many hours of pleasure watching these birds build their nest and feed their babies.

What a clever addition to the nest box by Julie's partner! The pardalotes tried something new and it worked! Of course, successful nesting and raising of young is an important aspect of adaptation to urban environments. The ability to invent a new behaviour in new surrounds and the ability to perform an existing behaviour (raising young) would be very useful to an urban bird.

To help your urban bird, try to provide a range of nesting sites in your backyard. This can be through growing a range of trees, shrubs, vines and tall grasses at different heights. By providing a range of places to build their nests, you may attract different types of birds to your garden. Eucalypts are ubiquitous across Australian landscapes; but they are declining in urban environments. The physical structure of eucalypt trees—the dense foliage, bark crevices, hollows and cavities—together with fallen limbs (logs) and foliage (leaf litter) on the ground, means shelter, refuge or breeding sites for large numbers of birds. So, if you have a dead tree or tree limbs, don't be so quick to remove them, You can even create nesting holes using a brace to enlarge existing holes. These holes should face away from the sun and direct cold wind.

The development of suitable hollows in trees takes many decades, the number and variety of hollows increasing with tree size and age.

In urban areas, remnant patches of eucalypts play a key role in maintaining wildlife populations in otherwise unsuitable environments. Cavity-nesting birds will use nest boxes, so consider installing a few around your garden. You can purchase or even construct your own nest box if you don't have access to dead or falling limbs. If you do want to make your own nest box, use western red cedar, redwood or plywood, as they are lightweight and durable. Don't paint the inside of your nest box and only treat the exterior with non-toxic wood finish. For cross-ventilation and to allow rain to escape, drill several holes near the roof and in the floor. The size of the entrance hole will determine what birds can use it, so have an idea what bird you are hoping to attract. Position the entrance of the hole near the top of the box to prevent predators from reaching in[6].

Birds such as rosellas and cockatoos could be a target bird for our nest box as they need to compete for limited resources associated with trees, like forks in eucalypts or hollows in trunks or limbs. Success in urban areas requires an understanding of the availability of urban resources, particularly food and shelter[7]. Tree hollows can be a key limiting resource in human-modified landscapes, while competition for nesting cavities can affect population abundance and species diversity at a local and regional scale.

In several Australian cities, native hollow-nesting sulphur-crested cockatoos have modified their behaviour to exploit urban environments and as a result can dominate use of large, urban tree hollows. The expansion in the range of this bird is associated with increases in their abundance in urban coastal areas over the past 45 years[8]. It is paradoxical given the scarcity of tree hollows in this environment and shows what smart adapters they are.

Olive-backed sunbirds, also known as yellow-bellied sunbirds, were originally from mangrove habitat but have adapted well to humans, partly due to their broad diet[7]. The sunbirds will take nectar from a mixture of native and exotic vegetation but will also take moths and spiders which are dismembered while the bird hovers in front of webs[9,10]. Their long narrow tongue, frayed at the tip like a brush, can be projected far beyond the bill so that the bird can lap or suck pollen from deep inside flowers, and catch smaller insects[9]. As a result of having a broad diet and nesting abilities, the birds are common even in fairly densely populated areas, building their nests in human dwellings—as Barb and Danny found out!

THE BIRDS HAVE MOVED IN

Barb and Danny Schmidt

Green frogs in the toilets, white-tail rats and pythons in the shed, goannas and wallabies regularly visiting, bush turkeys in abundance, and now sunbirds nesting in the kitchen! Welcome to suburbia, Tropical North Queensland style.

The latest addition to our wildlife menagerie is a pair of olive-backed sunbirds that have built a nest and taken up residence in our kitchen. Mr and Mrs Birdy, as they are affectionately known, have chosen to build their nest from a hanging ornament smack-bang in the middle of the entrance between our kitchen and living room. As our windows and doors are always open, they can come and go whenever they like.

How the nest maintains its structure and withstands the weight of the birds and their young and the windy conditions that sweep through the house is remarkable. Their saliva or whatever is used as the glue must be the same stuff that holds the Hoover Dam together.

We love sitting at the kitchen bench watching Mrs and Mr Birdy whizz past our ears to feed their babies. In no time at all, the mother and chicks are strong enough to leave the nest to embrace the big wide world. We have never been home to see this momentous occasion. We just come home to find them suddenly gone.

What is interesting about this story is that the birds constructed the nest in the same way as they would have done in a more natural setting. The sunbirds' nest can be suspended from a sapling, vine, low branch or building, or other artificial structure such as a clothesline[10]. This hanging adaptation is a nesting alternative to hollows or forks in trees. Because the birds are so light, their nests can be hung nearly anywhere, from vines to clotheslines—a very handy adaptation that can be used in urban areas. This pair adapted their nest by hanging it in Barb and Danny's kitchen.

> It is now nearing the end of March and the birds are back hovering around that nest and a few others they have built in the past around the house. They will no doubt make a choice for this year's nest very soon. Now that they have survived my wife's cooking, the accidental head-butting of the nest by unaware visitors, and the ever-present watchful eye of our tortoiseshell cat, they may well choose the kitchen suite again. We certainly hope so and look forward to welcoming them back!

The sunbirds did not see Barb and Danny as a threat. This story shows the birds displaying a rich diversity of behavioural flexibility in order to successfully raise young. Innovative nesting could be more risky than feeding, as nesting habitats are often specialised. In addition, a bird has more to lose as nesting takes time and effort. However, if a bird watches others' success in innovative nesting, it might copy it. Individuals will often have a choice of information sources, for example they can choose to observe others in their group, and to observe different species. While social information from group members may be the most relevant, relying solely on information from group members can also lead to increased competition for limited resources such as nesting sites.

If nesting is more tightly constrained than feeding, stories of birds showing innovation in nesting are clear signs of behaviour flexibility. Associating with other species may also affect the structure of the social network, which may positively influence the rate of information spread. For instance, the addition of new individuals in an area may increase the speed of an innovative adaption throughout a population. The combined mixed-species social network (for example, a mixed group of king parrots, rosellas and galahs) could have higher influence on the spread of information about food in a social network. When these individuals who have been mixing with others rejoin groups (fission–fusion), they can pass on what they learned from another species.

As we have talked about, finding food that is scattered patchily across Australia means listening to others about where food has been found. We expect that information about food is more likely to travel faster between individuals from the same group than between those outside the group. Associating with and acquiring information from different types of individuals may have greater benefit, such as by increasing the pool of local knowledge. Birds that incorporate a new food into their diet display food-type innovation.

Diet switching and the ability to recognise new food and consume that food is an important survival trait for living in Australia. Could the ability of birds to use the beak in a variety of ways help the bird exploit different types of food? Many Australian birds have evolved a flexible learning brain to allow for increased behavioural flexibility, enabling them to learn such things. This allows birds to cope with and respond to novel challenges, assisting them to live in new areas, including urban environments.

Let's have a closer look at diet switching or food switching. Food-switchers appear to be very common in Australia with birds feeding on a range of food, including exotic fruits. Adult currawongs are frugivores (fruit-eaters) and also semi-nomadic[11]. However, their offspring first grow up entirely on a diet of invertebrates and switch to fruit once fledged. Common koel young are largely raised by insectivorous hosts, with the female switching the young bird's diet to fruit once she collects them[12].

Brown cuckoo-doves and satin bowerbirds, for example, have been recorded feeding on both native and introduced plants such as lantana, privet and tobacco plants. High abundance of invasive fleshy-fruited exotic trees and shrub species, including camphor laurel, large- and small-leaved privet and lantana, could boost availability of food to opportunistic frugivorous birds but not to selective fruit-specialists[13]. Brown cuckoo-doves and white-headed pigeons grind ingested seeds and can therefore derive nutrition from seeds as well as fruit pulp[14]. Birds with seed-grinding digestion may therefore be less restricted in their sources of energy than non-grinding fruit-specialists such as rainforest pigeons (Wompoo, rose-crowned and superb fruit doves), which rely on the nutritional quality of the fruit[13]. Common urban plants like camphor laurel and privets can bear fruit in winter, allowing seed-grinding birds to increase as well as more general frugivores; for example, green catbirds, little wattlebirds and black-faced cuckoo-shrikes who eat a wide range of fruits[15].

An example of birds adapting to a new food type concerns the introduced cane toad. Cane toads are a toxic anuran native to South and Central America. The toads were introduced into northeastern Queensland in 1935, spreading since then across tropical and subtropical Australia. The primary impact of cane toads on Australian ecosystems is the poisoning of native species. The parotoid gland on either side of the head of the toad secretes bufadienolides that is toxic to most animals and birds.

As well as birds socially learning how to eat these toads, they are culturally transmitting predation techniques. Torresian crows and currawongs appear to have developed a technique to kill and eat cane toads by flipping the toads on their backs and consuming only the internal organs and part of the thighs[16]! The crows may learn how to perform the technique by imitating and replicating the behaviour of others[17]. Could this be a result of cultural transmission of predation among the crows? A number of other birds seem to have adjusted to the presence of cane toads through learned behavioural adaptations, again reflecting plasticity in behavioural change; for example, black kites and whistling kites have learned to eat only the tongue of the toad, leaving the rest behind[18]. This minimises the quantity of toxin ingested.

New food appears to be the most common form of innovation in birds who are ecological generalists. A higher overall innovation rate of trying a new food type, compared to dietary specialists, could result in generalist birds having greater success. This is one of the reasons why generalist species are more likely than specialists to become successfully established in urban environments, as our next story shows.

SMART AUSTRALIAN RAVEN

Kay Watson

The school playground can be a popular place for opportunistic birds after recess and lunch. Rainbow lorikeets and noisy miners become quite bold in their search for abandoned pieces of fruit that might litter eating areas. But it is the Aussie ravens that raid the garbage bins. These bins are those ubiquitous tall grey bins with lids, and each of these particular bins is lined with a black plastic bin bag. Bins are often left open (teenage girls don't like touching garbage bin lids!) but because the bins are quite deep, it is difficult for scavenging birds to reach the tasty food scraps at the bottom. I have watched as a raven, undeterred, positioned itself on the top rim of an open bin so that it could grasp the bin liner with its beak. It proceeded to pull the liner up bit by bit until the contents at the bottom became accessible. Then, by securing the bunched up liner with its feet, the raven enjoyed the fruits of its labour, scoring top marks for problem solving!

Birds that have a higher overall innovation rate could succeed in urban areas due to their feeding flexibility and their ability to produce appropriate behaviours; to get at the food even when it is hidden from view, as Kay's story shows. Human activities offer novel opportunities to a species which is able to exploit these opportunities[19].

Many birds introduced to Australia already had experience with the changes that came with living in human-altered landscapes[20]. We unintentionally selected birds (e.g. blackbirds, house sparrows) that are capable of thriving in cities and released them into the new cities of Australia. Many of our cities are often located within a mosaic of natural habitats, meaning that birds can fly between habitats. Our introduced birds seem to have the opportunity to expand to more pristine habitats but they do not; they stay close to us. One possible reason is the importance of habitat disturbance as a concept for successful invasion. By altering natural environments, we may be creating new disturbed opportunities for introduced birds who already had the knowledge of adapting to humans[21]. It is likely that well-established native birds in the more undisturbed pristine habitat have established niches[22]. It can be hard for a new species to learn how to penetrate without our help[23].

For instance, artificial selection for frequent reproduction in their domestic ancestors is thought to allow feral pigeons to increase offspring productivity. This allows for the bird to compensate for the high mortality rate associated with starvation and car accidents[23]. With the rapid urbanisation Australia underwent, we lost so many of our native birds. While there are many reasons why this happened, one may be that a number of native birds did not have enough time to adapt to efficiently exploit and use the new resources. An additional problem that birds had was the introduction of new predators (foxes, dogs and cats) and other birds who are competitively superior.

A bird that is competitively superior means it may be better at exploiting a resource than another individual or species. For example, introduced birds, house sparrows and spotted doves, could be easier to bully from an important resource such as food. While introduced birds seem to rely on us for food, native birds appear to show optimistic behaviour, possibly only taking human food when it suited. Behaving optimistically means the bird will take food when it comes across it. That is, change its behaviour to meet the needs of the environment, such as moving into urban areas in search of water during a drought. However, more research is needed to support this statement.

Introduced birds such as spotted doves and house sparrows will live close to us and use resources derived from human activities. This is consistent with the view that introduced birds exploit the abundant food accidentally or deliberately produced by human activities. This in turn may result in high population densities of introduced species. The fact that most introduced birds occur in urban environments indicates that they perhaps significantly rely on humans for their own survival. This is in contrast with native urban birds that could easily return to pre-1788 Australia.

It is important not to assume that introduced birds pose little risk for native species. Extinction can take time and birds were introduced into Australia less than 300 years ago. It is possible that some bird introductions are too recent for the impact to be observed[19]. A bigger threat for our native birds in urban areas could be the loss of habitat as we cut down trees in our gardens. It is easier to blame the introduced myna for the local extinction of parrots than of the removal of trees from the backyard to improve the view!

Chapter 17
THE LOVED BIRD

As I am writing this last chapter of the book in inner-city Melbourne, I am interrupted by the sound of a warbling magpie. I rarely hear this magpie so close to my house. I had just glimpsed him around the neighbourhood and named him Rascal. I immediately down tools and go outside to see if I can spot the magpie. Sure enough, there is Rascal in a nearby tree and he spots me too. I call him over to land on my birdbath next to me using exaggerated eye pointing and head pointing towards the bath. I think to myself, 'There is no way he will come over to me; he doesn't know me.'

Well, I am stopped mid-thought as the magpie flies over to me and lands on the birdbath. 'Wow!' is all I can say. The magpie is so big and brave and I feel a little intimidated. This bird is not afraid of me, but is looking at me square in the eye. I know what he wants: food. Like thousands of other people who can't resist interacting with these birds, I oblige. It is a magical moment between me and the ultimate Aussie bird, loved by most and feared by some. This encounter sets me up for the day. I still can't believe I could call the bird over just by looking him in the eye and gesturing for him to come over—and he did, then demanded a reward for doing so!

The magpie is one of the most researched and best known birds in the country, so it is no surprise that love for the bird is widespread. It also appears to be a favourite bird to provide food for. Obviously magpies are big birds and hard to miss, and they ooze intelligence as they interact with us.

I want to share a few quotes I received on why people provide food for magpies: 'They are sort of family members, as we have given them names'; 'They provide songs and interaction, and the magpies know us so no more swooping our dogs or us!'; 'It gives me great pleasure to see them, and the magpies that use the pond are like family'; and, 'I feel very connected to our juvenile magpie. I now know her distinctive squawks and I really enjoy watching her intelligence as she considers where to perch and how to avoid being noticed by other birds and possible predators.'

Are we connected with urban birds because they share so much of their lives with us? As we have discussed, birds such as magpies appear to show signs of taming and warming to humans as companions. Is part of the attraction that these birds remain free-ranging and self-sufficient, yet choose to befriend humans[1]? Many people have a strong personal attachment to the birds that visit them, as many of the stories in this book have shown.

As we have touched on, one of the main ways we interact with birds is through providing food for them. This activity goes deep into our history with them. We have fed them for hundreds, if not thousands, of years. Even today we hate wasting food, and some of it we give to birds. Read Maggie's story in which she explains why her mum provides food for birds.

WHY SHE FEEDS BIRDS

Maggie Pavlou

My mother is 94 years old. She started putting food scraps out for the birds several years ago as, having survived the 1941 famine in Greece, she couldn't bear to see food being thrown out or any creature going without. Along came her magpie couple who took full advantage of the new 'restaurant'. When the service is not up to their expectations, they fly over to whichever part of the house they think she is in and belt out that beautiful, but loud, warble. Not good at first light, but her neighbours are thankfully gracious about the early morning melodies.

In Europe, the practice of feeding birds was considered a humane response to the plight of hungry birds during the winter months. In Britain and Ireland, forests are transformed into farms and gardens, resulting in birds losing habitat. The likes of tits, robins and thrushes adapted to these changes, moving into gardens and farms. My own experience with bird feeding started when I was four. I remember my grandfather teaching me how to cut fat off meat in the shape of worms to feed to his robin. A male European robin will stay on its territory, often a backyard, throughout his life. As with the Aussie magpie, people form connections with the small red-breast birds, who are a constant presence, and once trust is formed they will take food directly from your hand. My grandfather's robin would perch on the handle of his lawnmower, watching on as he did his gardening. Worms were often thrown to the robin who would catch them midair! It was amazing, at such a young age, to witness the connection that can form between a man and a bird.

Working with birds to help eliminate pests such as cutworms that can kill crops provided a motivation to reward them. Like my grandfather, farmers provided food for birds as reward for eating invertebrate pests that would otherwise damage crops and even cause them to fail. By feeding birds, farmers were also ensuring that birds would survive the winter and be ready for work come spring. Farmers and gardeners still work with birds today, as Kay's story tells.

THE GARDENER'S FRIEND

Kay Waston

While I was making a veggie garden and in the process of digging and turning up the odd worm here and there, along came a yellow-breasted robin that perched on the post. Spying the worms as they wriggled around in the freshly dug soil, it would quickly fly down and grab them. It was so close to me it seemed to have no fear, so I would throw it worms and we got along in our mutual project. It became my favourite bird to visit my yard.

As urbanisation increased, birds lost more habitat. A series of severely cold weather spells in early 20th-century America resulted in thousands of birds freezing to death. The sight of their little bodies littering the streets resulted in a mass 'outreach to the birds'. This was when bird feeding really took off. Today, research has found bird feeding to be an important activity for large numbers of people and an important connection to nature. In fact, attracting birds by providing food is probably one of the most widespread and popular forms of human–wildlife interaction.

But in Australia we worry that our birds will become dependent on the food we provide, stop searching for natural food and become lazy and reliant on humans. Dependence is a really interesting issue as it causes significant concern for the public. While we need to do research into this area, I am not convinced that this is the major concern that many people have. Remember, we discussed diet switching in the last chapter? I feel that birds use us to get access to food and are smart enough to use our cues to know when we are going to provide food. This would help explain why birds seem to know when you are home from work or making your morning coffee. They see you moving about your house and hang around in the hopes you remember to feed them.

What do people who feed birds think the bird is getting out of it? In my own research into bird feeding, nearly 40 per cent of my participants thought that their feeding was supplementing the bird's diet. Comments I received included: 'a little extra because of reduced habitat'; 'a reliable source of appropriate, good quality food for the birds which visit my garden'; 'a reliable supply of food at the end of the day'; 'a source of food to supplement what they find naturally'; 'a supplement to the local diet, especially in times of stress (drought, etc)'. We are so quick to help them when they appear to be in need! Are we underestimating our birds? Birds long ago adapted to finding new food sources. Take this story from Judy about her magpies betraying her for a better meal.

OUR MAGPIES

Judy Margolis

Our magpies are partial to toast crumbs, pieces of bread and biscuits, especially crumbs of scotch fingers and butternut snaps. In an endeavour to provide something more nutritious than bread and bikkies, we began offering dry chook pellets, grudgingly accepted until our magpies simply deserted us for greener pastures. Where? On a visit to a neighbour, what did we find but our opportunistic, faithless magpies, enjoying bread and biscuit crumbs at another table!

One of the major problems associated with bird feeding is that people are feeding human food to birds: meat, cheese, bread and even rice. This is never going to be good for birds, just as it is injurious to dogs and cats. If you want to feed magpies, kookaburras and butcherbirds, consider using the insectivore food available at www.wombaroo.com.au. Your bird is probably going to complain about this change in food, but stick with it! This food, so much better for meat-eating birds, is used by wildlife carers and zoos across the country.

You can experiment with the mix by adding a bit of meat or cheese to the powder to entice your bird. Over time increase the powder and decrease the meat or cheese. Once you start feeding them, birds can become persistent, as Jan reports.

BUTCHERBIRDS AND MAGGIES WORKING AS A TEAM!

Jan Gorrel

Every morning we have either a magpie or grey butcherbird sitting on this chair awning and looking through the door waiting for us to get up. If we are late, the other magpies and grey butcherbirds gather on the verandah and start carolling until we come out into the kitchen. I am sure they take it in turns to stand guard, as one in particular will not make a sound when I get some minced meat and hand-feed him. Another one, as soon as he sees me at the fridge, will start calling the others in. When the butcherbird is on watch, he usually takes a few pieces of meat then calls the others in. It really seems that the two types of bird work together, taking turns in who will stand watch.

If you do choose to feed birds, as with providing water, ensure that you keep your feeding areas clean. Wash and scrub the area and containers you are providing food in with hot soapy water followed by a good rinse to ensure no residue. To help protect against predators, have your feeding area elevated. As disease can be spread through many birds at the same feeding areas, consider having a few spots around your garden where you provide food. While providing seed is ideal for parrots and cockatoos, provide mealworms for fairy-wrens and willy wagtails.

Since the arrival of Europeans (and no doubt well before), Aussie birds have both amazed and challenged people. Instead of working with the farmer, as the little English bird did, the native birds visited and ate newly planted crops in huge numbers. The birds watched the changes brought by Europeans, and those who could adapted to them.

I want to go back to how the early Europeans described so many of the native birds as tame. Of the willy wagtail, John Gould reported that, 'In its disposition this little bird is one of the tamest imaginable allowing of a near approach without evincing the slightest timidity and will even enter the house of persons resident in the bush in pursuit of gnats and other insects.'

William Saville-Kent noted in *The Naturalist in Australia* (1897) that 'laughing kookaburras and various species of Queensland Shrike genus are very readily tamed and being in captivity inveterate mimics with marked whistling and talking tendencies are in considerable favour as domestic pets'.

John Gould reported magpie larks as having a 'tame and familiar disposition . . . [which] must even obtain for it the friendship and protection of settlers whose verandahs and house-tops it constantly visits running along the latter like the pied wagtail of our own island; in fact, the two birds except in size are very similar'. Gould went on to report that he suspected that 'future research will, in all probability, establish the fact of this bird being universally dispersed over the greater portion of Australia'.

Remember, it is believed that the degree of tolerance to humans in urban populations is a result of learning over time about the risks attached. Were birds such as wagtails, magpies and bowerbirds already accustomed to changes in human behaviour because of an established relationship with Australia's first peoples?

We know Aboriginal Australians inhabited the continent for more than 65,000 years before Europeans arrived, and that birds could be important totems for them. We can see evidence of this in the huge number of Dreamtime stories about birds. For example, the Noongar Aboriginal people of Western Australia call the wagtail 'Chitty Chitty' because of its trademark chatter, and it was said to be a gossip and was driven away from important tribal meetings. Children were told not to chase wagtails because they'd be led into the bush and lost forever. Another Noongar story in the Dreaming has the wagtail as a great hunter 'who was one day robbed of his catch by Wardong the crow and Dwerda the dingo'[2]. They say that the wagtail never forgot this crime and this is why it still angrily attacks crows and dogs much bigger than itself.

Another lovely story from the Noongar Aboriginal people tells why magpies sing in the morning. According to the Noongar Dreaming[2], 'the sky was once so close to the ground that trees could not grow, people had to crawl and all the birds were forced to walk everywhere. Working together they managed to prop up the sky with sticks but it threatened to break the sticks and collapse to earth again—with potentially disastrous consequences. The clever magpies, however, took a long stick in their beaks and pushed it up and up until the sky suddenly sprang upwards by itself, revealing the sun and creating the first sunrise. Coolbardie the magpie's boastful singing each morning is to remind everybody of its important role in creation.'

I have to share one more story with you: how the joyous cry of the twenty-eight parrot (Australian ringneck) and its cheeky tail-wagging meant that it was always welcomed as a bringer of happiness by the Noongar people who called the bird Darlmoorluk[2]. It was said that when Darlmoorluk was around, the camp was safe from evil spirits that roamed the bush. Although these parrots were good to eat, the Noongar only hunted them in desperate times.

There is no doubt that Aboriginal Australians held sophisticated ecological, environmental and faunal knowledge. There were connections across groups that were maintained through trade and exchange networks. Alliances were built that could be abandoned and rebuilt. Having established networks and understandings between these groups of Aboriginal people was vital in the Australian environment, and the same could be said of the many birds who lived in groups.

At the root of it, we are social animals with a fundamental need to belong and to affiliate, to connect with others. Our constant drive to get along with others and to gain social acceptance is functional at a day-to-day level. Do we connect with urban birds because they are also social creatures and want to connect also? Even though they remain wild, they share their lives with us. We can see elements of our own behaviour in them, such as cheating, grieving, playing, and even displaying compassion, as this next story from Vivien shows.

THE PRIVILEGE OF A RELATIONSHIP WITH A DYING KING PARROT

Vivien Davidson

Living right up against the southern edge of Morton National Park means we have the opportunity to meet many birds, including king parrots. The king parrots are confident birds and easy to build connections with, but we had no particular 'pets'.

Last year among the flock gathering for grain, we noticed one male that seemed a bit slow, and seemed to wander across the courtyard and even stop and fall asleep. We hadn't seen this happen before and I discovered that this probably meant he was dying. He hung around and the next morning I discovered he had roosted on my kitchen window all night.

We put the cage on the front verandah where he could be warmed by the sun and there was wind and rain protection in the shed part of the cage. We gave him seed and water. He was surprisingly tame and easygoing.

> The rest of his flock came to visit him during the day, even though they normally hang out at the back of the house. Mind you, they also shared his seed, scattered on the cement! We then left his cage door open and he wandered out, just walking, not trying to fly, pottering about the garden, in front of the house, enjoying the afternoon sunshine.
>
> When it started to cool off, my husband told him it was time for bed, and he followed him back, slowly walking into his enclosure unassisted. We went to check on him early the next morning, but he had died in his sleep. We felt amazed and privileged that he had sought our care and trusted us with his last days of life.

We have been taught that evolution is a slow process occurring over millions of years, not something that can occur in the short time span of human history. We are now starting to realise this might not be so. Due to rapid, human-induced climate change and urbanisation, evolution can be fast in terms of behaviour change. A group member may try a new behaviour to get food or to nest and it works; other group members learn from this individual and the new behaviour can spread.

Our impact on the environment is so great that birds are forced to change their behaviour to adapt and even thrive in habitats that were originally created by humans for humans. For the first time in history, the number of people living in urban areas outnumbers those living in rural areas. Birds and humans are being forced closer to each other as urbanisation increases.

Birds learn that there are nice humans and not-so-nice ones. Just like them, we differ in our personality types—and we are everywhere. They need to understand us, and they do this through noticing us and even talking about us among themselves. They watch us to learn about us and our daily lives, to learn about what we might provide for them and, most importantly, to discover whether they can trust us. When they do choose to trust us, the relationship is magic, as Marion tells in our next story.

ALL IN A LINE

Marion Oates

We had quite a few magpies living on the property and they quickly learned that the horsefeed pellets were very palatable. We used to throw some of the softened pellets towards them which they would catch in midair.

One Saturday morning I went out to feed the horse, accompanied by three cats. I mixed the feed and began the walk down to the feeding trough along a well-trodden path. Something made me look behind and it was one of those moments when one wishes for a camera. Walking along behind me was a magpie followed by a cat then another magpie followed by another cat then another magpie and another cat, brought up behind by the last magpie. There was no aggravation; they all just strolled along the path one by one. One of the best moments of my life.

I would like to finish by revisiting my interaction with Rascal from the start of the chapter. I really felt I had communicated with this bird. I had an idea in my head that I wanted to share with him. That idea was that food would be provided if he came over. I shared this idea with Rascal through looking him in the eye and moving my eyes to the birdbath as well as pointing my head towards the bath. I repeated the actions a few times while thinking there was no way he was going to come over to me. To my utter astonishment, Rascal interpreted my actions. He flew from his tree and onto my birdbath. Rascal watched as I kept my end of the agreement and went back inside to get food that he took straight from my hand. He has done this before, I thought.

What I found so amazing about this experience was that I used the knowledge I gained while researching this book to communicate with a bird who did not know me—to communicate that food would be provided if he came into my garden. We both held up our parts of the agreement and trust formed. I was honoured with visits on the following days.

As this book has shown, what I experienced with Rascal was not unique. Instead, it was the personal experience I had with Rascal that made me feel special. I had a chat with a bird and we shared food and a drink.

POSTAMBLE

One of my missions for this book was to combine science with knowledge of bird personalities from stories I was sent by the public to help answer a question: can a bird have a personality? Through working in cooperative societies, our urban birds are showing intelligence and innovative, flexible behaviour to enable them to adapt to the urban world. In the pursuit of my mission, I found evidence that a bird *can* show individuality, and that led to another question: does a bird see itself as an individual? Sandie and Bruce's story is clearly a demonstration of personality!

MAGPIE VERSUS KOOKABURRA

Sandie and Bruce

Out of the kitchen window is a clothesline, and then an old fence (virtually just posts). The birds like to sit on these posts whilst they survey the landscape for bugs, worms, etc. One day a kookaburra was sitting on the post watching a magpie walking on the ground. Magpies here are very territorial and will swoop the other birds away

> regardless of their size. Well, this kookaburra sat contemplating this magpie walking up and down 'his' patch and . . . all of a sudden—kookie took off, head forward, beak extended—arrowing in on the magpie—hitting him full force and knocking him over. We sat watching in awe and said, 'Three cheers! You (kookaburra) have had your revenge!'

When we start talking of birds showing behaviours that we believe are uniquely human, we are accused of anthropomorphising. Why is such anthropomorphising so offensive to some? Are we as humans trying to hold on to a belief in our uniqueness, and that our uniqueness comes from individuality? Why are humans the only species thought to have a soul, as many people seem to believe? We put our needs before the needs of nature as our population continues to expand, and we can forget that we need nature to survive—but nature does not need us. To help answer these questions we need to look back at our own behavioural evolution, this time to a belief shared the world over: that our welfare and needs are more important than nature's.

I am going to talk about religion now! I feel our way of thinking about nature has been deeply influenced by religion. Christianity began as a Jewish sect in the mid-1st century arising out of Jesus of Nazareth's teaching. One of the Christian beliefs was of man's transcendence and rightful mastery over nature[1]. Nature was conceived primarily as a symbolic system through which God spoke to men. In the late 11th century there began a massive movement to translate Arabic and Greek scientific works into Latin. With the fall of the Eastern Roman Empire in 1453, the church replaced it as the head of a unified force in Europe. It was not until the late 18th century that the hypothesis of God became unnecessary to many scientists.

What did Christianity tell people about their relations with the environment? Very broadly, an all-powerful God created light and darkness, the heavenly bodies, the earth and all its plants, animals, birds and fishes. Man then named all the animals and established his dominance over them. Man is not *part* of nature; instead he is made in the image of God. For the first time in our evolutionary history, we began to think of ourselves as separate from nature, even masters over it.

The victory of religion over paganism can be described as 'the greatest psychic revolution in the history of our culture'[2]. By destroying pagan beliefs about working in harmony with and respecting nature, Christianity made it possible to exploit nature by casting man as superior to it. In combination with the development of agriculture, Christian dogma generated a profound change in the relationship between people and nature. Formerly we had been part of nature, living with it; now we were the exploiter of nature.

Humans have occupied the planet for several million years, but for almost all of that period we have lived as hunter-gatherers. It is only in the last 12,000 years that we started herding animals and cultivating grains and seeds. Interestingly, this change in lifestyle happened almost simultaneously in several areas of the world[3]. This suggests that global climatic changes were an important factor given that the development of agriculture coincided with the end of the Ice Age. Glaciers retreated, temperatures rose, and patterns of precipitation became more predictable. In parts of southwest Asia, grasslands replaced forests, in turn leading to an increased use of seeds for food, especially barley and wheat varieties.

Agriculture resulted in animal domestication and herding, in the clearing of woodlands, in the draining of swamps and wetlands, and in the turning, planting and tilling of soil. With the cultivation of grains and domestication of livestock, there were now relatively predictable supplies of food available. People started to abandon the hunter-gatherer lifestyle to settle in villages and take up farming. In time, villages gave way to towns and then towns to cities, eventually forming nation-states. The ability to produce food and other products from domesticated plants and animals resulted, in some instances, in a surplus of food. This led to population increase and possibly the opening of economic exchange[3], as farming resulted in food being available to non-food producers. This allowed for the emergence of other classes of people, such as priests, warriors, lords and kings. Our history progressed into the industrial era, and has now progressed further into the current technological era. At each step, we have become more removed from nature such that we have started to challenge its very survival.

Very broadly, belief in Christianity led countries to explore the world in order to spread the word of God beyond their shores. When conflicts of beliefs arose, the result was often war. More European forests were cut down but this time for building ships, not to extend farmland. The building of fine sailing ships gave several European countries—Britain, Holland, France, Spain and Portugal—the ability to travel vast distances. As we know, the British Empire was particularly successful in finding new lands, which soon led it to establish new settlements and to secure overseas possessions and trading posts. Once a country was 'claimed', the new religion of Christianity was forced on its people, along with allegiance to the British Crown.

By the time the British Empire claimed Australia as its own, it was for the purpose of solving the problem of a high crime rate brought on by overpopulation, in particular in London. With the American War of Independence won in 1783, America would no longer take convicts from England. Soon, overcrowding in prisons spawned the need to find somewhere new to send undesirable criminals, and Australia was the solution. The Empire was keen to spread its religion and to gain the cooperation of people they encountered. As long as things were done the British way, the proper civilised way, and in the name of God and the Crown, all would be peaceful.

One aspect of the Aboriginal Dreamtime that confused the European Christian men and women was the apparent lack of a higher power, a god who must be worshipped. They looked for a common god who was worshipped in Aboriginal culture, believing that Christianity could easily destroy all other gods as Christianity claimed the one true God. No evidence of gods was found; instead it was reported that 'None of the tribes believed in a supreme being. None had the faintest conception of any individual who might in any way be described as a High God of the Mysteries. Unable to see that the Aborigines were religious at all, I think conclusively that the Central Australian natives have nothing whatever in the way of a simple pure religion.'[4] Not only that, they did not even have a king or other kind of leader! Goodness me!

To make things more shocking to the English, there was no writing down of the spoken word, instead they came together to dance, sing, share food and stories, and interact with the Dreamtime. While each tribe had their own language, their nomadism encouraged learning from other tribes. To ensure survival of the culture, tribes came together at certain times to share knowledge through corroboree. The lack of a god to praise made the Aboriginal culture appear inferior and in dire need of British enlightenment through religion and settlement.

Today we understand how wrong the colonisers were. We now know of the profound relationship with and connection to country experienced by Aboriginal people. We acknowledge that a common belief in the laws of the Dreamtime allowed Aboriginal people to live successfully for 65,000 years. As Bill Gammage declared: 'In 1788 people never depended on farming. Mobility was much more important. It let people tend plants and animals in regions impossible for farmers today and manage Australia more sustainably than their dispossessors. It was the critical difference between them and farmers . . . Europeans think farming explains the difference between them and Aborigines.'[5] Hiding behind Christianity, the colonisers started to do unthinkable damage to the Dreamtime culture and its people in the name of God and the Crown.

A critical resource issue became apparent in the 17th and 18th centuries as Europeans observed the damage they were causing, especially in Australia where Europeans described how they were making things worse: 'In Australia thousands of years of grass and soil changed in a few years. The spongy soil grew hard, the run-off accelerated and different grasses dominated. The rivers flooded higher than the Aboriginals had ever seen.'[6] Long-lived, deep-rooted and tall perennial species such as curly windmill-grass (*Enteropogon acicularis*) and kangaroo grass (*Themeda australis*) declined and were replaced with heavily grazed areas with annual grasses[7]. Charles Darwin argued in *The Voyage of the Beagle* (1845) that the introduction of greyhounds was sure to cause extinction of some species. Things got worse, with George Bennett reporting the impact of farming:

> In October 1858 the territory of NSW suffered severely from the devastation occasioned by Aphides, and all the Cruciferous vegetables, as Cabbages, &c., were almost entirely destroyed by them throughout the colony, when probably some of the soft-billed birds, recklessly killed or driven away, might have prevented the evil . . . the birds do mischief occasionally among ripe corn there can be no doubt; but the harm they may cause in autumn is amply compensated by the good they do in spring, from the havoc they make among the insect tribes. The quantity of grubs and caterpillars annually destroyed by rooks and various small birds must be immense.

For a long time we believed that the resources vital to sustaining life on the planet were either infinite or infinitely substitutable[8]. We are starting to realise that this is not so. One of the basic laws of ecology is that everything is connected to everything else. You cannot change just one thing in nature. The simple biological fact is that nature does not need humans, but humans need nature[9]. Our own ultimate future depends upon that understanding. It has been suggested that 'conservation should give up its infatuation with parks and focus on mixing people and nature in mutually conducive ways that can offer positive results'[10].

We live in a time of rapid social change, widespread movement of people, and multicultural societies[11]. Many people did not grow up in the places where they live today, where there are no birds from their previous homes. Locally non-native or introduced species can often help people feel at home in a new place. I will put my hand up here: the song of the blackbird in the early morning, singing his heart out in my little garden in inner-city Melbourne, always reminds me of home, Ireland. While I would rather have the song of the magpie, I can't help but love the song of the blackbird. People will often see the species that they grew up with as particularly important. When people grow up with non-native species, for instance, it is these birds that matter to them and that they engage with emotionally and through their actions.

One way we can connect with nature is in our gardens; they are important for this very reason. According to some, 'experiencing urban biodiversity will be the key to halt the loss of global biodiversity. This is because people are most likely to take action for biodiversity if they have direct contact with nature.'[12] Much of the urban landscape consists of backyards such that people's primary experience of urban nature may be through their own gardens[13]. This is why it is so important to ensure your backyard is as wildlife friendly as possible. As our next story shows, watching birds can reveal all kinds of amusing encounters!

BABY MAGGIE HAS A NAP

Lowana Chapman

I had a baby magpie in my garden a long time ago. The parents always came and then when the babies were old enough they came along too. One day I had some undies draped over a rack on the back lawn, and this dear little baby maggie lay down beside it and gently pulled a pair of knickers over itself so it could have a rest.

In fact, research has found that a lack of early connection to nature in children might result in a lack of motivation to protect nature. This is because gardens can represent the main source of nature with which children interact in their daily lives[14]. For children, backyards seem particularly important in establishing a lifelong connection to nature[15]. Just like the young birds who play and feel safe in their territory, a preference for gardens being close to home has been reported in a study of children's use of neighbourhoods. Children's fondness for gardens makes them an important resource for supporting their connection to nature, particularly given that the main demonstration of biodiversity children encounter is in their home garden[16]. Indeed, one study found that school gardening programs improved children's ability to name species[17].

Making your garden more wildlife-friendly will help attract birds, but it can also help other urban wildlife. Providing water for birds in different spots and at different heights when water is scarce can create oases for lizards, echidnas, kangaroos and wallabies, for instance. Urban ecology is starting to combine natural and social science to understand what drives people to interact with nature in towns and cities. As we have talked about, bird feeding is often discouraged in Australia while it is celebrated as a national pastime in America and the UK. People's decision not to feed birds can be environmentally motivated by the belief that they are not helping birds and even causing damage by providing food. However there is no evidence to support this and bird feeding is an important activity as people seek to connect with urbanised nature[18].

Before science emerged as a profession, keen amateurs or naturalists used the natural world around them to help understand weather changes and other biological phenomena. The scientific revolution which started in the 17th century and lasted until roughly the 19th century saw the creation of the first scientific societies and academies. By the 18th century, scientific authority began to displace religious authority. Writers and thinkers with a background in the sciences contributed to scientific advancement, which led in turn to the privileging of free speech and thought over religion.

Instead of 'reading' the country around us and listening to those who know the land and work it, we apply rigorous scientific testing to answer questions. Sometimes it works but sometimes maybe not. A person can get to know his or her own habitat and who shares it with them. They may see behaviours and interactions between species that scientists have not considered, or for which no evidence has yet been shown. As this book has illustrated, there is a wealth of information about bird behaviour out there. Citizen science is the practice of engaging the public in scientific projects, led usually by a university. These studies are especially important for tracking wildlife in urban areas and gardens. Cameras and the GPS capability of mobile phones allow citizen scientists to gather a range of data in large quantities that can add greatly to our knowledge.

It is important for academics to share the outcomes of their studies with citizen scientists to ensure a two-way sharing of knowledge. While the end goal of the research may be to publish the results in a peer-reviewed journal, it is important to write another version that is accessible to participants in the study. This is where science communication comes in. Academics are encouraged to write more accessibly to ensure the public can understand the findings of the study. Two-way sharing of knowledge in citizen science studies ensures respect, because without participants, the study may not have even been possible. Our final story tells of a connection between Dale and the birds he watched during one of our bird surveys.

VISITING BIRDS

Dale Rabbett

I had the privilege of caring for my terminally ill partner for three years at home before her death. Activities at this time were limited because of her illness *but* we could enjoy the birds together and participate in bird surveys. We made friends with, in particular, a group of grey strike-thrushes, we enjoyed their song and they became so accustomed to our presence on the verandah that one of them would frequently land on our knees. My partner died this March past, and although I miss her terribly her birds still visit and in some small way I still feel connected.

Anyone who has felt this connection to a bird will know it can be profound. Birds are so different in appearance from us, yet can show similar behaviour as a result of living in a social world. While writing this book, I have been constantly tormented and inspired by my obstreperous cockatiel, Link.

While my two house cats ignore me until feeding time, Link is constantly interacting with me. Link is just delighted that I am spending my days at home writing. She will spend hours happily calling to me in different tones and sounds, depending on what she wants. She will tell me when she wants to move to a different area by changing her state. Link will yawn and stretch a wing and/or leg while vocalising at me. Something we have talked about throughout this book is how a bird communicates with another bird or even with a group, when it is ready go somewhere else. By changing body state, Link demands I pay attention and move her to where she desires to go.

She has a completely different relationship with my husband, whom she just tolerates. Link has different levels of mateship with me, with my husband, and even with my two cats. One cat she likes and will tolerate; the other cat she attacks. Did this cat attack her at some stage? Not that I know of! Interestingly, this is the cat that is the more submissive of the two, so maybe Link is just showing her dominance over it.

When I am not in the same room as her, Link uses a contact call to stay in touch. I answer 'Yes Link', and she immediately answers back. Less than 30 seconds later, she calls again. I'll reply, 'Yes Link, I am still here.' This can go on for quite a while! Link makes me feel cared about; she notices when I am not in the house by behaving differently. She spends more time in her cage roosting and acts more anti-social. This is despite my husband's best efforts to try to engage her in head rubs. Link will playfully attack his finger and try to engage my husband to play instead.

Link shows excitement when I come home, wanting scratches around her head and on her back to reaffirm our bond. Like so many birds that visit us, Link will use her head, beak and eye orientation to point to what she wants. This helps her communicate with me, and she knows that I often understand. Her calls can get more rapid and louder if I ignore her.

Despite the best efforts of myself and my hubby, Link still won't mimic songs or words. As in the wild, female cockatiels and budgies don't usually mimic, because there is no motivation for them to copy your words. Why? Because they are female! It is the male that needs to mimic their calls. This is why it is the males of the species that are more likely to pick up our words and songs.

Link will smile at me by bending her eyes slightly, tilting her head and gently grinding her beak as she looks happily at me. If I delve any deeper into her demonstrations of personality, I could easily be drawn into the anthropomorphising debate . . . I might just be spending too much time with her while writing about birds!

ACCOUNTS OF BIRDS FROM EARLY BRITISH EXPLORERS

Quotes in this book from early European visitors were sourced from their journals found at the Biodiversity Heritage Library at www.biodiversitylibrary.org. This website is an amazing resource to discover more about Australia's first European explorers, who often alluded to the questions we ask in this book. Within these journals is insight into the importance of birds in the lives of the people of the colony. As George Bennett in *Wanderings in New South Wales* reported about parrots: 'These birds are evidently gifted with the bump of talkativeness, it was once asserted that ladies kept birds to converse with when alone which served a double purpose that of being to them both practice and amusement.'[1]

In these journals, we get a taste of early Australia first-hand as Bennett goes on to write:

> No-one can walk the streets of Sydney and any of the villages of the colony or enter an inn or dwelling house without seeing this

> class of birds hung about in cages and having his ears assailed by the screeching babbling and whistling noises which issue from their vocal organs. It is street music of the colony and pretty polly, sweet polly are tender sounds which issue from that exterior as well as interior of every dwelling[1].

Would you have guessed that parrots were the street music of a young Sydney or Parramatta?

George Bennett would have made a great citizen scientist as he describes the behaviour of a pair of tawny frogmouths: 'For no less a period than five years, these two tawny frogmouths occupied the position of familiar household pets, and rewarded all the care and attention bestowed upon them by the concession of an undreamt of insight into their most marvellously Protean moods and tenses.' In the next part of this story, the description of the bond between the male frogmouth and Bennett is almost dog-like! 'An attitude which was commonly assumed by the male bird by way of a greeting to the writer at first sight of him on his returning home after some days absence. The bird's manifestation of pleasurable excitement under the foregoing condition were on all occasions most unmistakeable demonstrated.'

On one of his travels back to England, Bennett brought a firetail finch with him that showed remarkable persistence as the finch displayed 'a marked partiality for a lady acquaintance who possessed the, to him, irresistible attraction of a tiny gold mine in one of her front teeth. The ambition to attain access to, and to exploit the profundities of that glittering El Dorado, of which his keen eyes would detect the most momentary display, was his one endeavour and with that end in view his pertinacious attentions were somewhat embarrassing.'

Magpies and butcherbirds (family artamidae) were incorrectly classified as part of the corvid family at this time. A reason for this misclassification could have been that they looked and behaved similarly to European crows, ravens and magpies. Ravens were already known for their ability to mimic and play when in captivity. William Saville-Kent, another good example of an early citizen scientist, recorded various behaviours in a butcherbird in *The Naturalist in Australia*:

> A Young Queensland Shrike was obtained by the writer and . . . developed early its special whistling properties and these were so trained that within a few weeks he rehearsed the first stanzas of the Cambrian air 'The Rising of the Lark' with a vigour and correctness that would have won for him honourable mention if not a prize at a Welsh Eisteddfod. This became the customary merry reveille with which from his cage in the verandah he was accustomed to rouse the household in the early morning.

Saville-Kent describes the personality of the bird that is so familiar to anyone who interacts with these birds: 'The courage and spirit of these birds is notable; they will readily attack and drive away hawks, piping crows and almost any large birds that happen to poach upon its territory.' He goes on to report how the birds 'evince the strongest likes and dislikes to individual people with children became a special subject of hostility'. That is a sure sign of personality there! Saville-Kent describes another behaviour: 'Jealousy was with this Shrike a ruling passion and provided his ruin.' The next part of this story tells of an intriguing behaviour: 'With the arrival of a magpie, the butcher-bird's peace of mind received a shock though unrecognised at the time from which it never recovered. No sooner did he commence a bar of his favourite air than the Magpie would at once overpower it with a louder and for the occasion harsher note.'

I wonder what was going on in the mind of the magpie—was it intentionally trying to outcompete the butcherbird?

What happens next in this saga is sad but it also shows the effect birds had on the early Europeans who arrived on these shores: 'This unfriendly stratagem, continually repeated, had began to mope and lost his appetite and more winning ways. The recognised cause of his discomfiture was removed but unfortunately too late. All attempts to resuscitate his health proved fruitless and affectionately responding to our caresses to the last he peacefully passed away.'

And what did this man of God think happened to the bird after death? 'Surely, as the elder Agassize has previously suggested, there will be a resurrection for our departed dumb friends, for heaven without them would lack to many the highest potentiality of happiness.' I agree with you, William Saville-Kent!

FOR FULL TEXT:

Bennett, George (1804–1893) *Wanderings in New South Wales, Batavia, Pedir Coast, Singapore and China; being the Journal of a Naturalist in those countries, during 1832, 1833, and 1834.* Published in 1834. Doi:10.5962/bhl.title.39887. Available at: www.biodiversitylibrary.org/bibliography/39887#/summary

Bennett, George (1804–1893) *Gatherings of a naturalist in Australasia: being observations principally on the animals and vegetable productions of New South Wales, New Zealand, and some of the Austral Islands.* Published in 1860. Doi:10.5962/10.5962/bhi.title.115620. Available at: www.biodiversitylibrary.org/bibliography/115620#/summary

Darwin, Charles (1809–1882) *The Voyage of the Beagle.* Published in 1845. Doi:10.5962/bhl.title.98662. Available at: www.biodiversitylibrary.org/bibliography/98662#/summary

Gould, John (1804–1881) *Handbook to The Birds of Australia: Volume 1 and 2.* Published in 1865. Doi:10.5962/bhl.title.8367. Available at www.biodiversitylibrary.org/bibliography/8367#/summary

Saville-Kent, William (1845–1908) *The Naturalist in Australia.* Published in 1897. Doi:10.5962/bhl.title.18339. Available at: www.biodiversitylibrary.org/bibliography/18339#/summary

Tench, Watkin (1759–1833) *A Complete Account of the Settlement at Port Jackson. Including An Accurate Description of the Situation of the Colony; of the Natives; and Of Its Natural Productions.* University of Sydney Library. Available at: http://setis.library.usyd.edu.au/ozlit/pdf/p00044.pdf

ACKNOWLEDGEMENTS

This book was inspired by the people who notice and even become friends with the birds in their backyards. I would like to thank everyone who contributed to its writing by sending their stories about the birds they interact with. This book would not have been possible without your insightful contributions and compelling questions. Working with your stories to write a book was a joy and I hope I have answered some of your questions!

ENDNOTES

PREAMBLE

1. Bolhuis J.J. and Wynne C.D.L (2009) Can evolution explain how minds work? *Nature* 458, 832–833; doi:10.1038/458832a
2. Darwin C. (1882) *The Descent of Man and Selection in Relation to Sex.* Murray, London
3. Petkov C.I. and Jarvis E.D. (2012) Birds, primates and spoken language origins: behavioural phenotypes and neurobiological substrates. *Fronts in Evolutionary Neuroscience* 4:12; doi:10.3389/fnevo.2012.00012
4. Kaplan G. (2016) *Bird Minds: Cognition and Behaviour of Australian Native Birds.* CSIRO Publishing, Melbourne
5. Kaplan G. (2004) *Australian Magpie: Biology and Behaviour of an Unusual Songbird.* CSIRO Publishing, Melbourne
6. Rumbaugh D.M. (1977) *Language Learning by a Chimpanzee.* Academic Press, New York
7. Shettleworth S.J. (2010) *Cognition, Evolution and Behaviour.* Oxford University Press, New York
8. Prather J., Peters S., Nowicki S. and Mooney R. (2008) Precise

auditory-vocal mirroring in neurons for learned vocal communication. *Nature* 451, 305–310; doi:10.1038/nature06492

9. Peters S., Searcy W.A. and Nowicki S. (2014) Developmental stress, song-learning and cognition. *Integrative and Comparative Biology* 54:4, 555–567; doi:10.1093/icb/icu020
10. Riebel K. (2003) The 'mute' sex revisited: vocal production and perception learning in female songbirds. pp. 49–86. In: *Advances in the Study of Behaviour* Vol 33. Slater P.J.B., Rosenblatt J.S., Roper T.J., Snowdon C.T., Naguib M. (editors) Elsevier Academic Press, Massachusetts
11. Brainard M.S. and Doupe A.J. (2013) Translating birdsong: songbirds as a model for basic and applied medical research. *Annual Review of Neuroscience* 36, 489–517; doi:10.1146/annurev-neuro-060909-152826
12. Funabiki Y. and Konishi M. (2003) Long Memory in Song Learning by Zebra Finches. *The Journal of Neuroscience* 23:17, 6928–6935; doi:10.1523/JNEUROSCI.23-17-06928.2003
13. Bolhuis J.J., Okanoya K. and Schaff C. (2010) Twitter evolution: converging mechanisms in birdsong and human speech. *Neuroscience Biology* 11, 747–759; doi:10.1038/nrn2931
14. Doupe A.J. and Kuhl P.K. (1999) Birdsong and human speech: common themes and mechanisms. *Annual Review of Neuroscience* 22:1, 567–631; doi:10.1146/annurev.neuro.22.1.567
15. Marler P. (1997) Three models of song learning: Evidence from behaviour. *Journal of Neurobiology* 33:5, 501-516; doi:10.1002/(SICI)1097-4695(19971105)33:5<501::AID-NEU2>3.0.CO;2-8
16. Hauser M.D., Chomsky N. and Fitch W.T. (2002) The faculty of language: what is it, who has it and how did it evolve? *Science* 298:5598, 1569–1579; doi:10.1126/science.298.5598.1569
17. Humphrey N. (1976) The social function of intellect. pp. 303–317. In: *Growing points in theology.* Bateson P.P.G., Hinde R.A. (editors). Cambridge University Press, Cambridge

18. Emery N.J. (2006) Cognitive Ornithology; the evolution of avian intelligence. *Philosophical Transactions of the Royal Society B: Biological Sciences* 361:1465, 23-43; doi:10.1098/rstb.2005.1736
19. Cockburn A. (2006) Prevalence of different modes of parental care in birds. *Proceedings of the Royal Society B: Biological Sciences* 273:1592, 1375–1383; doi:10.1098/rspb.2005.3458
20. Gowaty P.A., Drickamer L.C. and Schmid-Holmes S. (2003) Male house mice produce fewer offspring with lower viability and poorer performance when mated with females they do not prefer. *Animal Behaviour* 65:1, 95–103; doi:10.1006/anbe.2002.2026
21. Ihle M., Kempenaers B. and Forstmeier W. (2015) Fitness Benefits of Mate Choice for Compatibility in a Socially Monogamous Species. *PLoS Biology* 13:9, e1002248; doi.org/10.1371/journal.pbio.1002248
22. Forstmeier W. and Birkhead T.R. (2004) Repeatability of mate choice in the zebra finch: consistency within and between females. *Animal Behaviour* 68:5, 1017–1028; doi:10.1016/j.anbehav.2004.02.007
23. Schuett W., Tregenza T. and Dall S.R.X. (2010) Sexual selection and animal personality. *Biological Reviews* 85:2, 2017–2046; doi:10.1111/j.1469-185X.2009.00101.x
24. Schuett W., Dall S.R.X. and Royle N.J. (2011) Pairs of zebra finches with similar 'personalities' make better parents. *Animal Behaviour* 81:3, 609–618; doi:10.1016/j.anbehav.2010.12.006
25. Fraser O.N. and Bugnyar F. (2011) Ravens reconcile after aggressive conflicts with valuable partners. *PLos One* 6:3, e18118; doi.org/10.1371/journal.pone.0018118
26. Braun A. and Bugnyar T. (2012) Social bonds and rank acquisition in raven nonbreeder aggregation. *Animal Behaviour* 84:6, 1507–1515; doi:10.1016/j.anbehav.2012.09.024

CHAPTER 1: THE FRIENDLY BIRD

1. Ashley M. (2016) *The Birdman's Wife*. Affirm Press, Melbourne
2. Cockburn A., Osmond H.L., Mulder R.A., Green D.J. and Double M.C. (2003) Divorce, dispersal and incest avoidance in the cooperatively breeding superb fairy-wren *Maurus cyaneus*. *Journal of Animal Ecology* 72:2, 189–202; doi: 10.1046/j.1365-2656.2003.00694.x
3. Sol D., Timmermans S. and Lefebvre L. (2002) Behavioural flexibility and invasion success in birds. *Animal Behaviour* 63:3, 495–502; doi:10.1006/anbe.2001.1953
4. Emery N.J. (2006) Cognitive ornithology; the evolution of avian intelligence. *Philosophical Transactions of the Royal Society B: Biological Sciences* 361:1465, 23-43; doi:10.1098/rstb.2005.1736
5. Kaplan G. (2016) *Bird Minds: Cognition and Behaviour of Australian Native Birds*. CSIRO Publishing, Melbourne
6. Kaplan G. (2004) *Australian Magpie: Biology and Behaviour of an Unusual Songbird*. CSIRO Publishing, Melbourne
7. Shettleworth S.J. (1998) *Cognition, Evolution and Behavior*. Oxford University Press, New York
8. Pepperberg I.M. (2002) The Alex Studies: Cognitive and Communicative Abilities of Grey Parrots. *Current Directions in Psychological Science* 11:3, 83–87; doi:10.1111/1467-8721.00174
9. Emery N.J. and Clayton N.S. (2005) Evolution of the avian brain and intelligence. *Current Biology* 15:23, R946–R950; doi:10.1016/j.cub.2005.11.029
10. Cracraft J. (2001) Avian evolution, Gondwana biogeography and the Cretaceous-Tertiary mass extinction event. *Proceedings of the Royal Society B: Biological Sciences* 268:1466, 459–469; doi:10.1098/rspb.2000.1368
11. Humphrey N. (1976) The social function of intellect. pp. 303–317. In: *Growing points in theology*. Bateson P.P.G., Hinde R.A. (editors). Cambridge University Press, Cambridge

12. Wolf J.B. and Moore A.J. (2010) Interacting phenotypes and indirect genetic effects. pp. 225–245. In: *Evolutionary Behavioural Ecology*. Westneat D.F. and Fox C.W. (editors). Oxford University Press, New York

13. Silk M.J., Croft D.P., Tregenza T. and Bearhop S. (2014) The importance of fission–fusion social group dynamics in birds. *IBIS* 156:4, 701–715; doi:10.1111/ibi.12191

CHAPTER 2: THE COOPERATIVE BIRD

1. Kaplan G. (2016) *Bird Minds: Cognition and Behaviour of Australian Native Birds*. CSIRO Publishing, Melbourne

2. Aplin L.M., Farine D.R., Mann R.P. and Sheldon B.C. (2014) Individual-level personality influences social foraging and collective behaviour in wild birds. *Proceedings of The Royal Society B: Biological Sciences* 281:1789; doi.org/10.1098/rspb.2014.1016

3. Cockburn A. and Russell A.F. (2011) Cooperative Breeding: A Question of Climate? *Current Biology* 215:5, R195–R197; doi:10.1016/j.cub.2011.01.044

4. Hills R.S. (2004) Origins of the southeastern Australian vegetation. *Transactions of the Royal Society* 359:1450, 1537–1549; doi:1098/rstb.2004.1526

5. White M.E. (1994) *After the Greening: The Browning of Australia*. Kangaroo Press, New South Wales

6. Cook R., Bird G., Catmur C., Press C. and Heyes C. (2014) Mirror neurons: from origin to function. *Behavioral and Brain Sciences* 37:2, 177–192; doi:10.1017/S0140525X13000903

7. Ramachandran V.S. (2009) The neurons that shaped civilization. Available at www.ted.com/talk/vs_ramachandran_the_neurons_that_shaped_civilization.html

8. Heyes C. (2010) Where do mirror neurons come from? *Neuroscience and Biobehavioral Review* 34:4, 575–583; dio:10.1016/j.neubiorev.2009.11.007

9. Heyes C. (2011) Automatic imitation. *Psychological Bulletin* 137:3, 463–483; doi:10.1037/a0022288
10. Ferrari P.F. and Rizzolatti G. (2014) Mirror neuron research: the past and the future. *Philosophical Transactions of the Royal Society B: Biological Sciences* 369:164; doi:10.1098/rstb.2013.0169
11. Rizzolatti G. and Craighero L. (2004) The Mirror-Neuron System. *Annual Review of Neuroscience* 27, 169–192; doi:10.1146/annurev.neuro.27.070203.144230
12. Brainard M.S. and Doupe A.J. (2013) Translating Birdsong: Songbirds as a model for basic and applied medical research. *Annual Review of Neuroscience* 36, 489–517; doi:10.1146/annurev-neuro-060909-152826
13. Fitch W.T. (2000) The evolution of speech: a comparative review. *Trends in Cognitive Sciences* 4:7, 258–267; doi:10.1016/S1364-6613(00)01494-7
14. Funabiki Y. and Konishi M. (2003) Long Memory in Song Learning by Zebra Finches. *The Journal of Neuroscience* 23:17, 6928–6935; doi:10.1523/JNEUROSCI.23-17-06928.2003
15. Lakin J.L., Jefferis V.E., Cheng C.M. and Chartrand T.L. (2003) The chameleon effect as social glue: evidence for the evolutionary significance of nonconscious mimicry. *Journal of Nonverbal Behaviour* 27:3, 145–162; doi:10.1023/A:1025389814290
16. Yabar Y., Johnston L., Miles L. and Peace V. (2006) Implicit Behavioural Mimicry: Investigating the Impact of Group Membership. *Journal of Nonverbal Behavior* 30:3, 97–113; doi:10.1007/s10919-006-0010-6
17. Couzin I.D., Krause J., Franks N.R. and Levin S.A. (2005) Effective leadership and decision-making in animal groups on the move. *Nature* 433, 513–516; doi:10.1038/nature03236
18. Emery N.J. (2000) The eyes have it: The neuroethology, function and evolution of social gaze. *Neuroscience Behaviour Review* 24:6, 581–604; doi:10.1016/S0149-7634(00)00025-7

19. Kaplan G. (2011) Pointing gesture in a bird—merely instrumental or a cognitively complex behaviour? *Current Zoology* 57:4, 453–467; doi:10.1016/S0149-7634(00)00025-7
20. King A.J., Johnson D.D.P. and Va Vugt M. (2009) The Origins and Evolution of Leadership. *Current Biology* 19:19, R911–R916; doi:10.1016/j.cub.2009.07.027
21. Wright J., Stone R.E. and Brown N. (2003) Communal roosts as structured information centres in the raven, *Corvus corax*. *Journal of Animal Ecology* 72:6, 1003–1014; doi:10.1046/j.1365-2656.2003.00771.x
22. Van Vugt M. (2006) Evolutionary Origins of Leadership and Followership. *Personality and Social Psychology Review* 10:4, 354–371; doi:10.1207/s15327957pspr1004_5
23. Mesoudi A. (2008) An experimental simulation of the 'copy-successful-individuals' cultural learning strategy: adaptive landscapes, producer-scrounger dynamics and informational access costs. *Evolution and Human Behaviour* 29:5, 350–363; doi:10.1016/j.evolhumbehav.2008.04.005
24. Kaplan G. (2011) Ponting gesture in bird—merely instrumental or a cognitively complex behaviour? *Current Zoology* 57:4, 453–467; doi:10.1093/czoolo/57.4.453
25. Cockburn A. (1996) Why do so many Australian birds cooperate: social evolution in the Corvida? pp. 451–472. In: *Frontiers of population ecology*. Floyd R.B., Sheppard A.W. and de Barrow P.J. (editors) CSIRO Publishing, Melbourne

CHAPTER 3: THE NETWORKING BIRD

1. Conradt L. and Roper T.J. (2005) Consensus decision making in animals. *Trends in Ecology and Evolution* 20:8, 449–456; doi:10.1016/j.tree.2005.05.008
2. Couzin I.D. (2006) Social Organization in Fission–Fusion Societies. *Current Biology* 16:7, R169–R171; doi:10.1016/j.cub.2006.02.042

3. Falls J.B. (1982) Individual recognition by sound in birds. pp. 237–278. In: *Acoustic Communication in Birds Vol 2.* Academic Press, New York
4. Balsby T.J.S. and Adams D.M. (2011) Vocal similarity and familiarity determine response to potential flockmates in orange-fronted conures. *Animal Behaviour* 81:5, 983–991; doi:10.1016/j.anbehav.2011.01.034
5. Dean L.G., Kendal R.L., Schapiro S.J., Thierry B. and Laland K.N. (2012) Identification of the Social and Cognitive Processes Underlying Human Cumulative Culture. *Science* 335:6072, 1114–1118; doi:10.1126/science.1213969
6. Whiten A. and Mesoudi A. (2008) Establishing an experimental science of culture: animal social diffusion experiments. *Philosophical Transactions of the Royal Society B: Biological Sciences* 363:1509, 3477–3488; doi:10.1098/rstb.2008.0134
7. Aplin L.M., Farine D.R., Morand-Ferron J., Cockburn A., Thornton A. and Sheldon B.C. (2015) Experimentally induced innovations lead to persistent culture via conformity in wild birds. *Nature* 518, 538–541; doi:10.1038/nature13998
8. Hatchwell B.J. (2009) The evolution of cooperative breeding in birds: kinship, dispersal and life history. *Philosophical Transactions of the Royal Society B: Biological Sciences* 364:1533, 3217–3227; doi:10.1098/rstb.2009.0109
9. Painter J.N., Crozier R.H., Poiani A., Robertson R.J. and Clarke M.R. (2000) Complex social organization reflects genetic structure and relatedness in the cooperatively breeding bell miner, *Manorina melanophrys. Molecular Ecology* 9:9, 1339–1347; doi:10.1046/j.1365-294x.2000.01012.x
10. Peake T.M. and Terry A. (2001) Male great tits eavesdrop on simulated male-to-male vocal interactions. *Proceedings of the Royal Society B: Biological Sciences* 268:1472, 1183–1187; doi:10.1098/rspb.2001.1648

11. Mennill D.J., Radcliffe L.M. and Boag P.T. (2002) Females eavesdropping on male song contests in songbirds. *Science* 296:5569, 873–874; doi:10.1126/science.296.5569.873
12. Valone T.J. (1993) Patch Information and Estimation: A Cost of Group Foraging. *OIKOS* 68:2, 258–266; doi:10.2307/3544838
13. McGregor P.K. and Peake T.M. (2000) Communication networks: social environments for receiving and signalling behaviour. *Acta Ethologica* 2:2, 71–81; doi:10.1007/s102110000015
14. Stamps J., Clark A., Arrowood P. and Kus B. (1985) Parent-Offspring Conflict in Budgerigars. *Behaviour* 94:1, 1–39; doi:10.1163/156853985X00253
15. Baltz A.P. and Clark A.B. (1997) Extra-pair courtship behaviour of male budgerigars and the effect of an audience. *Animal Behaviour* 53:5, 1017–1024; doi:10.1006/anbe.1996.0354
16. Heinrich B. (1989) *Ravens in winter.* Summit Books, New York
17. Szipl G., Ringler E. and Bugnyar T. (2018) Attacked ravens flexibly adjust signalling behaviour according to audience composition. *Proceedings of the Royal Society B: Biological Sciences* 285:1880; doi:10.1098/rspb.2018.0375
18. Boeckle M. and Bugnyar T. (2012) Long-Term Memory for Affiliates in Ravens. *Current Biology* 22:9, 801–806; doi:10.1016/j.cub.2012.03.023
19. Massen J.J.M., Ritter C. and Bugnyar T. (2015) Tolerance and rewards equity predict cooperation in ravens (*Corvus corax*). *Scientific Reports* 5:15021; doi:10.1038/srep15021
20. Heinrch B. and Marzluff J.M. (1991) Do common ravens yell because they want to attract others? *Behavioural Ecology and Sociobiology* 28:1, 13–21; doi:10.1007/BF00172134

CHAPTER 4: THE DINOSAUR BIRD

1. Kaplan G. (2016) *Bird Minds: Cognition and Behaviour of Australian Native Birds.* CSIRO Publishing, Melbourne

2. Low T. (2014) *Where Song Began*. Penguin, Melbourne
3. Hills R.S. (2004) Origins of the southeastern Australian vegetation. *Philosophical Transactions of the Royal Society B: Biological Sciences* 359:1450, 1537–1549; doi:10.1098/rstb.2004.1526.
4. Groves R.H. (1994) *Australian Vegetation*. Cambridge University Press, Cambridge
5. Cracraft J. (2001) Avian evolution, Gondwana biogeography and the Cretaceous-Tertiary mass extinction event. *Proceedings of the Royal Society B: Biological Sciences* 268:1466, 459–469; doi:/10.1098/rspb.2000.1368
6. White N.E. et al. (2011) The evolutionary history of cockatoos (Aves: Psittaciformes: Cacatuidae). *Molecular Phylogenetics and Evolution* 59:3, 615–622; doi:10.1016/j.ympev.2011.03.011
7. Frith C.B. and Frith D.W. (2001) Nesting biology of the spotted catbird, *Ailuroedus melanotis*, a monogamous bowerbird (*Ptilonorhynchidae*). *Australian Journal of Zoology* 49:3, 279–310; doi:10.1071/ZO00061
8. Nicholls J.A. and Goldizen A.W. (2006) Habitat type and density influence vocal signals design in satin bowerbirds. *Journal of Animal Ecology* 75:2, 549–558; doi:10.1111/j.1365-2656.2006.01075.x
9. Kusmierski R., Borgia G., Uy A. and Crozier R.H. (1997) Labile evolution of display traits in bowerbirds indicates reduced effects of phylogenetic constraint. *Proceedings of the Royal Society B: Biological Sciences* 264:1380, 307–313; doi:10.1098/rspb.1997.0044
10. Borgia G. (1985) Bower quality, number of decorations and mating success of satin bowerbirds (*Ptilonorhynchus violaceus*): an experimental analysis. *Animal Behaviour* 33:1, 266–271; doi:10.1016/S0003-3472(85)80140-8
11. Endler J.A. (2012) Bowerbirds, art and aesthetics; Are bowerbirds artists and do they have an aesthetic sense? *Communicative and Integrative Biology* 5:3, 281–283; doi:10.4161/cib.19481
12. Frith C.B. and Frith D.W. (2004) *The Bowerbird, Ptilonorhynchidae*. Oxford University Press, New York

13. Patricelli G.L., Coleman S.W. and Borgia G. (2006) Male satin bowerbirds, *Ptilonorhynchus violaceus*, adjust their display intensity in response to female startling: an experiment with robotic females. *Animal Behaviour* 71:1, 49–59; doi:10.1016/j.anbehav.2005.03.029

14. Collis K. and Borgia G. (1993) The cost of male display and delayed plumage maturation in the satin bowerbird (*Ptilonorhynchus violaceus*). *Ethology* 94:1, 59–71; doi:10.1111/j.1439-0310.1993.tb00547.x

15. Maxwell P.S., Robson T.E. and Goldizen A. (2004) Home range size and bower visitation patterns of immature male Satin Bowerbirds (*Ptilonorhynchus violaceus*). *Emu: Austral Ornithology* 104:1, 75–77; doi:10.1071/MU03018

16. Vellenga R. (1970) Behaviour of the male satin bower-bird at the bower. *Australian Bird Bander* 1, 3–11

17. Uy J.A.C., Patricelli G.L. and Borgia G. (2001) Loss of preferred mates forces female satin bowerbirds (*Ptilonorhynchus violaceus*) to increase mate searching. *Proceedings of the Royal Society B: Biological Sciences* 268:1467, 633–638; doi:10.1098/rspb.2000.1413

18. Uy J.A.C. and Borgia G. (2000) Sexual selection drives rapid divergence in bowerbird display traits. *Evolution* 54:1, 273–278; doi:10.1111/j.0014-3820.2000.tb00027.x

19. Coleman S.W., Patricelli G.L. and Borgia G. (2004) Variable female preferences drive complex male displays. *Nature* 428, 742–745; doi:10.1038/nature02419

20. Borgia G. and Keagy J. (2006) An inverse relationship between decoration and food colour preferences in satin bowerbirds does not support the sensory drive hypothesis. *Animal Behaviour* 72:5, 1125–1133; doi:10.1016/j.anbehav.2006.03.015

21. Madden J.R. and Tanner K. (2003) Preferences for coloured bower decorations can be explained in a nonsexual context. *Animal Behaviour* 65:6, 1077–1083; doi:10.1006/anbe.2003.2126

22. Loffredo C.A. and Borgia G. (1986) Male courtship vocalizations as cues for mate choice in the satin bowerbird (*Ptilonorhynchus violaceus*). *The Auk* 103:1, 189–195

CHAPTER 5: THE 1788 BIRD

1. White N.E. et al. (2011) The evolutionary history of cockatoos (Aves: Psittaciformes: Cacatuidae). *Molecular Phylogenetics and Evolution*. 59:3, 615–622; doi:10.1016/j.ympev.2011.03.011
2. Homberger D.G. (2003) The comparative biomechanics of the pre-predator relationship: The adaptive morphologies of the feeding apparatus of Australian black cockatoos and their food as a basis for the reconstruction of the evolutionary history of the Psittaciformes. pp. 203–228. In: *Vertebrate Biomechanics and Evolution*. BIOS Scientific, United Kingdom
3. Rowley I. (1997) Family Cacatuidae (cockatoos). pp. 246–279. In: *Handbook of the birds of the world*. de Hoyo J., Elliott A. and Sargatal, J. (editors) Lynx Edicions, Barcelona
4. Bradbury J.W. (2003) Vocal communication in wild parrots. In: *Animals social complexity: intelligence, culture and individualized societies*. de Waal F.B.M. and Tyack P.L. (editors) Harvard University Press, Cambridge
5. Couzin I.D. (2006) Behavioural ecology: Social organization in fission–fusion societies. *Current Biology* 16:5, R169–R171; doi:10.1016/j.cub.2006.02.042
6. Bradbury J.W. and Balsby T.J.S. (2016) The functions of vocal learning in parrots. *Behavioural Ecology and Sociobiology* 70:3, 293–312; doi:10.1007/s00265-016-2068-4
7. Fitch W.T. (2000) The evolution of speech: a comparative review. *Trends in Cognitive Sciences* 4:7, 258–267; doi:10.1016/S1364-6613(00)01494-7
8. Sueur C. et al. (2011) Collective decision-making and fission–fusion

dynamics: a conceptual framework. *OIKOS* 120:11, 1608–1617; doi:10.1111/j.1600-0706.2011.19685.x

9. Ward P.I. and Zahavi A. (1973) Importance of certain assemblages of birds as information centres for food finding. *IBIS* 115:4, 517–534; doi:0.1111/j.1474-919X.1973.tb01990.x

CHAPTER 6: THE NECTAR-LOVING BIRD

1. Martin P.G. and Dowd J.M. (1988) A molecular evolutionary clock of angiosperms. *Taxon* 37:2, 364–377; doi:10.2307/1222145
2. Cracraft J. (2001) Avian evolution, Gondwana biogeography and the Cretaceous-Tertiary mass extinction event. *Proceedings of the Royal Society B: Biological Sciences* 268:1466, 459–469; doi:10.1098/rspb.2000.1368
3. Orians G.H. and Milswski A.V. (2007) Ecology of Australia: the effects of nutrient-poor soils and intense fires. *Biological Review* 82:3, 393–423; doi:10.1111/j.1469-185X.2007.00017.x
4. Flannery T. (2005) *The Future Eaters: An Ecological History of the Australasian Lands and People.* Reed New Holland, Sydney
5. Gammage, B. (2012) *The Biggest Estate on Earth: How Aborigines made Australia.* Allen and Unwin, Sydney
6. Ford H.A., Paton D.C. and Forde N. (1979) Birds as pollinators of Australian plants. *New Zealand Journal of Botany* 17:4, 509–519; doi:10/1080/0028825X.1979.10432566
7. Gartrell B.D. (2000) The Nutritional, Morphologic and Physiological Bases of Nectarivory in Australian Birds. *Journal of Avian Medicine and Surgery* 14:2, 85–94
8. Christidis L., Schodde R., Shaw D.D. and Maynes S.F. (1991) Relationships among the Australo-Papuan Parrots Lorikeets and Cockatoos (Aves: Psittaciformes): Protein Evidence. *The Condor* 93:2, 302–317; doi:10.2307/1368946
9. Holyoak D.T. (1973) Comments on taxonomy and relationships in

the parrot subfamilies Nestorinae, Loriinae and Platycercinae. *Emu—Austral Ornithology* 73:4, 157–176; doi:10.1071/MU973157

10. Longmore W. (1991) *Honeyeaters and their allies of Australia* HarperCollins Publishers, Sydney
11. Gardner J.L., Trueman J.W.H., Ebert D., Joseph L. and Magrath R.D. (2010) Phylogeny and evolution of the Meliphagoidea the largest radiation of Australasian songbirds. *Molecular Phylogenetics and Evolution* 55:3, 1087–1102; doi:10.1016/j.ympev.2010.02.005
12. Higgins P.J., Peter J.M. and Steele W.K. (2001) *Handbook of Australian, New Zealand and Antarctic Birds. Tyrant-flycatchers to Chats, Vol 5.* Oxford University Press, Melbourne
13. Krauss S.L., Phillips R.D., Karron J.D., Johnson S.D., Roberts D.G. and Hopper S.D. (2017) Novel consequences of bird pollination for plants mating. *Trends in Plant Science* 22:5, 395–410; doi:10.1016/j.tplants.2017.03.005
14. Pyke G.H. (1989) Effects of removal on abundance and behaviour of honeyeaters in heathland near Sydney. *Australian Journal of Ecology* 14:4, 415–421; doi:10.1111/j.1442-9993.1989.tb01451.x
15. McGoldrick J.M. and MacNally R. (1998) Impact of flowering on bird community dynamics in some central Victorian eucalypt forests. *Ecological Research* 13:2, 125–139; doi:10.1046/j.1440-1703.1998.00252.x
16. McFarland D.C. (1986) The organization of a honeyeater community in an unpredictable environment. *Austral Ecology* 11:2, 107–120; doi:10.1111/j.1442-9993.1986.tb01382.x
17. Ford H.A. and Tremont S. (2000) Life history characteristics of two Australian honeyeaters (Meliphagidae). *Australian Journal of Zoology* 48:1, 21–32; doi:10.1071/ZO99030
18. Bennetts R.E. and Kitchens W.M. (2000) Factors Influencing Movement Probabilities of a Nomadic Food Specialist: Proximate Foraging Benefits or Ultimate Gains from Exploration. *OIKOS* 91:3, 459–467; doi:10.1034/j.1600-0706.2000.910306.x

19. Sulikowski D. and Burke D. (2015) Noisy miners plan ahead: cryptic signalling of reward location impairs search for nectar, but not for invertebrates. *Animal Behaviour* 102, 149–155; doi:10.1016/j.anbehav.2015.01.005
20. Garrison J.S.E. and Gass C.L. (1999) Response of a traplining hummingbirds to changes in nectar availability. *Behavioural Ecology* 10:6, 714–725; doi:10.1093/beheco/10.6.714
21. Sulikowski D. and Burke D. (2011) Movement and memory: different cognitive strategies are used to search for resources with different natural distributions. *Behavioural Ecology and Sociobiology* 65:4, 621–631; doi:10.1007/s00265-010-1063-4
22. Lihoreau M. et al. (2012) Radar tracking and motion-sensitive cameras on flowers reveal development of pollinator multi-destination routes over large spatial scales. *PLoS Biology* 10:9, e1001392; doi.org/10.1371/journal.pbio.1001392
23. Saunders A.S.J., Burgin S. and Jones H. (2003) The importance of eucalypt nectar in the diet of large honeyeaters. *Journal of the Australian Bird Study Association* 27:1, 1–12
24. Martin T.G. and Catterall C.P. (2001) Do fragmented coastal heathlands have habitat value to birds in eastern Australia? *Wildlife Research* 28:1, 17–31; doi:10.1071/WR99096
25. French K., Major R.E. and Hely K. (2005) Use of native and exotic garden plants by suburban nectarivorous birds. *Biological Conservation* 121:4, 545–559; doi:10.1016/j.biocon.2004.06.004
26. Sewell S.R. and Catterall C.P. (1998) Bushland modification and styles of urban development: their effects on birds in south-east Queensland. *Wildlife Research* 25:1, 41–63; doi:10.1071/WR96078

CHAPTER 7: THE BATHING BIRD

1. Ford D.E. and Thornton K.W. (1989) Water Resources in a changing climate. pp. 26–47. In: *Global Climate Change and Freshwater*

Ecosystem. Firth P. and Fisher S.G. (editors) Spinger-Verlag, New York; doi: 10.1007/978-1-4612-2814-1

2. Chan K. (2001) Partial migration in Australian landbirds: a review. *Emu: Austral Ornithology* 101:4, 281–292; doi:10.1071/MU00034
3. Woinarski J.C.Z., Connors G. and Franklin D. (2000) Thinking honeyeater: nectar maps for the Northern Territory Australia. *Pacific Conservation Biology* 6:1, 61–80; doi:10.1071/PC000061
4. Schneider N.A. and Griesser M. (2009) Influence and value of different water regimes on avian species richness in arid inland Australia. *Biodiversity Conservation* 18:2, 457–471; doi:10.1007/s10531-008-9501-6
5. McKechnie A.E. and Wolf B.O. (2010) Climate change increases the likelihood of catastrophic avian mortality events during extreme heat waves. *Biology Letters* 6:2, 253–256; doi: 10.1098/rsbl.2009.0702
6. McKechnie A.E., Hockey P.A.R. and Wolf B.O. (2012) Feeling the heat: Australian landbirds and climate change. *Emu: Austral Ornithology* 112:2, i–vii; doi:10.1071/MUv112n2_ED
7. Tucker V.A. (1968) Respiratory exchange and evaporative water loss in the flying budgerigar. *Journal of Experimental Biology* 48:1, 67–87
8. Serventy D.L. (1971) Biology of desert birds. Chapter 7, pp. 287–339. In: *Avian biology Vol 1*. Farner D.S. and King J.R. (editors) Academic Press, New York
9. Dawson W.R. (1982) Evaporative losses of water by birds. *Comparative Biochemistry and Physiology Part A: Physiology* 71:4, 495–509; doi: 10.1016/0300-9629(82)90198-0
10. Wyndham E. (1980) Diurnal cycles: behaviour and social organization of the Budgerigar *Melopsittacus undulatus. Emu: Austral Ornithology* 80:1, 25–33; doi:10.1071/MU9800025
11. Trillmich F. (1976) Spatial proximity and mate-specific behaviour in a flock of budgerigars (*Melopsittacus undulatus*: Aves, Psittacidae). *Ethology* 41:3, 307–331; doi:10.1111/j.1439-0310.1976.tb00485.x

12. Malecki I. and Martin G.B. (2002) Fertile period and clutch size in the Emu (*Dromaius novaehollandiae*). *Emu: Austral Ornithology* 102:2, 165–170; doi:10.1071/MU01067

13. Farine D.R. and Milburn P. (2013) Social organisation of Thornbill-dominated mixed-species flocks using social network analysis. *Behavioural Ecology and Sociobiology* 67:2, 321–330; doi:10.1007/s00265-012-1452-y

CHAPTER 8: THE TALKING BIRD

1. Rizzolatti G., Fogassi L. and Gallese V. (2001) Neurophysiological mechanisms underlying the understanding and imitation of action. *Nature Review Neuroscience* 2:9, 661–670; doi:10.1038/35090060

2. Fitch W.T. (2000) The evolution of speech: a comparative review. *Trends in Cognitive Sciences* 4:7, 258–267; doi:10.1016/S1364-6613(00)01494-7

3. Gergely G. and Csibra G. (2006) Sylvia's recipe: the role of imitation and pedagogy in the transmission of cultural knowledge. pp. 229–255. In: *Roots of human sociality: culture, cognition and interaction.* Enfield N.J. and Levinson S.C. (editors) Berg Publishers, Oxford

4. Dunbar R.I. and Shultz S. (2010) Bondedness and sociality. *Behaviour* 147:7, 775–803; doi:10.1163/000579510X501151

5. Miller M.L., Gallup A.C., Vogel A.R., Vicario S.M. and Clark A.B. (2012) Evidence for contagious behaviours in budgerigars (*Melopsittacus undulatus*): An observational study of yawning and stretching. *Behavioural Processes* 89:3, 264–270; doi:10.1016/j.beproc.2011.12.012

6. Clayton N.S. (1987) Song tutor choice in zebra finches. *Animal Behaviour* 35:3, 714–721; doi:10.1016/S0003-3472(87)80107-0

7. Clayton N.S. (1988) Song discrimination learning in zebra finches. *Animal Behaviour* 36:4, 1016–1024; doi:10.1016/S0003-3472(88)80061-7

8. Low P.S., Shank S.S., Sejnowski T.J. and Margoliash D. (2008) Mammalian-like features of sleep structure in zebra finches. *Proceedings of the National Academy of Sciences of the United States of America* 105:25, 9081–9086; doi:10.1073/pnas.0703452105
9. Vorster A.P. and Born J. (2015) Sleep and memory in mammals, birds and invertebrates. *Neuroscience and Biobehavioral Reviews* 50, 103–119; doi:10.1016/j.neubiorev.2014.09.020
10. Margoliash D. and Brawn T.P. (2012) Sleep and Learning in Birds: Rats! There's More to Sleep. Chapter 6, pp. 109–146. In: *Sleep and Brain Activity*. Marcos G.F. (editor) Elsevier; doi:10.1016/B978-0-12-384995-3.00006-x
11. Diekelmann S., Wilhelm I. and Born J. (2009) The whats and whens of sleep-dependent memory consolidation. *Sleep Medicine Review* 13:5, 309–321; doi:10.1016/j.smrv.2008.08.002
12. McGaugh J.L. (2000) Memory—a Century of Consolidation. *Science* 287:5451, 248–251; doi:10.1126/science.287.5451.248
13. Emery N.J., Seed A.M., von Bayern A.M.P. and Clayton N.S. (2007) Cognitive adaptations of social bonding in birds. *Philosophical Transactions of the Royal Society B: Biological Sciences* 362:1480; doi:10.1098/rstb.2006.1991
14. Kaplan G. (2016) *Bird Minds: Cognition and Behaviour of Australian Native Birds*. CSIRO Publishing, Melbourne
15. Kaplan G. (2004) *Australian Magpie: Biology and Behaviour of an Unusual Songbird*. CSIRO Publishing, Melbourne
16. Sewall K.B., Young A.M. and Wright T.F. (2016) Social calls provide novel insights into the evolution of vocal learning. *Animal Behaviour* 120, 163–172; doi:10.1016/j.anbehav.2016.07.031
17. Hoeschele M. and Bowling D.L. (2016) Sex Differences in Rhythmic preferences in the Budgerigar (*Melopsittacus undulatus*): A Comparative Study with Humans. *Frontiers in Psychology* 7:1543, 1–10; doi:10.3389/fpsyg.2016.01543

18. Bradbury J.W. and Balsby T.J.S. (2016) The functions of vocal learning in parrots. *Behavioural Ecology and Sociobiology* 70:3, 293–312; doi:10.1007/s00265-016-2068-4

19. Fitch W.T. (2013) Rhythmic cognition in humans and animals: distinguishing meter and pulse perception. *Frontiers in Systems Neuroscience* 7:68; doi:10.3389/fnsys.2013.00068

20. Heinsohn R., Zdenek C.N., Cunningham R.B., Endler J.A. and Langmore N.E. (2017) Tool-assisted rhythmic drumming in palm cockatoos share key elements of human instrumental music. *Science Advance* 3:6, e1602399; doi:10.1126/sciadv.1602399

21. Laland K., Wilkins C. and Clayton N. (2016) The evolution of dance. *Current Biology* 26:1, R5–R9; doi:10.1016/j.cub.2015.11.031

22. Dalziell A.H., Peters R.A., Cockburn A., Dorland A.D., Maisey A.C. and Magrath R.D. (2013) Dance choreography is coordinated with song repertoire in a complex avian display. *Current Biology* 23:12, 1132–1135; doi:10.1016/j.cub.2013.05.018

23. Mulder R.A. and Hall M.L. (2013) Animal behaviour: A Song and Dance about Lyrebirds. *Current Biology* 23:12, R518-R519; doi:10.1016/j.cub.2013.05.009

24. Curtis H.S. (1972) The Albert Lyrebird in display. *Emu: Austral Ornithology* 72:3, 81–84; doi:10.1071/MU972081

25. Anderson J.R. and Gallup G.G. (2015) Mirror self-recognition: a review and critique of attempts to promote and engineer self-recognition in primates. *Primates* 56:4, 317–326; doi:10.1007/s10329-015-0488-9

26. Janik V.M. and Slater P.J.B. (2000) The different roles of social learning in vocal communication. *Animal Behaviour* 60:1, 1–11; doi:10.1006/anbe.2000.1410

27. Seki Y., Osmanski A.S. and Dooling R.J. (2018) Failure of Operant Control of Vocal Learning in budgerigars. *Animal Behaviour and Cognition* 5:1, 154–168; doi:10.26451/abc.05.01.11.2018

28. ten Cate C. (2018) The comparative study of grammar learning mechanisms; birds as models. *Current Opinion in Behavioral Sciences* 21, 13–18; doi:10.1016/j.cobeha.2017.11.008

29. Huber L., Troje N.F., Loidolt M., Aust U. and Grass D. (2000) Natural categorization through multiple feature learning in pigeons. *The Quarterly Journal of Experimental Psychology* 56B:4, 341-357; doi:10.1080/713932733

CHAPTER 9: THE PERSONALITY BIRD

1. Aplin L.M., Farine D.R., Mann R.P. and Sheldon B.C. (2014) Individual-level personality influences social foraging and collective behaviour in wild birds. *Proceedings of the Royal Society B: Biological Sciences* 281:20141016; doi:10.1098/rspb.2014.1016

2. Dingemanse N.J. and Wolf M. (2013) Between-individual differences in behavioural plasticity within populations: causes and consequences. *Animal Behaviour* 85:5, 1031–1039; doi.org/10.1016/j.anbehav.2012.12.032

3. Jolles J.W., Fleetwood-Wilson A., Nakayama S., Stumpe M.C., Johnstone R.A. and Manica A. (2014) The role of previous social experience on risk-taking and leadership in three-spined stickleback. *Behavioural Ecology* 25:6, 1395–1401; doi.org/10.1093/beheco/aru146

4. Kaplan G. (2004) *Australian Magpie: Biology and Behaviour of an Unusual Songbird.* CSIRO Publishing, Melbourne

5. Kaplan G. (2011) Pointing gesture in a bird—merely instrumental or a cognitively complex behaviour? *Current Zoology* 57:4, 453–467; doi:10.1093/czoolo/57.4.453

6. Ghalambor C.K., Angeloni L.M. and Carroll S.C. (2010) Behavior as Phenotypic Plasticity. pp. 90–107. In: *Evolutionary Behavioral Ecology.* Westneast D.F. and Fox C.W. (editors) Oxford University Press, New York

7. Dukas R. (1998) Constraints on information processing and their effects on behaviour. Chapter 3, pp. 89–128. In: *Cognitive Ecology: The*

Evolutionary Ecology of Information Processing and Decision-Making. Dukas R. (editor) University of Chicago Press, Chicago IL

8. Moczek A.P. et al. (2011) The role of developmental plasticity in evolutionary innovation. *Proceedings of the Royal Society B: Biological Sciences* 278:1719, 2705–2713; doi:10.1098/rspb.2011.0971
9. Wolf M., van Doorn S. and Weissing F.J. (2008) Evolutionary emergence of responsive and unresponsive personalities. *Proceedings of the National Academy of Sciences of the United States of America.* 105:41, 15825–15830; doi: 1073/pnas.0805473105
10. Michelena P., Jeanson R., Deneubourg J.L. and Sibbald A.M. (2010) Personality and collective decision-making in foraging herbivores. *Proceedings of the Royal Society B: Biological Sciences* 277:1684, 1093–1099; doi:10.1098/rspb.2009.1926
11. Coppens C.M., de Boer S.F. and Koolhaas J.M. (2010) Coping styles and behavioural flexibility: towards underlying mechanisms. *Philosophical Transactions of the Royal Society B: Biological Sciences* 365:1560, 4021–4028; doi:10.1098/rstb.2010.0217
12. Morand-Ferron J. and Quinn J.L. (2011) Larger groups of passerines are more efficient problem solvers in the wild. *Proceedings of the National Academy of Sciences of the United States of America* 108:38, 15898–15903; doi:10.1073/pnas.1111560108
13. Cole E.F., Cram D.L. and Quinn J.L. (2011) Individual variation in spontaneous problem-solving performance among wild great tits. *Animal Behaviour* 81:2, 491–498; doi.org/10.1016/j.anbehav.2010.11.025
14. Croft D.P. et al. (2003) Mechanisms underlying shoal composition in the Trinidadian guppy, *Poecilia reticulate. OIKOS* 100:3, 429–438; doi:10.1034/j.1600-0706.2003.12023.x
15. Pika S. and Bugnyar T. (2011) The use of referential gestures in ravens (*Corvus corax*) in the wild. *Nature Communication* 2:560; doi:10.1038/ncomms1567

16. Luef E.M., Maat A.T. and Pika S. (2017) Vocal similarity in long-distance and short-distance vocalizations in raven pairs (*Corvus corax*) in captivity. *Behavioural Processes* 142, 1–7; doi:10.1016/j.beproc.2017.05.013
17. Zollinger S.A. and Brumm H. (2015) Why birds sing loud songs and why they sometimes don't. *Animal Behaviour* 105, 289–295; doi:10.1016/j.anbehav.2015.03.030
18. Scheid C. and Noe R. (2010) The performance of rooks in a cooperative task depending on their temperament. *Animal Cognition* 13:3, 545–553; doi:10.1007/s10071-009-0305-1
19. Groothuis T.G.G. and Carere C. (2005) Avian personalities: characterization and epigenesist. *Neuroscience and Biobehavioral Reviews* 29:1, 137–150; doi:10.1016/j.neubiorev.2004.06.010
20. Sih A., Bell A.M., Johnson C. and Ziemba R.E. (2004) Behavioural syndromes: an integrative overview. *The Quarterly Review of Biology* 79:3, 241–279; doi:10.1086/422893

CHAPTER 10: THE SELF-AWARE BIRD

1. Deregnaucourt S. and Bovet D. (2016) The Perception of Self in Birds. *Neuroscience and Biobehavioural Reviews* 69, 1–14; doi:10.1016/j.neubiorev.2016.06.039
2. Holveck M.J. and Riebel K. (2009) Low-quality females prefer low-quality males when choosing a mate. *Proceedings of the Royal Society B: Biological Sciences* 277 153–160; doi:10.1098/rspb.2009.1222
3. Farine D.R. et al. (2015) The role of social and ecological processes in structuring animal populations: a case study for automated tracking of wild birds. *Royal Society Open Science* 2:150057; doi:10.1098/rsos.150057
4. Snijders L., Naguib M. and van Oers K. (2017) Dominance rank and boldness predict social attraction in great tits. *Behavioral Ecology* 28:2, 398–406; doi:10.1093/beheco/arw158

5. Kusayama T., Bischof H.J. and Watanabe S. (2000) Responses to mirror-image stimulation in jungle crows (*Corvus macrorhynchos*). *Animal Cognition* 3:1, 61–64; doi:10.1007/s100710050051
6. Diamond J. and Bond A. (1989) Note on the lasting responsiveness of a Kea *Nestor notabilis* toward its mirror image. *Avicultural Magazine* 95:2, 92–94
7. Henry L., Le Cars K., Mathelier M., Bruderer M. and Hausberger M. (2008) The use of a mirror as a 'social substitute' in laboratory birds. *Ethology* 331:7, 526–531; doi:10.1016/j.crvi.2008.04.005
8. Salzen E.A. and Cornell J.A. (1967) Self-Perception and Species Recognition in Birds. *Behaviour* 30:1, 44–64; doi:10.1163/156853968X00171
9. Holland B. and Rice W.R. (1998) Perspective. Chase-away sexual selection: antagonistic seduction versus resistance. *Evolution* 52:1, 1–7; doi:10.1111/j.1558-5646.1998.tb05132.x
10. Forstmeier W. and Birkhead T.R. (2004) Repeatability of mate choice in the zebra finch: consistency within and between females. *Animal Behaviour* 68:5, 1017–1028; doi:10.1016/j.anbehav.2004.02.007
11. Little A.C., Burt D.M., Penton-Voak I.S. and Perrett D.I. (2001) Self-perceived attractiveness influences human female preferences for sexual dimorphism and symmetry in male faces. *Proceedings of the Royal Society B: Biological Sciences* 268 39–44; doi:10.1098/rspb.2000.1327
12. Buston P.M. and Emlen S.T. (2003) Cognitive processes underlying human mate choice: the relationship between self-perception and mate preference in Western society. *Proceedings of the National Academy of Sciences of the United States of America* 100:15, 8805–8810; doi:10.1073/pnas.1533220100
13. Todd P.M., Penke L., Fasolo B. and Lenton A.P. (2007) Different cognitive processes underlie human mate choices and mate preferences. *Proceedings of the National Academy of Sciences of the United States of America.* 104:38, 15011–15016; doi:10.1073/pnas.0705290104

14. Otter K. and Ratcliffe L. (1996) Female initiated divorce in a monogamous songbird: abandoning mates for males of higher quality. *Proceedings of the Royal Society B: Biological Sciences* 263:1368, 351–355; doi:10.1098/rspb.1996.0054
15. Riebel K., Holveck M.J., Verhulst S. and Fawcett T. (2010) Are high-quality mates always attractive? State-dependent mate preferences in birds and humans. *Communicative and Integrative Biology* 3:3, 271–273; doi:10.4161/cib.3.3.11557
16. Burley N.T. and Foster V.S. (2006) Variation in female choice of mates: condition influences selectivity. *Animal Behaviour* 72:3, 713–719; doi:10.1016/j.anbehav.2006.01.017
17. Cotar C., McNamara J.M., Collins E.J. and Houston A.I. (2008) Should females prefer to mate with low-quality males? *Journal of Theoretical Biology* 254:3, 561–567; doi:10.1016/j.jtbi.2008.06.015
18. McNamara J.M., Forslund P. and Lang A. (1999) An ESS model for divorce strategies in birds. *Philosophical Transactions of the Royal Society B: Biological Sciences* 354:1380, 223–236; doi:10.1098/rstb.1999.0374

CHAPTER 11: THE CUCKOOED BIRD

1. Davies N.B. (2010) *Cuckoos, cowbirds and other cheats.* T & AD Poyser Ltd, London
2. Langmore N.E. et al. (2005) The evolution of egg rejection by cuckoo hosts in Australia and Europe. *Behavioural Ecology* 16:4, 686–692; doi:10.1093/beheco/ari041
3. Feeney W.E. et al. (2013) Brood Parasitism and the Evolution of Cooperative Breeding in Birds. *Science* 342:6165, 1506–1508; doi:10.1126/science.1240039
4. Cockburn A., Sims R.A., Osmond H.L., Green D.J., Double M.C. and Mulder R.A. (2008) Can we measure the benefits of

help in cooperatively breeding birds: the case of superb fairy-wrens *Malurus cyaneus*? *Journal of Animal Ecology* 77:3, 430–438; doi: 10.1111/j.1365-2656.2007.01351.x

5. Mulder R.A. (1995) Natal and breeding dispersal in a co-operative, extra-group mating bird. *Journal of Avian Biology* 26:3, 234–240; doi:10.2307/3677324
6. Brooker M.G., Brooker L.C. and Rowley I. (1988) Egg Deposition by the Bronze-Cuckoos *Chrysococcyx basalis* and *Ch. lucidus*. *Emu: Austral Ornithology* 88:2, 107–109; doi:10.1071/MU9880107
7. Payne R.B., Payne L.L. and Rowley I. (1985) Splendid wren *Malurus splendens* response to cuckoos: an experimental test of social organization in a communal bird. *Behaviour* 94:1, 108–126; doi:10.1163/156853985X00299
8. Feeney W.E. and Langmore N.E. (2013) Social learning of a brood parasite by its host. *Biology Letters* 9:4; doi:10.1098/rsbl.2013.0443
9. Feeney W.E. et al. (2013) Brood parasitism and the evolution of cooperative breeding in birds. *Science* 342:6165, 1506–1508; doi:10.1126/science.1240039
10. Colombelli-Negrel, D. et al. (2012) Embryonic learning of vocal passwords in super fairy-wrens reveals intruder cuckoo nestlings. *Current Biology* 22:22, 2155–2160; doi:10.1016/j.cub.2012.09.025
11. Gosper D.G. (1997) Aspects of breeding of the common koel *Eudynamys scolopacea* and One of its Biological Hosts, the Magpie-lark *Grallina cyanoleuca*. *Australian Field Ornithology*, 17:1, 11–19
12. Davies N.B. (2011) Cuckoo adaptations: trickery and tuning. *Journal of Zoology* 284:1, 1–14; doi:10.1111/j.1469-7998.2011.00810.x
13. Kilner R.M., Noble D.G. and Davies N.B. (1999) Signals of need in parent-offspring communication and their exploitation by the common cuckoo. *Nature* 397, 667–672; doi:10.1038/17746
14. Langmore N.E., Stevens M., Maurer G., Heinsohn R., Hall M.L., Peters A. and Kilner R.M. (2011) Visual mimicry of host nestlings by

cuckoos. *Proceedings of the Royal Society B: Biological Sciences* 278:1717, 2455–2463; doi:10.1098/rspb.2010.2391

15. Welbergen J.A. and Davies N.B. (2011) A parasite in wolf's clothing: hawk resemblance reduces mobbing of cuckoos by hosts. *Behavioral Ecology* 22:3, 574–579; doi:10.1093/beheco/arr008
16. Campobello D., Sealy S.G. and Welbergen J.A. (2017) Anti-brood Parasite Defences: The Role of Individual and Social Learning. pp. 421–436. In: *Avian Brood Parasitism. Fascinating Life Sciences.* Soler M. (editor) Springer, Cham; doi:10.1007/978-3-319-73138-4_23
17. Lotem A. (1993) Learning to recognize nestlings in maladaptive for cuckoo *Cuculus canorus* hosts. *Nature* 362, 743–745; doi:10.1038/362743a0
18. Langmore N.E., Cockburn A., Russell A.F. and Kilner R.M. (2009) Flexible cuckoo chick-rejection rules in the superb fairy-wren. *Behavioural Ecology* 20:5, 978–984; doi:10.1093/beheco/arp086
19. Langmore N.E., Hunt S. and Kilner R.M. (2003) Escalation of a coevolutionary arms race through host rejection of brood parasitic young. *Nature* 422, 157–160; doi:10.1038/nature01460
20. Campobello D. and Hare J.F. (2007) Information transfer determined by association of neighbours in European bee-eater (*Merops apiaster*) colonies. *Ethology Ecology Evolution* 19:3, 237–243; doi:10.1080/08927014.2007.9522565
21. Heyes C.M. (1994) Social learning in animals: categories and mechanisms. *Biological Review* 69:2, 207–231; doi: 10.1111/j.1469-185X.1994.tb01506.x
22. Johnson F.R., McNaughton E.J., Shelley C.D. and Blumstein D.T. (2003) Mechanisms of heterospecific recognition in avian mobbing calls. *Australian Journal of Zoology* 51:6, 577–585; doi:10.1071/ZO03031
23. Magrath R.D., Pitcher B.J. and Gardner J.L. (2007) A mutual understanding? Interspecific responses by birds to each other's aerial alarm calls. *Behavioural Ecology* 18:4, 944–951; doi:10.1093/beheco/arm063

24. Magrath R.D., Pitcher B.J. and Gardner J.L. (2009) An avian eavesdropping network: alarm signal reliability and heterospecific response. *Behavioural Ecology* 20:4, 745–752; doi:10.1093/beheco/arp055

25. Magrath R.D., Pitcher B.J. and Gardner J.L. (2009) Recognition of other species' aerial alarm calls: speaking the same language or learning another? *Proceedings of the Royal Society B: Biological Sciences* 276:1657, 769–774; doi:10/1098/rspb.2008.1368

CHAPTER 12: THE CHEATING BIRD

1. Mulder R.A. and Langmore N.E. (1993) Dominant males punish helpers for temporary defection in superb fairy-wrens. *Animal Behaviour* 45:4, 830–833; doi:10.1006/anbe.1993.1100

2. Cockburn A., Osmond H.L., Mulder R.A., Green D.J. and Double M.C. (2008) Demography of male reproductive queues in cooperatively breeding fairy wrens *Malurus cyaneus*. *Journal of Animal Ecology* 77:2, 297–304; doi:10.1111/j.1365-2656.2007.01335.x

3. Dunn P.O. and Cockburn A. (1999) Extrapair mate choice and honest signalling in cooperatively breeding superb fairy-wrens. *Evolution* 53:3, 938–946; doi:10.1111/j.1558-646.1999.tb05387.x

4. Zottl M., Heg D., Chervet N. and Taborsky M. (2013) Kinship reduces alloparental care in cooperative cichlids where helpers pay-to-stay. *Nature Communications* 4:1341; doi:10.1038/ncomms2344

5. Kramer J., Klauke N., Bauer M. and Schaefer H.M. (2016) No evidence for enforced alloparental care in a cooperatively breeding parrot. *Ethology* 122:5, 389–398; doi:10.1111/eth.12486

6. Legge S. and Cockburn A. (2000) Social and mating system of cooperatively-breeding laughing kookaburras (*Dacelo novaeguineae*). *Behavioural Ecology and Sociobiology* 47:4, 220–229; doi:10.1007/s002650050659

7. Emlen S.T. (1997) Predicting family dynamics in social vertebrates. Chapter 10, pp. 228–253. In: *Behavioural Ecology: An Evolutionary*

Approach (4th Edition). Krebs J.R. and Davies N.B. (editors) Blackwell Publishing, Oxford

8. Emlen S.T. (1982) The evolution of helping. I. An ecological constraints model. *American Naturalist* 119:1, 29–39; doi:10.1086/283888
9. Boland C.R.J., Heinsohn R. and Cockburn A. (1997) Experimental manipulation of brood reduction and parental care in cooperatively breeding white-winged choughs. *Journal of Animal Ecology* 66:5, 683–691; doi:10.2307/5921
10. Heinsohn R.G., Cockburn A. and Cunningham R.B. (1988) Foraging, delayed maturity and cooperative breeding in white-winged choughs, *Corcorax melanorhamphos*. *Ethology* 77:3, 177–186; doi:10.1111/j.1439-0310.1988.tb00202.x
11. Heinsohn R.G. (1991) Kidnapping and reciprocity in cooperatively breeding white-winged choughs. *Animal Behaviour* 41:6, 1097–1100; doi:10.1016/S0003-3472(05)80652-9
12. Mitchell J.S. (2003) Social correlates of reproductive success in false clown anemonefish: subordinate group members do not pay-to-stay. *Evolutionary Ecology Research* 5, 89–104
13. Ekman J., Baglione V., Eggers S. and Griesser M. (2001) Delayed dispersal: living under the reign of nepotistic parents. *The Auk: Ornithological Advances* 118:1, 1–10; doi:10.1642/0004-8038(2001)118[0001:DDLUTR]2.0.CO;2
14. Canestrari D., Marcos J.M. and Baglione V. (2005) Effect of parentage and relatedness on the individual contribution to cooperative chick care in carrion crows *Corvus corone corone*. *Behaviour Ecology and Sociobiology* 57:5, 422–428; doi:10.1007/s00265-004-0879-1
15. Baglione V., Canestrari D., Chiarati E., Vera R. and Marcos J.M. (2010) Lazy group members are substitute helpers in carrion crows. *Proceedings of the Royal Society B: Biological Sciences*; doi.org/10.1098/rspb.2010.0745

16. Vander Wall S.B. and Smith K.G. (1987) Cache-protecting behaviour of food-hoarding animals. pp. 611–645. In: *Foraging Behaivour.* Kamil A.C., Kerb J.R. and Pulliam H.R. (editors) Springer, Boston; doi:10.1007/978-1-4613-1839-2_22_
17. Hampton R.R. and Sherry D.F. (1994) The effect of cache loss on choice of cache sites in black-capped chickadees. *Behavioural Ecology* 5:1, 44–50; doi:10.1093/beheco/5.1.44
18. Bugnyar T. and Kotrschal K. (2002) Observational learning and the raiding of food caches in ravens *Corvus corax*: is it 'tactical' deception? *Animal Behaviour* 64:2, 185–195; doi:10.1006/anbe.2002.3056
19. Raihani N., Thornton A. and Bshary R. (2012) Punishment and cooperation in nature. *Trends in Ecology and Evolution* 27:5, 288–295; doi:10.1016/j.tree.2011.12.004
20. Clutton-Brock T.H. and Parker G.A. (1995) Punishment in animal societies. *Nature* 373, 209–216; doi:10.1038/373209a0
21. Machiavelli Niccolo, *The Prince* (1532), Penguin, New York, 1981

CHAPTER 13: THE GRIEVING BIRD

1. Marzluff J. and Angell T. (2012) *Gifts of the Crow: how perception, emotion and thought allow smart birds to behave like humans.* ATRIA Paperback, New York
2. Iglesias T.L., Stetkevich R.C. and Patricelli G.L. (2014) Dead heterospecifics as cues of risk in the environment: Does size affect response? *Behaviour* 151:1, 1–22; doi:10.1163/1568539X-00003120
3. Lima S.L. and Dill L.M. (1990) Behavioural decisions made under the risk of predation a review and prospectus. *Canadian Journal of Zoology* 68:4, 619–640; doi:10.1139/z90-092
4. Curio E. (1978) Adaptive significance of avian mobbing I Teleonomic hypotheses and prediction. *Ethology* 48:2, 175–183; doi: 10.1111/j.1439-0310.1978.tb00254.x
5. Flasskamp A. (1994) The adaptive significance of avian mobbing

V: an experimental test of the 'move on' hypothesis. *Ethology* 96:4, 322–333; doi:10.1111/j.1439-0310.1994.tb01020.x

6. Hamilton W.B. (1971) Geometry for the selfish herd. *Journal of Theoretical Biology* 31:2, 295–311; doi:10.1016/0022-5193(71)90189-5
7. Griffin A.S. (2004) Social learning about predators: a review and prospectus. *Animal Learning & Behavior* 32:1, 131–140; doi:10.3758/BF03196014
8. Swift K.A. and Marzluff J.M. (2015) Wild American crows gather around their dead to learn about danger. *Animal Behaviour* 109, 187–197; doi:10.1016/j.anbehav.2015.08.021
9. Rowley I. (1973) The comparative ecology of Australian corvids II Social organisation and behaviour. *Wildlife Research* 18:1, 25–65; doi:10.1071/CWR9730025

CHAPTER 14: THE PLAYFUL BIRD

1. O'Hara M. and Auersperf A.M.I. (2017) Object play in parrots and corvids. *Current Opinion in Behavioural Science* 16, 119–125; doi:10.1016/j.cobeha.2017.05.008
2. Kaplan, G. (2016) *Bird Minds: Cognition and Behaviour of Australian Native Birds*. CSIRO Publishing, Melbourne
3. Marzluff, J. and Angell, T. (2012) *Gifts of the Crow: how perception, emotion and thought allow smart birds to behave like humans.* ATRIA Paperback, New York
4. Spinka M., Newberry R.C. and Bekoff M. (2001) Mammalian Play: training for the unexpected. *The Quarterly Review of Biology* 76:2, 141–168; doi:10.1086/393866
5. Burghardt G.M. (2005) *The Genesis of Animal Play: Testing the Limits.* MIT Press, Cambridge MA
6. Pellegrini A.D. and Smith P.K. (1998) Physical Activity Play: The Nature and Function of a Neglected Aspect of Play. *Child Development* 69:3, 577–598; doi:10.1111/j.1467-8624.1998.tb06226.x

7. Emery N.J. and Clayton N.S. (2004) The Mentality of Crows: Convergent Evolution of Intelligence in Corvids and Apes. *Science* 306:5703, 1903–1907; doi:10.1126/science.1098410
8. Heinrich B. and Smolker R. (1988) Play in common ravens (*Corvus corax*). Chapter 2 pp. 27–44. In: *Animal Play: Evolutionary, Comparative and Ecological Perspectives.* Bekoff M. and Byers J.A. (editors) Cambridge University Press, Cambridge
9. Heinrich B. and Bugnyar T. (2007) Just How Smart are Ravens? *Scientific American* 296, 64–71; doi:10.1038/scientificamerican0407-64
10. Frohlich M. et al. (2016) Unpeeling the layers of language: Bonobos and chimpanzees engage in cooperative turn-taking sequences. *Scientific Reports* 6:25887; doi:10.1038/srep25887
11. Kaplan G. (2004) *Australian Magpie: Biology and Behaviour of an Unusual Songbird.* CSIRO Publishing, Melbourne
12. Pellis S.M. (1981) Exploration and Play in the behavioural Development of the Australian Magpie *Gumnorhina tibicen. Bird Behaviour* 3:1-2, 37–49; doi:10.3727/015613881791560900

CHAPTER 15: THE URBAN BIRD

1. Sol D. and Maspons J. (2016) Life History, Behaviour and Invasion Success. Chapter 5, pp. 63–81. In: *Biological Invasions and Animal Behaviour.* Weis J.S. and Sol D. (editors) Cambridge University Press; doi:10.1017/CB09781139939492
2. Miranda A.C., Schielzeth H., Sonntag T. and Partecke J. (2013) Urbanization and its effects on personality traits: a result of microevolution or phenotypic plasticity. *Global Change Biology* 19:9, 2634–2644; doi:10.1111/gcb.12258
3. Sol D., Griffin A.S., Bartomeus I. and Boyce H. (2011) Exploring or Avoiding Novel Food Resources? The Novelty Conflict in an Invasive Bird. *PLoS One* 6:5, e19535; doi:10.1371/journal.pone.0019535
4. Liker A. and Bokony V. (2009) Larger groups are more successful

in innovative problem solving in house sparrows. *Proceedings of the National Academy of Science* 106:19, 7893–7898; doi:10.1073/pnas.0900042106

5. Black A. (2015) Range expansion of the Crested Pigeon, *Ocyphaps lophotes*, in South Australia. *South Australian Ornithologist* 40:2, 45–61
6. Moller A.P. (2008) Flight distance of urban birds, predation, and selection for urban life. *Behavioural Ecology and Sociobiology* 63, 63–75; doi:10.1007/s00265-008-0636-y
7. Moller A.P. and Erritzoe J. (2014) Predator-prey interactions, flight initiation distance and brain size. *Journal of Evolutionary Biology* 27:1, 34–42; doi:10.1111/jeb.12272
8. Perals D., Griffin A.S., Bartomeus I. and Sol D. (2017) Revisiting the open-field test: what does it really tell us about animal personality? *Animal Behaviour* 123, 69–79; doi:10.1016/j.anbehav.2016.10.006
9. Gendall J., Lill A. and Bechman J. (2015) Tolerance of disturbance by humans in long-time resident and recent colonist urban doves. *Avian Research* 6:7; doi:10.1186/s40657-015-0018-x
10. Boyd R. and Richerson P.J. (1995) Why Culture is common, but Cultural Evolution is Rare. *Proceedings of the British Academy* 88, 77–93
11. Evans K.L., Hatchwell B.J., Parnell M. and Gaston K.J. (2010) A conceptual framework for the colonisation of urban areas: the blackbird *Turdus merula* as a case study. *Biological Review* 85:3, 643–667; doi: 10.1111/j.1469-185X.2010.00121.x
12. Ostling A. (2005) Neutral theory tested by birds. *Nature* 436, 635–636; doi:10.1038/436635a
13. Chaine S.A. and Clobert J. (2012) Dispersal. Chapter 5, pp. 63–79. In: *Behavioural Responses to a Changing World.* Candolin U. and Wong B. (editors) Oxford University Press, Oxford
14. Sol D., Bartomeus I. and Griffin A.S. (2012) The paradox of invasion in birds: competitive superiority or ecological opportunism. *Oecologia* 169:2, 553–564; doi:10.1007/s00442-011-2203-x

15. Kaplan G. (2018) *Tawny Frogmouth.* CSIRO Publishing, Melbourne
16. Moller A.P. and Erritzoe J. (2015) Brain size and urbanization in birds. *Avian Research* 6:8; doi:10.1186/s40657-015-0017-y
17. Temeles E.J. (1994) The role of neighbours in territorial systems: when are they dear enemies? *Animal Behaviour* 47:2, 339–350
18. Fisher J.B. (1954) Evolution and bird sociality. pp. 71–83. In: *Evolution as a Process.* Huxley J., Hardy A.C. and Ford E.B. (editors) Allen and Unwin, London
19. Muller C.A. and Manser M.B. (2007) 'Nasty neighbours' rather than 'dear enemies' in a social carnivore. *The Royal Society Publishing Proceedings B: Biological Sciences* 274:1612, 959–965; doi:10.1098/rspb.2006.0222
20. Bruintjes R., Lynton-Jenkins J., Jones J.W. and Radford A.N. (2006) Our-Group Threat Promotes within-group affiliation in a cooperative fish. *The American Naturalist* 187:2, 274–282; doi:10.1086/684411

CHAPTER 16: THE INNOVATIVE BIRD

1. Greenberg R. and Mettke-Hofmann C. (2001) Ecological Aspects of Neophobia and Neophilia in Birds. Chapter 3, pp. 119–178. In: *Current Ornithology Vol 16.* Nolan Jr V. et al. (editors) Kluwer Academic/Plenum Publishers, New York
2. Lefebvre L., Reader S.M. and Sol D. (2004) Brains, Innovations and Evolution in Birds and Primates. *Brain, Behavior and Evolution* 63, 233–246; doi:10.1159/000076784
3. Reader S.M. and Laland K.N. (2002) Social intelligence, innovation and enhanced brain size in primates. *Proceedings of the National Academy of Sciences of the United States of America* 99:7, 4436–4441; doi:10.1073/pnas.062041299
4. Laland K.N. and Kendal J.R. (2003) What the models say about social learning. Chapter 2, pp. 33–55. *The Biology of Traditions: Models and Evidence.* Fragaszy D.M. and Perry S. (editors) Cambridge University Press, Cambridge

5. Aplin L.M., Farine D.R., Morand-Ferron J., Cockburn A. and Thornton B.S. (2015) Experimentally induced innovations leads to persistent culture via conformity in wild birds. *Nature* 518, 538–541; doi:10.1038/nature13998
6. Gibbons P. and Lindenmayer D.B. (2002) *Tree Hollows and Wildlife Conservation in Australia.* CSIRO Publishing, Melbourne
7. Shochat E. (2004) Credit or debit? Resource input changes population dynamics of city-slicker birds. *OIKOS* 106:3, 622–626; doi:10.1111/j.0030-1299.2004.13159.x
8. Higgins P.J. (1999) *Handbook of Australian, New Zealand and Antarctic Birds. Vol 4: Parrots to Dollar Birds.* Oxford University Press, Oxford
9. Paton D.C. and Collins B.G. (1989) Bills and tongues of nectar-feeding birds: A review of morphology, function and performance with intercontinental comparisons. *Austral Ecology* 14:4, 473–506; doi:10.1111/j.1442-9993.1989.tb01457.x
10. Olsen P. and Joseph L. (2011) *Stray Feathers, Reflections on the Structure, Behaviour and Evolution of Birds.* CSIRO Publishing, Melbourne
11. Barker R.D. and Vestjens W.J.M. (1990) *The food of Australian Birds 2: Passerines.* CSIRO Division of Wildlife and Ecology, Canberra
12. Moran C., Catterall C.P., Green R.J. and Olsen M.F. (2004) Fates of feathered fruit-eaters in fragmented forests. pp. 699–721. In: *Conservation of Australia's Forest Fauna (second edition).* Lunney D. (editor) Royal Zoological Society of New South Wales, Mosman, NSW
13. Frith H.J. (1982) *Pigeons and Doves of Australia.* Rigby, Adelaide
14. Blakers M., Davies S.J.J.F. and Reilly P.N. (1984) *The Atlas of Australian Birds.* Melbourne Press, Melbourne
15. Donato D.B. and Potts R.T. (2004) Culturally transmitted predation and consumption techniques by Torresian crows *Corvus orru* on cane toads *Bufo marinus. Australian Field Ornithology* 21:3, 125–126
16. Debus S.J.S. (2012) Stone the crows! Could corvids be Australia's

smartest export? Available at https://theconversation.com/stone-the-crows-could-corvids-be-australias-smartest-export-4346

17. Beckmann C. and Shine R. (2011) Toad's tongue for breakfast: exploitation of a novel prey type, the invasive cane toad, by scavenging raptors in tropical Australia. *Biological Invasion* 13:6, 1447–1455; doi:10.1007/s10530-010-9903-8
18. Sol D., Bartomeus I. and Griffin A.S. (2012) The paradox of invasion in birds: competitive superiority or ecological opportunism? *Oecologia* 169:2, 553–564; doi:10.1007/200442-011-2203-x
19. Diamond J.M. and Veitch C.R. (1981) Extinctions and introductions in the New Zealand avifauna: cause and effect? *Science* 211:499, 499–501; doi:501 10.1126/science.211.4481.499
20. Sol D., Gonzalex-Lagos C., Lapiedra O. and Diaz M. (2017) Why are exotic birds so successful in urbanized environments? In: *Ecology and Conservation of birds in Urban Environments.* Murgui E. and Hedblom M. (editors) Springer, Cham; doi:10.1007/978-3-319-43314-1_5
21. Case T.J. (1996) Global patterns in the establishment and distribution of exotic birds. *Biological Conservation* 78:1-2, 69–96; doi:10.1016/0006-3207(96)00019-5
22. Shea K. and Chesson P. (2002) Community ecology theory as a framework for biological invasions. *Trends in Ecology and Evolution* 17:4, 170–176; doi:10.1016/S0169-5347(02)02495-3
23. Janiga M. (1991) Interclutch interval and territoriality in the feral pigeon, Columba livia Gm. 1789. *Biologia* 46:961–966

CHAPTER 17: THE LOVED BIRD

1. Kaplan G. (2004) *Australian Magpie: Biology and Behaviour of an Unusual Songbird.* CSIRO Publishing, Melbourne
2. Hancock P. (2014) Ancient tales of Perth's fascinating birds. *Sydney Morning Herald.* Available at www.smh.com.au/entertainment/ancient-tales-of-perths-fascinating-birds-20140405-3650p.html

POSTAMBLE

1. White L. (1967) The Historical Roots of Our Ecologic Crisis. *Science* 155:3767, 1203–1207
2. Oelschlaeger M. (1991) *The idea of wilderness from prehistory to the age of ecology.* Yale University Press, London
3. Reed C.A. (1977) *Origins of Agriculture.* The Hague, Mounton
4. Charlesworth M., Morphy H., Bell D. and Maddock K. (1986) *Religion in Aboriginal Australia. An Anthology.* Library of the University of Queensland, University of Queensland Press
5. Gammage B. (2012) *The Biggest Estate on Earth: How Aborigines made Australia.* Allen and Unwin, Sydney
6. Pascoe B. (2014) *Dark Emu Black Seeds: agriculture or accident?* Magabala books, Western Australia
7. Ludwig J., Tongway D., Freudenberger D., Noble J. and Hodgkinson K. (1997) *Landscape ecology, function and management: principles from Australia's rangelands.* CSIRO, Melbourne
8. Dunlap R.E. and Van Liere K.D. (1978) The New Environmental Paradigm. *The Journal of Environmental Education.* 9:4, 10–19; doi:10.1080/00958964.1978.10801875
9. Wilson E.O. (2016) *Half Earth: Our Planet's Fight for Life.* Liveright, New York
10. Fletcher R. and Büscher B. (2016) Why E. O. Wilson is wrong about how to save the Earth. Available at www.aeon.co/opinions/why-e-o-wilson-is-wrong-about-how-to-save-the-earth11.
11. Wilson E.O. (2016) *Half Earth.* Available at www.aeon.co/essays/half-of-the-earth-must-be-preserved-for1030nature-conservation 10311032
12. Muller N., Werner P. and Kelcey J.G. (2010) *Urban Biodiversity and Design.* Wiley-Blackwell, Oxford
13. Millard A. (2010) Cultural Aspects of Urban Biodiversity. In: *Urban*

Biodiversity and Design. Muller N., Werner P. and Kelecey J.G. (editors) Wiley-Blackwell, Oxford

14. Hand K.L. et al. (2017) The importance of urban gardens in supporting children's biophilia. *Proceedings of the National Academy of Sciences of the United States of America* 114:2, 274–279; doi:10.1073/pnas.1609588114
15. Wells N.M. and Lekies K.S. (2006) Nature and the life course: pathways from childhood nature experiences to adult environmentalism. *Child Youth Environmentalism* 16:1, 1–24
16. Min B. and Lee J. (2006) Children's neighbourhood place as a psychological and behavioural domain. *Journal of Environmental Psychology* 26:1, 51–71; doi:10.1016/j.jenvp.2006.04.003
17. Benkowitz D. and Kohler K. (2010) Perception of biodiversity—the impact of school gardening. Chapter 22, pp. 425–440. In: *Urban Biodiversity and Design.* Muller N., Werner P. and Kelcey J.G. (editors) Wiley-Blackwell, Oxford
18. Jones D.N. and Reynolds S.J. (2008) Feeding birds in our town and cities: a global research opportunity. *Journal of Avian Biology* 39:3, 265–271; doi:10.1111/j.0908-8857.2008.04271.x

LIST OF ILLUSTRATIONS

INDEX